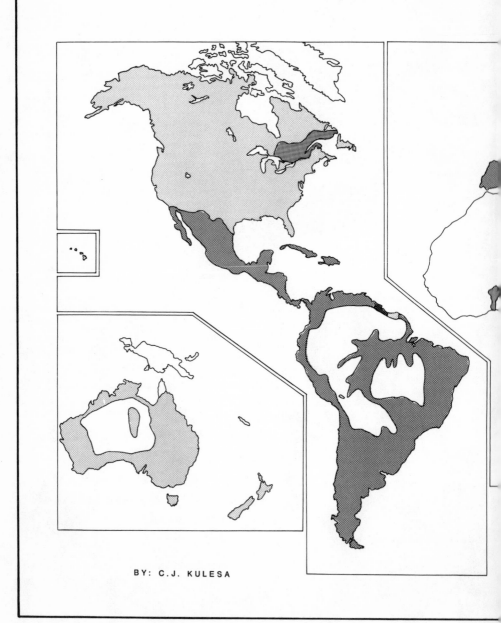

BY: C.J. KULESA

An **Introduction** *to the*

Southern Illinois University Press

Carbondale and Edwardsville

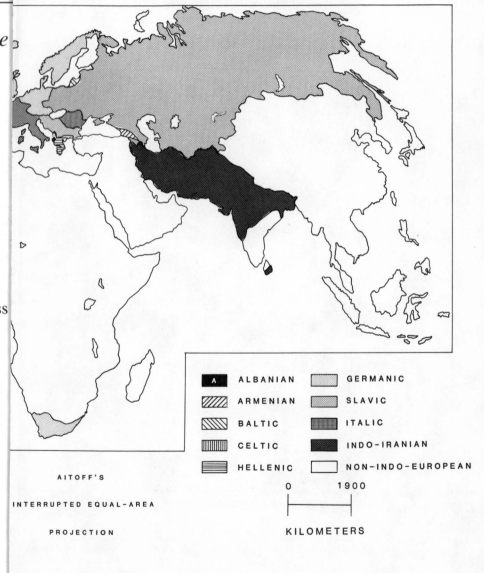

INDO-EUROPEAN STOCKS

A	ALBANIAN		GERMANIC
	ARMENIAN		SLAVIC
	BALTIC		ITALIC
	CELTIC		INDO-IRANIAN
	HELLENIC		NON-INDO-EUROPEAN

AITOFF'S

INTERRUPTED EQUAL-AREA

PROJECTION

0   1900

KILOMETERS

Indo-European Languages

By Philip Baldi

Library of Congress Cataloging in Publication Data

Baldi, Philip.
  An introduction to the Indo-European languages.

  Bibliography: p.
  Includes indexes.
  1. Indo-European languages. I. Title.
P561.B3 1983   410   82–19218
ISBN 0–8093–1090–2
ISBN 0–8093–1091–0 (pbk)

87 86 85 84 83 5 4 3 2 1

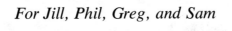

For Jill, Phil, Greg, and Sam

CONTENTS

ILLUSTRATIONS

Tables

Figure

PREFACE

This book began as a chapter of a much larger work that I undertook in the fall of 1979. That work, "An Introduction to Indo-European Comparative Linguistics," is still underway.

My original plan was to include in the larger volume a treatment of the Indo-European stocks that provided more information than the usual cursory mention found in most introductory works. In attempting to avoid such a superficial treatment in my own volume, I discovered that in the process I had written a book that surveyed the Indo-European stocks. I believe that the present volume fills a long-standing need in Indo-European and general linguistic studies for a comprehensive linguistic survey of the Indo-European groups that synthesizes the vast amount of information available in the specialized handbooks of the individual stocks.

This book is intended primarily for students, and it is my hope that it will prove useful in general courses in Indo-European languages and linguistics. And though little in this volume will be new information for specialists in the field of Indo-European studies, I believe that the synthesis of information available on the different stocks, together with the extensive bibliography, makes it something more than a classroom text.

I am pleased to thank the following people who aided me throughout the production of this book: Gordon Fairbanks of the University of Hawaii, who helped me with details of Indo-Iranian; Rama Sharma of the University of Hawaii, who shared his immeasurable knowledge of Indic, especially Sanskrit; Walter Maurer of the University of Hawaii, who provided much-needed information on the Avestan text; Alfred Bammesberger of the Katholische Universität Eichstätt, who helped with some details of Old Irish; Ernst Ebbinghaus of The Pennsylvania State University, who read and commented on a draft of the manuscript and provided invaluable assistance on Germanic; Antanas Klimas of the University of Rochester, who clarified points of Baltic; and finally William R. Schmalstieg, also of The Pennsylvania State University, who read and criticized the manuscript, gave me special help with the Baltic and Slavic sections, and whose erudition and dedication stand as a model for the members of our profession.

I also express my gratitude to the Department of Linguistics, University of Hawaii, where I spent a six-month sabbatical leave in 1980 and completed a great deal of the research on this book. Special thanks to Byron Bender, Chairman, for making it possible for me to work in the most beautiful place in the world, and to The Pennsylvania State University for granting that leave.

Thanks also are due to the Office of Research of the College of the Liberal Arts of the Pennsylvania State University (Thomas F. Magner, Dean) for financial support for this endeavor; to my wife, Jill, and to my student, Beverley Goodman, both of whom assisted in the editing; and to Connie Moore, who patiently and faithfully typed a difficult manuscript.

P. B.

State College, Pa.
January, 1982

An Introduction *to the*
Indo-European Languages

ABBREVIATIONS

A. Languages

A-I, Attic-Ionic
Alb., Albanian
Arm., Armenian
AS, Anglo-Saxon
Av., Avestan
Bryth., Brythonic
Dor., Doric
Eng., English
Falisc., Faliscan
Gaul., Gaulish
Germ., German
Gk., Greek
Gmc., Germanic
Goth., Gothic
Hitt., Hittite
IE, Indo-European
Ir., Irish
Lat., Latin
Latv., Latvian
Lith., Lithuanian
NGmc., North Germanic
OCS, Old Church Slavic

OE, Old English
OFris., Old Frisian
OHG, Old High German
OIc., Old Icelandic
OIr., Old Irish
OLat., Old Latin
OLith., Old Lithuanian
OPers., Old Persian
OPruss., Old Prussian
OS, Old Saxon
Osc., Oscan
OWel., Old Welsh
PIE, Proto-Indo-European
PGmc., Proto-Germanic
Pol., Polish
Russ., Russian
Sab., Sabine
Skt., Sanskrit
Slav., Slavic
Toch., Tocharian
Umbr., Umbrian

B. Grammatical Terms

abl., ablative
acc., accusative
aor., aorist
adj., adjective
conj., conjunction
dat., dative
dec., declension
def., definite
emph., emphatic
gen., genitive
id., the same

indef., indefinite
indic., indicative
inf., infinitive
instr., instrumental
interr., interrogative
lit., literally
loc., locative
nom., nominative
opt., optative
part., participle
perf., perfect

pers., person
pl., plural
post., postposition
pres., present
prep., preposition
pret., preterite
prog., progressive

prt., particle
rel., relative
sg., singular
subj., subjunctive
vcd., voiced
vclss., voiceless
voc., vocative

C. Other Symbols and Abbreviations

cf. = compare
< = is developed from
> = develops into
→ = is replaced by
*   designates an unattested or reconstructed form

Introduction   I

Background   1.0.

The scientific study of language began late in the eighteenth century with the discovery of Sanskrit in India by Europeans. The beginning is clearly signaled by the excessively quoted, but still important, lines of Sir William Jones, a British judge in India, in 1786:

> The Sanscrit language, whatever be its antiquity, is of a wonderful structure; more perfect than the Greek, more copious than the Latin, and more exquisitely refined than either; yet bearing to both of them a stronger affinity, both in the roots of verbs and the forms of grammar, than could possibly have been produced by accident; so strong indeed that no philologer could examine them all three without believing them to have sprung from some common source, which, perhaps, no longer exists; there is a similar reason, though not quite so forcible, for supposing that both the Gothick and Celtick, though blended with a different idiom, had the same origin with the Sanscrit; and the Old Persian might be added to the same family.

Following Jones' declaration about possible relationships among these distinct languages was a wealth of activity in the study and systematic comparison of Sanskrit, Greek, Latin, and the other languages of Europe. Studies were conducted throughout the nineteenth century by people whose names remain connected with the dawning of a science, the science of *comparative grammar:* Schlegel, Bopp, Whitney, Wackernagel, Bühler, Rask, Grimm, Brugmann, and many others far too numerous to mention. The foundations of much of what we know about historical grammar were laid in the nineteenth century. Just what was it that attracted these scholars?

The Concept of Indo-European   1.1.

As a first step in answering this question, let us consider the lists of words presented in table 1. At first glance, these lists seem to contain a dizzying array of individual words with only some superficial similarities. But it does not require excessive scrutiny to see that many of the words in the various columns are remarkably like each other (though this is more obvious for some than for others). How can these similarities be explained? There are several alternative explanations: first, it could be that the similarities are accidental; second, it could be that some or all of the languages borrowed the word in question from some other language; third, it could be that the similarities are only apparent and result from the way we are displaying the data; fourth and finally, it

TABLE 1

Collateral Words in Selected Languages

	'father'		'mother'		'brother'
Skt.	pitár-		mātár-		bhrā́tar-
Lat.	pater		māter		frāter
Gk.	patér		mátēr (Dor.)		phrā́tēr
OIr.	athir		māthir		brāthir
Goth.	faðar	OIc.	mōðir	Goth.	brōþar
Arm.	hayr		mayr		ełbayr
Toch. A	pācar		mācar		pracar
B	pātar		mātar		procer
		OCS	mati		bratrŭ

	'one'		'two'
Skt.	éka-	Skt.	d(u)vá
Lat.	ūnus	Av.	d(u)va
Gk.	oiné 'ace'	Lat.	duo
OIr.	ōen	Gk.	dúo
Goth.	áins	OIr.	dāu, dā
OPruss.	ainan (acc.)	OCS	dŭva

	'three'		'nine'
Skt.	tráya-	Skt.	náva-
Lat.	trēs	Lat.	novem
Gk.	treîs	Gk.	enné(w)a
OIr.	trī	OIr.	nōin-
Goth.	þriya	Goth.	niun
Toch. A	tri (fem.)	Toch. A	ñū
B	trai	B	ñū
OCS	trĭje		

could be that each of these languages has inherited the words in question from some source common to them all.

Our first exploratory set of illustrative data is chosen from basic kinship and lower numerals for several reasons. One is that each forms an interrelated set; it is inconceivable that so many languages could show such systematic similarity in these areas by accident. As for the second possible explanation of similarity, borrowing, we have strong evidence from elsewhere that languages resist borrowing in the areas of basic kinship and numerals; hence borrowing is not a reasonable explanation. As for the third possibility, that they are some sort of analytical artifacts due to an improper analysis of the data, we can only say that these words are morphologically transparent; there is little chance that they have been mistaken for something that they are not. Reason suggests that the final possibility, common parentage, is in fact the only real one and that the words on each list descend from some source that is the same for all.

Of course, exactly what this common source is or was is not yet answered, nor can we be absolutely certain, on the basis of only seven words, that we have sufficient evidence to make such a far-reaching claim concerning common ancestry. But we can add to our basic data here, and the array of similarities starts to mount up. Let us first simply expand our word list by drawing lexical items from a variety of different semantic fields (see table 2; to avoid overwhelming the reader, data from only a few representative languages are provided).

By this time the essential claim about common ancestry would seem to be quite securely made. But for the skeptic to be convinced, we shall have to move beyond the lexicon, which is notoriously unreliable and often deceptive because of its proclivity to change. In fact, during the early period of comparative linguistics, when the basic discoveries concerning the Indo-European family were first being made, many scholars were attending to matters other than lexical ones. Franz Bopp, for example (1816), concentrated his attention, not on the comparison of words, but rather on the comparison of inflectional endings, especially in the verbal systems of Sanskrit, Greek, Latin, and the Germanic languages. And, during the period 1819–1837, Jacob Grimm's monumental *Deutsche Grammatik* appeared; in it the author provided a comprehensive treatment of Germanic historical-comparative grammar based primarily on the systematic com-

TABLE 2

Collateral Words, Continued

	'foot'		'great'
Skt.	pád-	Skt.	mahā́nt-
Lat.	pēs	Lat.	magnus
Gk.	poús	Gk.	mégas
Goth.	fōtus	Goth.	mikils

	'dead'		'yoke'
Skt.	mr̥tá-	Skt.	yugá-
Lat.	mortuus	Lat.	iugum
Gk.	á-mbrotos 'immortal'	Gk.	zugón
OHG	mord 'murder'	Goth.	yuk

	'see, know'		'dog'
Skt.	vidmá 'we know'	Skt.	śván-
Lat.	videō	Lat.	can-is
Gk.	(w)ídmen 'we know'	Gk.	kúōn
OE	witon	Goth.	hunds

	'wolf'		'knee'
Skt.	vŕ̥ka-	Skt.	jā́nu-
Lat.	lupus	Lat.	genu
Gk.	lúkos	Gk.	gónu
Goth.	wulfs	Goth.	kniu

	'mind, remember'		'carry'
Skt.	matí-	Skt.	bhár-
Lat.	ment-is (gen.)	Lat.	ferō
Gk.	autó-matos 'self-acting'	Gk.	phérō
Goth.	(ga-)munan	Goth.	baíran

	'stand'		'mouse'
Skt.	sthā́-	Skt.	mū́ṣ-
Lat.	stō	Lat.	mūs
Gk.	hístāmi (Dor.)	Gk.	mûs
Goth.	standan	OHG	mūs

	'what'		'house'
Skt.	ká-	Skt.	dáma-
Lat.	quis	Lat.	domus
Lith.	kàs	Gk.	dómos
Goth.	hwas	OCS	domŭ

TABLE 2 Continued

	'be'		'woman'
Skt.	ábhūt 'was'	Gk.	gunḗ
Lat.	fuī 'was'	OHG	quena
Gk.	éphū 'grew'	Eng.	queen
OCS	byti	OCS	žena

	'heart'		'field'
Lat.	cord-is (gen.)	Skt.	ájra-
Gk.	kardía	Lat.	ager
Lith.	širdìs	Gk.	agrós
Goth.	haírtō	Goth.	akrs

	'widow'		'sit'
Skt.	vidhávā-	Skt.	sád-
Lat.	vidua	Lat.	sedeō
OPruss.	widdewū	OLith.	sḗdmi
Goth.	widuwō	OIc.	sitia

parison of sound systems and morphological patterns. Later scholars continued the practice of concentrating on phonological, morphological, and, to a lesser extent, syntactic analysis and comparison of the attested languages, and did not simply catalogue their lexical similarities. (Two outstanding syntacticians from a slightly later period were Delbrück, e.g., 1879, 1888, 1893–1900, and Wackernagel, e.g., 1926–1928; for an excellent review of the pioneer days of comparative grammar, see Pedersen 1959.)

We can see what kind of comparative morphological and phonological regularities these scholars observed by examining a few representative samples of data. Consider the sets of words presented in table 3. In these two representatives of the present tense of the verb 'to be', we find strong similarity not only in the verb root (which is lexical), but also, and more critically, in the grammatical markers indicating first and third person (-m, -mi and -t, -ti, respectively). If we are seeking to establish common ancestry rather than borrowing or accident, such systematic regularities in inflectional endings cannot be dismissed. In other words, a language might borrow the word for 'arrow', 'to sail', or 'wheel', but it is most unlikely that it will borrow the marker for 'plural', 'first person', or 'third person'.

We can push the point of grammatical endings a step further by noting the similarities in the morphemes marked out in the forms for 'horse' in the various cases (see table 4; cf. nom. sg. to nom. sg., gen. pl. to gen. pl., etc.). The reader will note the lack of concord in the number of cases in Greek, Latin, and Sanskrit. Sanskrit is believed by some to represent the original system with eight cases; it is commonly held that the old ablative, locative, and instrumental merged in Latin into the ablative; in Greek, the old genitive and ablative merged into the genitive, while the old dative, locative, and instrumental fell together into the dative.

When we add the correspondences of the nominal system from the nouns for 'horse', the evidence becomes simply overwhelming. And a closer analysis would reveal still greater similarity in the nouns than is apparent, because numerous sound changes and developments within the individual languages have altered the shapes of the original morphemes. If we were to extend our analysis beyond the physical forms themselves into the syntaxes of the different languages, we would find that they utilize these forms to serve similar grammatical functions. We would also find that the three languages in our noun data are all *inflecting* (as opposed to *analytic* or *agglutinating*) languages. Inflecting languages are those in which words are not neatly divisible into

TABLE 3

The First- and Third-Person Singular of 'To Be' in Selected Languages

	'I am'		'he/she is'
Skt.	ás-*mi*	Skt.	ás-*ti*
Lat.	su-*m*	Lat.	es-*t*
Gk.	ei-*mí*	Gk.	es-*tí*
Hitt.	eš-*mi*	Hitt.	(kuen-*zi* 'he strikes')
Arm.	e-*m*	OLith.	ēs-*ti*
Goth.	i-*m*	Goth.	is-*t*
OCS	jes-*mǐ*	OCS	jes-*tǐ*
Alb.	ja-*m*		
Osc.	sú-*m*		

discrete morphemes and in which the relationship between morphological markers and grammatical categories is highly complex. Agglutinating languages are those in which words are segmentable into strings of discrete morphemes, each with a different grammatical function. Inflecting languages tend to have significant amounts of morphophonemic variation at morpheme boundaries that blurs morpheme membership, whereas agglutinating

TABLE 4

Paradigms of the Word for 'Horse' in Sanskrit, Latin, and Greek

		Singular	Plural
Skt.	*áśva-*		
	Nom.	áśv-*as*	áśvās
	Gen.	áśvasya	áśvān-*ām*
	Dat.	áśvāya	áśvebhyas
	Acc.	áśv-*am*	áśv-*āṃs*
	Abl.	áśv-*ād*	áśvebhyas
	Voc.	áśva	áśvās
	Loc.	áśve	áśveṣu
	Instr.	áśvā	áśvais
Lat.	*equus*		
	Nom.	equ-*us*	equ-*ī* (-*oi* in earlier forms)
	Gen.	equī	equorum (cf. de-*um* 'of the gods')
	Dat.	equ-*ō* (cf. OLat. Numasi-*oi* 'to Numerius')	equ*īs*
	Acc.	equ-*um*	equ-*ōs*
	Abl.	equ-*ō* (cf. OLat. Gnaiv-*ōd* 'from Gnaivus')	equ*īs*
	Voc.	equ-*e*	equ-*ī*
Gk.	*híppos*		
	Nom.	hípp-*os*	hípp-*oi*
	Gen.	híppou	hípp-*ōn*
	Dat.	hípp-*ōi*	hípp-*ois*
	Acc.	hípp-*on*	hípp-*ous*
	Voc.	hípp-*e*	hípp-*oi*

languages show very little of this kind of alternation. Analytic languages, which are also known as isolating languages, have words that are fixed unanalyzable units.

Returning now to table 4, we find that the ending of the nominative case, for example, serves to mark subject of verb in each; the genitive form signals possession, partitive, and other common functions; the accusative morpheme indicates direct object, among other things. And note that even when forms differ there is often parallel distribution; for example, the dative and ablative plural share a common form in both Latin and Sanskrit, and the same is true for the nominative and vocative plurals in all three languages.

1.2.   Comparative Grammar

It was the contribution of Rasmus Rask, Jacob Grimm, and other scholars of the early nineteenth century to observe a system of comparison between the sounds of the various languages they were investigating. That is, when one compares material from two different but obviously related languages, it is usually the case that a given sound x in one will be predictably and systematically represented by a given sound y in the other. This regularity forms the basis of the *comparative method,* a technique of comparison by which linguists not only verify relatedness between languages, but also can reconstruct features of the ancestral parent of the related languages. Though this method cannot be dealt with in any detail here (see Anttila 1972 and Lehmann 1973 for detailed treatments), we should at the least look at some of the data in the way Grimm might have.

We shall proceed by recalling some of the earlier forms and by adding a few new ones, as presented in table 5. In these six words it is important to note not only the general similarity of the words in form and meaning, but also the fact that there is a regularity of sound correspondence evident in the different words. For example, in the first, *father,* the Skt. p = Lat. p = Gk. p = Goth. (Gmc.) f; the same equation holds in *master* and *nephew/grandson.* In *father* again, we find $r = r = r = r$, a pattern repeated in *red* and *carry* (the s of Goth. *raúps* is due to other factors). Note further that the n of *nephew/grandson* is represented by $n = n = n = n$, as it is in *nine.* In some cases these correspondence sets, as they are called, are not so neat, but linguists have developed highly sophisticated techniques since Grimm's day to explain the irregularities.

Thus we can see that the various languages that attracted the attention of the early scholars show remarkable similarity and comparability in the lexicon, morphology, phonology, and, to a lesser degree, syntax, though we have not pursued the similarities in this last area to any degree here. The conclusion of common ancestry is inescapable, and we can now identify the parent.

The language family to which our selected languages all belong is called the *Indo-European* family (Germ. *Indogermanisch*). They are all descendents of an ancestral language that we call *Primitive* or *Proto-Indo-European* (PIE). PIE was never written down, and we have consequently no direct records of it. Its former existence, however, can be established beyond a doubt from the evidence and systematic comparison of the descendent languages. The term 'Indo-European' is essentially a geographical label that indicates the eastern (India) and western (Europe)

TABLE 5

Forms in Several Languages Partially Aligned
for the Comparative Method

	'father'	'nephew, grandson'
Skt.	pitár-	nápāt-
Lat.	pater	nepōs
Gk.	patếr	anepsiós 'sister's son'
Goth.	faðar	OIc. nefe

	'red'	'master'
Skt.	rudhirá-	páti-
Lat.	ruber	potis
Gk.	eruthrós	pósis
Goth.	rauþs	-faþs

	'nine'	'carry'
Skt.	náva-	bhár-
Lat.	novem	ferō
Gk.	enné(w)a	phérō
Goth.	niun	baíran

reaches of the family at the time of its discovery. (New discoveries and modern language expansion would surely now suggest a new name, but the early usage is firmly rooted in the linguistic tradition.) Because of the passage of time and the social and geographical separation of speakers, the Indo-European languages became so different from each other that their common ancestry is readily apparent in only a relatively small number of words and forms such as those cited earlier. In most cases careful scrutiny and comparison is required to verify cognate elements.

The Indo-European language family is made up of eleven subgroups, though one hastens to add that various scholars see the issue of subgrouping differently, especially on the question of Balto-Slavic, Italo-Celtic, and some of the peripheral languages such as Venetic and Illyrian. In this volume we shall follow a neutral course on these issues; the groupings that follow in most cases do not reflect anything more than a synopsis of prevailing thought. The eleven major groups are Italic, Hellenic (= Greek), Indo-Iranian, Celtic, Germanic, Baltic, Slavic, Armenian, Anatolian, Albanian, and Tocharian. Other important, but largely fragmentary, languages that have been securely interpreted as Indo-European are Thracian, Phrygian, Ligurian, Messapic, Venetic, Illyrian, Lepontic, Sicel, and Raetic.

For a very long time it was common practice in comparative Indo-European linguistics to propose statements about the protolanguage on the basis of mainly three language groups, Italic, Hellenic, and Indo-Iranian, with the strongest secondary support from Germanic and Slavic. Of course, this practice is not scientifically sound, since it tends to relegate the other dialects to a silent secondary status, to be called forth when the need arises for a representative example of lexicon or morphology. Many scholars have condemned this practice (especially those with specializations in language areas other than these three), citing a historical conspiracy of the 'triumvirate' ('trilinguate'?) of Greek, Latin, and Sanskrit in historical reconstruction. This practice is criticized on yet other grounds, which relate to observed trends of language change. It has long been known that social and political change brings with it an accelerated rate of language change. The reasons for such change are easy enough to see (increased technology, trade with foreign peoples, heightened social stratification), and need not be discussed here. And what of Greek, Latin, and Sanskrit? Here we have three of the most sophisticated and advanced social groups within the Indo-European family! All were highly stratified socially, contributing to dialectal differences; all had extensive contacts with speakers of other languages, in many cases sharing common cultural patterns; and all were quite advanced socially, intellectually, and technologically in comparison with the other Indo-European peoples, especially the pastoral peoples of Central Europe. So why do we continue to rely so heavily on the data furnished by these languages? The principal reason is that they are the ones we know best, providing us with records reaching well back in time: Greek to at least 800 B.C., though Mycenaean goes back even further; Sanskrit to somewhere between 1200 and 1000 B.C. The Latin evidence from before the third century B.C. is inscriptional and not systematically helpful, but the evidence from then on is voluminous. The discovery and decipherment of Hittite has helped to change the picture a great deal, but it must be pointed out that the standard reference works in Indo-European linguistics were prepared before or in ignorance of the Hittite discoveries, which provide evidence to approximately 1500 B.C. And since the historical linguist relies heavily on written records, both as an older source and an inherently more conservative one, it seems that we have little choice but to continue our primary dependence on Greek, Latin, Sanskrit, and now Hittite, but with the thought in mind that they may not always be the most faithful to the original.

1.2.1. The Indo-Europeans

The systematic comparison of the Indo-European languages and the postulation of the reconstructed proto-language, Proto-Indo-European, raises as many questions as it answers. One of the most intriguing issues centers on the Indo-European people themselves: who were they, where did they come from, and how advanced were they socially? These questions have been hotly debated from the early days of comparative linguistics, and because of some fairly recent archaeological work by Gimbutas, we are now beginning to understand the origin of the Indo-European people much better.

Gimbutas has posited (e.g., 1970, 1973) that the Indo-European people had their original homeland in the area north of the Black Sea in what is now southern Russia. Though dating is hazardous, the best estimates for their presence in this area seem to suggest the period about 3000 B.C. This date is indicated not only by the linguistic evidence, but also by the apparent identity of the Indo-Europeans as the carriers of the so-called Kurgan Culture that Gimbutas has postulated for this area at that time. The hypothesis that the Indo-Europeans were the bearers of the Kurgan Culture has been well received by the linguistic and archaeological communities. It adds the archaeological evidence, primarily from the single graves in deep shafts that characterize the Kurgans, to the linguistically reconstructed material items such as 'wheel', 'axle', 'horse', 'sheep', and 'agriculture'. These reconstructible words indicate that the Indo-Europeans had knowledge of agriculture, worked metals, and domesticated animals.

At some unknown time after 3000 B.C., the Indo-European community broke up and spread out of the central area to the north and west into southern and western Europe, as well as to the east and south into India. That these wanderings most likely took place in waves is recorded and embedded in the linguistic histories of the descendent languages in the form of certain phonological developments and influences from other languages encountered by the conquering Indo-Europeans.

1.3.   A Brief Structural Sketch
of Proto-Indo-European

As already mentioned, PIE is a language that has been reconstructed on the basis of the evidence we find in the attested languages of the family. Needless to say, the reconstruction of a lost language is a difficult and even hazardous undertaking. This is so because the data we find in the descendent languages are not uniform and are often separated by enormous gaps in time (for example, there is approximately a 3,000-year gap between the oldest Hittite records and the oldest Lithuanian texts). Furthermore, that each of the Indo-European stocks has been subjected to a variety of influences from other languages, many of them non-Indo-European, further complicates the analysis and the reconstruction of the proto-language.

Many points of controversy surround the reconstruction of PIE, and indeed surround any reconstruction effort. Some are methodological questions (for example, how do we distinguish archaism from innovation?); some are philosophical (for example, what kinds of linguistic evidence are admissable in reconstruction?); some are simply differences of opinion based on the preconceptions and orientation of the investigator (for example, which is more archaic, Hittite or Sanskrit?). This book is not the place to resolve these issues. I mention them only to point out that the brief structural sketch offered below represents only one possible array of facts. Others would surely present the facts differently, and, of course, linguists skilled in the issues of reconstructed PIE will no doubt take issue with various points. It should simply be kept in mind that this is only a sketch designed to provide a framework for understanding what follows in the chapters on the individual stocks.

1.3.1. Phonology

1.3.1.1. Vowels

PIE had a vocalic system of the triangular type which employed functional distinctions of length. It assumes the following diagrammatic form:

$$\begin{matrix} \breve{\bar{\imath}} & & \breve{\bar{u}} \\ \breve{\bar{e}} & \partial & \breve{\bar{o}} \\ & \breve{\bar{a}} & \end{matrix}$$

This vocalic system is by no means universally accepted. Some specialists have proposed a system without original length distinctions, these being the result of the loss of segments from a still earlier stage in the language. Others assert that there is no basis for *ə, or for ĭ and ŭ. But, despite all the efforts of the past eighty or so years, the triangular system with contrastive length and phonemic *ə remains the most defensible.

We also postulate for PIE a series of diphthongs, *ai, ei, oi, au, eu, ou*. There is a possibility, though it is not strongly supported, that a set of long diphthongs also existed, namely, *āi, ēi, ōi, āu, ēu, ōu*.

The vowels *i* and *u* had consonantal counterparts (semivowels), *y* and *w* (often written *i̯* and *u̯*). We find these in such forms as Skt. *tráya-*, Gk. *treîs*, OCS *trĭje* 'three'; and Lat. *iuvenis*, Skt. *yúvan-* 'youth'.

An important feature of Indo-European morphophonology that is manifested in the vowel system is called *vowel alternation*, or *ablaut* (it is also known as *vowel gradation*). In the oldest stage of the language, verbs, and probably nouns as well, were differentiated in their various stem classes primarily by a modification of the stem vowel rather than by the addition of suffixes, the system we find predominating in the later language. Ablaut is an archaic feature that we find to one degree or another in most of the descendent stocks. Greek, Germanic, and Sanskrit preserve it most systematically (see chapters 4, 5, and 10 for details).

There were two basic types of ablaut, the qualitative and the quantitative. In qualitative ablaut the actual vowel quality was alternated, whereas in quantitative ablaut the alternation was one of length. The primary qualitative alternation was between *e : o : φ*. A few examples are the following: Gk. *peíth-ō (e)* 'I trust': *pé-poith-a (o)* 'I trusted': *é-pith-on (φ)*: 'I trusted'; cf. also Lat. *fīdō* 'I trust' (< *ei*): *foedus* 'agreement' (< *oi*): *fides* 'trust' (< *φi*); also Lat. *tegō* 'I cover': *toga* 'a covering'; Gk. *légō* 'I say': *lógos* 'word'. Modern English abounds in remnants of this process in such verbs as *drive, drove, driven; sing, sang, sung;* and so on. There were other ablaut series besides *e : o : φ;* they are best represented in Germanic.

The quantitative series was based on an alternation of vowel length, not vowel quality—for example, *o : ō, e : ē,* and so on. It is systematically represented in Sanskrit—for example, *pát-ati (a)* 'he falls', *pāt-áyati (ā)* 'he causes to fall', *pa-pt-imá (φ)* 'we fell'. Cf. also Gk. (nom.) *patḗr* 'father' *(ē)*, (acc.) *patéra (e)*, (gen.) *patrós (φ)*.

Accent in PIE is also a much disputed issue. The traditional position is that the accentual system was one based on pitch rather than on emphasis and that each word was characterized by high pitch on one syllable. The rules for the precise placement of the accent in PIE have never been worked out satisfactorily.

1.3.1.2. Consonants

As with the vowels, the consonants of PIE are a matter of debate. We shall begin with a listing of the secure sounds and then proceed to the disputed points.

It is reasonably clear that PIE had a series of liquids, one of nasals and one of syllabics. They are as follows:

Liquids	l	r			
Nasals	m	n			
Syllabics	l̥	r̥	m̥	n̥	(possibly also l̥̄ r̥̄ m̥̄ n̥̄)

In addition to these, the following obstruent phonemes are postulated for PIE:

	Labial	Dental	Palatal	Labio-velar	Velar
Stops					
Voiceless	p	t	k̑	kʷ	k
Voiced	b	d	g̑	gʷ	g
Voiced Aspirate	bh	dh	g̑h	gʷh	gh
Voiceless Aspirate	ph	th	k̑h	kʷh	kh
Fricative		s			

(*Laryngeals*   h, x, ɣ, ʔ)

The major points of controversy in the obstruent system are discussed below (1.3.1.2.a, b, and c).

a. Voiceless aspirated stops. From a typological standpoint, the reconstructed system *without* voiceless aspirates is unbalanced and indeed quite unusual. This is so primarily because, as studies of language universals have shown, the presence of a voiced member of a series implies the presence of the voiceless member; that is, *bh, dh, gh* implies *ph, th, kh*. The reverse, however, is not true. It is consistent with such a principle that we should postulate both the voiceless and the voiced aspirated series for PIE. However, the voiceless series is not well substantiated by the evidence of the descendent languages and is required only to cover those relatively few cases in which Skt. *ph, th,* and so on, correspond to Gk. *ph, th,* and so on—for example, Skt. *sphál-* 'quiver, burst', Gk. *sphállō* 'overthrow, cause to break'. Usually, the Greek voiceless aspirates *ph, th, kh* correspond to the Sanskrit voiced aspirates *bh, dh, gh*—for example, Skt. *bhrā́tar-* 'brother', Gk. *phrátēr* 'member of a clan'. Interestingly, only Sanskrit among the IE languages has both voiced and voiceless stops; all others have developed systems with either plain voiceless stops, voiceless fricatives, and plain voiced stops (e.g., Latin) or plain voiceless stops, plain voiced stops, and voiceless aspirated stops (e.g., Greek). Some scholars have tried to explain the Sanskrit voiceless aspirates as the result of the action of laryngeal phonemes in PIE (see 1.3.1.2.c below), but the issue remains unsettled.

b. Velars, palato-velars, and labiovelars. The reconstruction of the three independent series for PIE of velar, palato-velar (or palatal), and labiovelar phonemes is necessitated by the distribution of certain sounds in the attested languages. Because it is a requirement of the comparative method that there be systematic correspondences between sounds for orderly reconstruction to take place, there is a need to posit these three separate phonemic series even though no single language shows all three as inherited sounds.

The need for plain velars appears clear enough: cf. Lat. *cruor* 'blood', Gk. *kréas*, Skt. *kraví-* 'flesh', Lith. *kraūjas* 'blood' (*k : k : k : k < *k*); also Gk. *steíkhō* 'walk', Goth. *steigan* 'climb', Skt. *stígh-* 'mount', OCS *stignǫ* 'come' (*kh : g : gh : g < *gh*). However, velars in these languages usually do not line up so neatly. Much more common are the cases in which Latin or Greek velars correspond to Sanskrit or Lithuanian sibilants: cf. Lat. *centum*, Gk. *he-katón*, Skt. *śatám*, Lith. *šiṁtas* '100'; also Lat. *decem*, Gk. *déka*, Skt. *dáśa*, Lith. *dēšimt* '10'. In these examples the correspondence is *k : k : ś : š*.

The distribution of *velar : velar* and *velar : sibilant* has prompted some scholars of Indo-European to reconstruct two separate series for the proto-language, a plain velar and a palato-velar. What is assumed then is that the plain velars remained velars in all languages, while the palato-velars merged with the velars in some (the *centum* languages) and became sibilants in the others (the *satem* languages). (For further discussion of the *centum-satem* division, see 11.2.)

The distribution of the reflexes of the reconstructed labio-velars is similar, though considerably less skewed. Only Latin, Germanic, Mycenaean Greek, and Hittite actually have labio-velar phonemes (*qu, hw, q*, and *ku*, respectively, in the voiceless unaspirated series). Corresponding sounds in Greek have all merged with reflexes of other sounds, namely, *p, t*, and *k*, depending on the following vowel. In Sanskrit, the corresponding sounds are plain velars. Thus we find, for example, Lat. *quis*, Goth. *hwas*, Skt. *kás*, Hitt. *kuiš*, Gk. *tís* 'who' (*qu : hw : k : ku : t < *kʷ*); also Lat. *sequor* 'follow', Goth. *saíhwan* 'see', Skt. *sáce* 'follow', Hitt. *šakuwa* 'eyes', Gk. *hépomai* 'follow' (*qu : hw : c : ku : p*).

Thus, even though we find labiovelars physically present in only four stocks, the correspondences of these sounds with those in the other stocks compel us to assume labiovelars for PIE and to assume that they have merged with other sounds (usually plain velars or labials) in the other languages.

c. Laryngeals. It is very often the case that data in the descendent languages do not line up in the neat arrays that the comparative method requires. In one such instance certain features seem to have been unpredictably present in some languages where no visible explanation was possible. For some of these it was proposed in the latter part of the nineteenth century that the unpredicted sounds were due to the action of other sounds that had existed at some earlier stage in the language but were lost before the first written records of the language. These sounds left evidence of their former presence by modifying the sounds surrounding them in such ways as lengthening or changing a vowel, aspirating a consonant, and others. These lost sounds are called *laryngeals*. They are surely the most controversial point of reconstructed PIE phonology. Some scholars utterly reject them (e.g., Schmalstieg 1973), while others rely on them heavily (e.g., Lehmann 1952).

Proposals for the number of laryngeals for PIE range from as few as one to as many as twelve. The laryngeal theory was given strong support when Hittite was deciphered and shown to be an Indo-European language, for Hittite alone preserves these sounds. (For further discussion, see 12.3.)

1.3.2. Morphology

The grammatical basis of PIE as an inflectional language is quite secure, though there is ample evidence that at some earlier stage of pre-proto–Indo-European it was probably agglutinative. PIE made use of a three-gender system of masculine-feminine-neuter, though Hittite confounds this picture somewhat with its two-gender system of common and neuter. The language had a number system based on a distinction among singular-plural-dual, though it is possible that the dual is a later development.

The best evidence for the nominal inflectional system of PIE points to eight cases: nominative, genitive, dative, accusative, ablative, vocative, locative, and instrumental. This is a rather complex issue, however. Only Sanskrit has eight fully developed cases; we find seven in Baltic, six in Latin, five in Greek, four in Germanic, and so on down the line, with no cases surviving in many of the modern languages such as English. Case functions are relatively uniform, however. The nominative typically marks the subject of the sentence; the genitive is used to mark possession, partitive, and other functions; the dative signals indirect object, possession, and sometimes agency; the accusative marks the direct object, the goal, extent of time and space; the ablative signals location, separation, and sometimes agency; the vocative is the case used for direct address; the instrumental signals instrument-used; and the locative marks primarily stationary location. These functions by no means exhaust the list, but they do capture the essential generalities applicable to most of the stocks.

Adjectives follow noun patterns in declension, as do some of the lower numerals. Pronouns, however, have a quite different declensional basis from that of the nouns.

Noun groups are divided into two main classes: the *thematic type*, which is of the form *Root + Theme Vowel + Ending* (represented, for example, by nom. sg. Lat. *equ-u-s*, Skt. *áśv-a-s*, Gk. *hípp-o-s* 'horse'); and the *athematic type*, which is of the form *Root + ø + Ending* (represented, for example, by nom. sg. Lat. *vōx* (*vōk-s*), Skt. *vāk* (< *vāc-s*) 'voice'). Both types are well represented in the attested languages.

The analysis of the Indo-European verb is a complex issue. In the earliest language, it is likely that tense was not a grammatical category; temporal relations were marked by particles and adverbs. A more basic distinction was an aspectual one between perfective (completed) and imperfective (noncompleted) action. A further contrast between momentary and durative action may have also been a grammatical feature of PIE. In the later language tense predominates, though it is not clear what tenses actually existed in PIE beyond the simple present and preterite. There are as many as eight tenses in some Indo-European languages (e.g., Sanskrit), and as few as two in others (e.g., Germanic). The same uncertainty exists for mood categories. Sanskrit has an indicative, optative, and imperative; others have a subjunctive and other categories. Exactly which of these was present in the proto-language is an open question, though the indicative and imperative seem secure.

One aspect of the verbal system of which we are fairly confident is that of voice. PIE had two voices, active and mediopassive. The active marks the grammatical subject as the agent of the sentence. The mediopassive is a combined category that embraces two functions, the middle and the passive, one of which usually predominates in the individual languages. The middle function marks the subject of the sentence as both the agent and the recipient of the action. It is clearly indicated by the Skt. (active) *yájati* 'he makes a sacrifice (for others)', (middle) *yájate* 'he makes a sacrifice for himself'. The passive function is clearly marked by Lat. *homo amatur a femina* 'The man is loved by the woman'. In such uses the grammatical subject is the recipient of the action but is not the agent.

In most of the IE languages one or the other of these two uses of the mediopassive predominates. In Sanskrit it is clearly the middle (the native grammarians do not even recognize a passive). In Latin the passive predominates. In Greek both functions are in productive use, though here as in the other languages the two are very close formally.

1.3.3. Syntax

The syntax of PIE is currently a hotly debated topic. Despite some excellent work done in syntax around the turn of the century, especially by Delbrück, most Indo-European scholarship has been directed at the phonology, morphology, and lexicon. But in recent years some very innovative (and controversial) work by Lehmann (e.g., 1974) has brought a new approach to the study of syntax. Based on typology, the method owes much of its foundation to the earlier work of Greenberg (e.g., 1966). Other imaginative work has been carried out by Friedrich (1975) and others.

Lehmann's method allows us to proceed beyond morphology in the study of syntactic systems. It is clear that languages with rich inflectional systems carry out a great deal of their syntax in morphological terms. Case endings mark such functions as subject of sentence, direct object, and indirect recipient of action. But Lehmann's work has at least pointed the way beyond the nominal morphology. The approach is based on word-order typology, and it allows us to make inferences about the syntactic system of PIE on the basis of dominant patterns of word order in sentences. Lehmann has asserted, for example, that PIE was predominantly Subject-Object-Verb (SOV) in its unmarked sentence order. From this fact we can infer, among a number of interesting features, that it was also postpositional (as Hittite suggests), that it had relative clauses that preceded their head nouns, that it had impersonal sentences with optional subjects, and that (uninflected) adjectives preceded their nouns. Another distinguishing characteristic of PIE syntax is its use of absolute constructions, a feature found in many of the stocks, especially Greek, Italic, and Indo-Iranian (see chapters 2, 4, and 5 for details).

The issues involved in the study of PIE syntax are far too complex for an introductory sketch of this type. The reader should consult Lehmann (1974) for deeper discussion. Suffice it to say that, whether it is correct or not, this work has reopened the field of PIE syntax.

I have deliberately avoided citing extensive data for the simple reason that this is not a book about PIE, but about its descendent languages. Nothing short of a full-length treatment could do justice to this topic. It is my hope, however, that the evidence on which the foregoing sketch is based will emerge from the chapters that follow. After all, the attested languages form the basis of our hypotheses about the proto-language, not the other way around.

References

I. General Background

Allen 1953
Anttila 1972
Bynon 1977
Hoenigswald 1960

Lehmann 1973
Pedersen 1959
Sturtevant 1962a
Szemerényi 1972

II. General Indo-European Handbooks and Grammars

Adrados 1975
Brugmann 1897–1916
Brugmann 1903
Hirt 1921–1937
Krahe 1962
Kuryłowicz 1968

Meillet 1964
Meillet 1922 [1967]
Pisani 1961
Schmalstieg 1980
Szemerényi 1970
Watkins 1969

III. Dictionaries

Buck 1951
Pokorny 1951–1959

IV. Works Cited in the Text

Anttila 1972
Bopp 1816
Delbrück 1879
Delbrück 1888

Delbrück 1893–1900
Friedrich 1975
Gimbutas 1970
Gimbutas 1973

Greenberg 1966
Grimm 1819–1837
 (1870–1898)
Lehmann 1952
Lehmann 1973

Lehmann 1974
Pedersen 1959
Schmalstieg 1973
Wackernagel 1926–
 1928

2   Italic

2.0.   Introduction

Latin is only one of many dialects that were spoken in ancient Latium, where Rome was located. Because of the commanding social and political position that the speakers of Latin eventually enjoyed, it became the dominant language of the area and in the end suffocated all the others. The proto-Latins were basically a group of West Indo-European invaders who came into the area we now call Italy sometime before the tenth century B.C. But they did not find empty spaces; the area was already occupied by a variety of different tribes, some of whom were Indo-European and some of whom were not. Though the interpretation of the evidence, mostly archaeological and partly linguistic, is open to serious debate, we are now fairly certain that Italy was occupied by a variety of peoples before and during the first millenium B.C. The best known of these people are the Etruscans, whose own prehistory is clouded in uncertainty, but who were firmly entrenched in northern Italy by the seventh century B.C. and who controlled most of Latium and probably founded Rome, where a *vicus Tuscus* 'Etruscan quarter' remained into the Roman period.

The Etruscans were definitely non-Indo-European, and they exerted a profound influence on the Romans in cultural, religious, and political matters. This influence is directly visible in Roman nomenclature, military and religious terminology, and art, as well as in political and social vocabulary and organization. As they took firm control of the Italian peninsula, the Romans all but eliminated the Etruscan influence, banishing the last of the Etruscan kings, Tarquinius Superbus, in about 500 B.C. Considering the close contact of the two peoples, the overall linguistic influence of Etruscan on Latin is apparently not at all great, being confined to lexical items in fairly narrow areas. (A brief sample of Latin words from Etruscan: *histrio* 'actor', *persōna* 'mask', possibly also *amāre* 'love', as well as certain other words that reflect Etruscan influence, especially where *h* is written to indicate aspiration, e.g., *Gracchus, Cethegus,* and others.)

There is some evidence for a group of so-called Mediterranean languages (e.g., Pelasgian) spoken by native people who, in addition to the non-Indo-European Etruscans, occupied the land later invaded by the proto-Latins. The evidence for these languages is scanty, confined mostly to onomastic and situational data in the form of aberrant dialect forms.

Among the other, Indo-European languages in Italy we find Illyrian, Venetic, Messapic, Ligurian, Sicel, and Raetic. (Each of these will be taken up separately in chapter 13.) Latin is the principal member of the Italic family, which itself is usually divided into two groups, the Latin-Faliscan and the Oscan-Umbrian. We shall now focus on the Italic family proper and the relationship between its two main divisions.

Latin-Faliscan   **2.1.**

2.1.1. Faliscan

Since so little is known about Faliscan, a few words on the subject should suffice. The exact territorial boundaries of the Falisci are not known, but they most certainly were concentrated in southern Etruria, with Falerii as the capital (modern Città Castellana). When it was first discovered, some scholars believed that Faliscan was the 'missing link' between Latin and Oscan-Umbrian. The principal source for this dialect is a series of inscriptions found in the territory of Falerii, which provide some phonological evidence linking it more closely to Latin than to the Oscan-Umbrian dialects (e.g., parallel treatment of labiovelars as *qu,* whereas in Oscan-Umbrian these are realized as *p,* and several other features). The most important Faliscan material is a fourth-century inscription on a cup found in Rome, *Foied vino pipafo cra carefo,* which in Classical Latin would be *hodiē vīnum bibam crās carebō* 'Today I will drink wine, tomorrow I will do without'. The material of Faliscan is far too scant to advance our knowledge of the Italic group very far, however, and it is of practically no value in the overall Indo-European picture.

2.1.2. Latin

As the most important cultural, hence linguistic, group in ancient Italy, the Romans left behind a vast treasure of linguistic resources. The oldest known monument of Latin, dating from the sixth century B.C., is the celebrated Praenestine fibula containing a brief inscription, *Manios med fhefhaked Numasioi* (= Lat. *Mānius mē fēcit Numeriō* 'Manius made me for Numerius'). This old inscription shows many archaic features characteristic of early Latin (nom. in *-os*, reduplicated perf. in the verb *fhefhaked*, older dat. in *-ōi*, among other things), but unfortunately it stands almost alone as a monument of the older period (and its authenticity has been seriously challenged; see Ridgway 1981). This so-called Praenestine Latin and representatives of other local varieties of older Latin do show some important differences from later Roman Latin (compare the following preliterary forms with their classical counterparts: *rēcei: rēgī* 'for the king'; *iouxmenta: iūmenta* 'beasts of burden'; *sakros: sacer* 'holy'), but for all practical purposes the first significant monuments of Latin are no older than the third century B.C. Among them we find abundant texts reflecting an earlier, pastoral society (Latin vocabulary is full of terms that reflect an early preoccupation with farming, e.g., *pecūnia* 'money'; cf. *pecus* 'cattle'). And the wealth of fairly continuous and linguistically consistent material that the emerging Latin literature provides, despite the fact that it is modeled largely on Greek, has been indispensable in the task of discovering the nature of the Indo-European parent language.

2.2.   A Brief Structural Sketch of Latin

2.2.1. Phonology

2.2.1.1. Vowels

Latin has a vocalic system similar to that of many other early Indo-European languages. It continues the Indo-European system of distinctive vowel length, utilizing a triangular vowel system. There are probably some phonetic differences between the long and short varieties besides the length, but I have ignored them here:

$$\breve{\bar{\imath}} \qquad \breve{\bar{u}}$$
$$\breve{\bar{e}} \qquad \breve{\bar{o}}$$
$$\breve{\bar{a}}$$

The diphthongs *ai* (later *ae*), *ei* (later *ī*), *oi* (later *ū*), *au, ou, eu* (later *ū*) round out the list of vowels.

One characteristic of Latin vowel phonology is the reduction of many vowels to *i* in certain unstressed environments (stress itself is not distinctive). A few examples are *faciō* 'do', *conficiō* 'complete', *cadō* 'fall', *occidō* 'beat', *ratus* 'reckoned', and *irritus* 'invalid'.

The Indo-European system of vowel gradation, or ablaut (best preserved in Greek verbal forms such as *pétomai* 'fly': *poté* 'flight'; *leípō: léloipa: élipon* 'leave, left', where the vowels *e, o,* and *ø* alternate in different grammatical environments; cf. also English forms such as *sing: sang: sung*), is in general greatly reduced. It is evident in its qualitative form in such Latin pairs as *tegō* 'cover': *toga* 'a covering'; *sequor* 'follow': *socius* 'associate'. The so-called quantitative ablaut system, based on differences in vowel length rather than quality is also greatly reduced and is recoverable in pairs such as *vocō* 'call': *vōx* 'voice', and some others. As a rule, Latin generalized one or the other of the original vowels in these pairs.

a. Semivowels. Latin has two semivowels (sounds that function as either vowels or consonants depending on phonetic environment). These are *y* and *w; j* is the typical written form of the consonantal variant of the former, *i* of the vowel; *v* frequently represents the consonant of the latter, *u* the vowel. A few examples of these are *jugum* 'yoke', *medius* 'middle', *vīdī* 'saw', *monuī* 'warned'.

2.2.1.2. Consonants

Latin has a fairly symmetrical consonantal system, which diverges from that of Indo-European primarily in its replacement of the aspirated series of consonants (**bh, *dh, *gh*) by a partial fricative series, as well as in certain other modifications. It takes the following form:

p	t	k	k^w
b	d	g	g^w
f	s	h	
m	n		
	l		
	r		

2.2.2. Morphology

Latin is distinguished by its highly developed inflectional system in both the noun and the verb. In matters of noun morphology, six cases are generally marked for each noun (nominative, genitive, dative, accusative, ablative, and vocative). A seventh case, the locative, is found in certain morpholexical classes and archaic forms (e.g., *domī* 'at home', *rūrī* 'in the country'). There are two numbers, singular and plural, with only relics of the earlier dual that is typically postulated for Indo-European (cf. *ambō* 'both', *duo* 'two', as well as dual pronoun types such as *uter* 'which of two?').

The Latin noun classes are divided into five inflectional groups, or declensions, each characterized by its own system of affixes. There are, in addition, three genders (masculine, feminine, and neuter) commonly associated with nouns on a partly natural, partly grammatical basis. Adjectives in Latin follow the same declensional patterns as nouns of the first three declensions.

The Latin verbal system is organized into four inflectional groups, or conjugations. All contain the same grammatical categories of voice, tense, aspect, and mood, their differences being based on purely formal matters. The primary divisions in the verb are aspectual, with a *perfectum,* or 'completed action', and an *infectum,* or 'noncompleted action'. There are also temporal distinctions within each aspect category of past, present, and future tense.

There are in addition three voices (reflecting the relationship of the subject to the action identified in the predicate). These are the active, passive, and middle, or deponent (see Baldi 1977a). The verb is further subdivided into four moods, the indicative, subjunctive, imperative, and infinitive. Derived forms such as the gerund, gerundive, and supine round out the verbal category.

2.2.3. Syntax

The system of syntax utilized in a language cannot possibly be captured in a few brief lines. Indeed, in highly inflected languages such as Latin and other members of the Indo-European family, because it is frequently difficult to determine the boundary between the syntax and the morphology, the job of a brief characterization is also made that much more difficult.

Latin is typologically an inflecting language, of course, wherein morphological endings signal most higher-order grammatical relations such as subject and object. Word order in Latin is for the most part free, though there is a statistical tendency toward Subject-Object-Verb (SOV) and the harmonic Noun-Adjective (Noun + Adj.) order. It is mostly prepositional, though a few postpositions survive in archaisms and in formulaic expressions (e.g., *mēcum* 'with me').

Probably the most distinctive feature of Latin syntax is its relative rigidity with respect to case selection and case functions. Where other languages show considerable flexibility as regards cases (for example, Sanskrit allows either the genitive or the dative to mark indirect object), Latin typically has only a single case in which constructions are realized (see Baldi 1977b, 1978).

A Sample Latin Text   2.3.

The following passage is taken from Cicero's *De Officiis* 1:122 and is offered to the reader as a representative sample of a connected text from Latin of the classical period (c. 90 B.C. to A.D. 14):

Est	igitur	adulescentis		maiores	natu
(It) is	therefore	(the duty) of a young man	those greater	with respect to age

vereri	exque	iis	deligere	optimos	et	probatissimos,
to respect	and from	them	to choose	the best	and	most approved

quorum	consilio	atque	auctoritate	nitatur;
of whom	by the counsel	and	authority	he might benefit

ineuntis	enim	aetatis	inscitia	senum	constituenda
of the beginning	for	of age	the ignorance	of the aged	strengthened

et	regenda	prudentia	est.
and	directed	by wisdom	is to be

'It is therefore the duty of a young man to respect his elders and to choose the best and most approved from among them, so that he might benefit from their counsel and authority. For the ignorance of youth must be strengthened and directed by the wisdom of elders.'

Oscan-Umbrian   2.4.

The origins of the Oscans and the Umbrians are extremely cloudy, and we shall have nothing to say on this issue. Though the two languages are by no means identical, Oscan and Umbrian are similar enough in matters of phonology, morphology, and syntax that we are certainly justified in grouping them together.

2.4.1. Oscan

Oscan (*lingua Osca*) is the name given by the Romans to the dialect spoken by the Osci in Campania. Our knowledge of the language is based almost entirely on about two hundred inscriptions from Campania, Samnium, northern Apulia, Lucania, Bruttium, and the city of Messana. The earliest, which are coin legends, may be as old as the fifth century B.C., but the bulk belongs to the period of 80–90 B.C. The most important Oscan document is the Tabula Bantina, which is a list of municipal regulations. After that, the Cippus Abellanus, which is another municipal document, provides the most data. Other evidence is in the form of private documents and military and election announcements. Oscan is held to be quite archaic (Buck 1928:18 calls it "the Gothic of the Italic dialects"), especially in its inherited vowel system.

2.4.2. Umbrian

Apart from scattered inscriptions, the principal source of ancient Umbrian data is the famous Iguvine Tables, a set of seven (originally nine) bronze tables discovered at Gubbio (ancient Iguvium) in the fifteenth century. The tables, which have been dated to the period 400–90 B.C., contain all together about four to five thousand words, including directions for and descriptions of various religious ceremonies performed by a group of priests called the Atiedian Brothers.

2.5.   A Brief Structural Sketch of Oscan and Umbrian

As mentioned above, Oscan and Umbrian are two distinct languages that show sufficient similarity to be grouped together. In the interest of brevity and clarity, I shall confine the structural discussion to features that characterize both languages. Following established practice, I shall present these features as they are contrasted with the corresponding Latin features.

2.5.1. Phonology

2.5.1.1. Vowels

Oscan-Umbrian has the same basic five-vowel system as Latin, marked by distinctive vowel length. But there are internal developments in both Oscan and Umbrian that are quite different from those in Latin, and it would therefore be imprecise to say that they are developmentally identical. The same is generally true of the diphthongal elements *ai, ei, oi, au, eu, ou,* except that in Umbrian all these have become monophthongs (cf. Lat. *quaestor,* Osc. *kvaísstur,* Umbr. *kvestur*).

While there are numerous internal developments in Oscan-Umbrian phonology which parallel those in Latin, there are many that are unknown in Latin. One major point of divergence between Oscan-Umbrian and Latin is the weakening of unstressed medial syllables mentioned in connection with Latin pairs such as *faciō: conficiō,* and so on. Such weakening is not found in Oscan-Umbrian, though syncope (complete loss of short vowels in medial syllables) is much more common (cf. Osc. *actud,* Lat. *agitō*). Overall, however, the accent system of Oscan-Umbrian is poorly understood.

As in Latin, the role of the Indo-European ablaut system is considerably diminished in both Oscan and Umbrian. In most cases the gradation can only be seen by comparison with Latin forms (cf. Umbr. *meřs* 'oath', Osc. *meddíss:* Lat. *modus, modestus*).

a. Semivowels. Though their internal distribution differs somewhat from that of Latin, the semivowels *y* and *w* with either vocalic or consonantal function are found in both Oscan and Umbrian.

2.5.1.2. Consonants

The consonantal systems of Oscan and Umbrian differ from that of Latin in several ways, mainly in the historical development of certain sounds from Indo-European. The major differences are the treatment of $*k^w$ and $*g^w$, which become *p* and *b,* respectively, in Oscan-Umbrian as opposed to *qu* and *u* (*gu* after *n*) in Latin. Cf. Osc. *pis,* Umbr. *pisi,* Lat. *quis* 'who'; Osc. *bivus,* Lat. *vīvī* 'living' (nom. pl. masc.); Umbr. *benust,* Lat. *venērit* 'will have come'. Other developments of earlier sounds and sound clusters distinguish Oscan-Umbrian from Latin, especially certain assimilations such as *ks* to *ss* and others (cf. Lat. *dextra est,* Osc. *destrst* 'it is right'). The overall consonantal system is as follows:

p	t	k	
b	d	g	
m	n		
f	s	h	z
	l		
	r		

2.5.2. Morphology

Oscan-Umbrian noun morphology is very similar to that found in Latin. There are five declensions (though the pattern in the Oscan-Umbrian third and fifth declensions is different from that of Latin), each showing the same cases as found in Latin, though with a more distinctive locative form.

On the matter of verb morphology, there is once again general agreement between Latin and Oscan-Umbrian, with four conjugations; there are some organizational differences, however, between the third and fourth conjugation verbs in each group. Moods, tenses, and voices are the same also, though the middle voice is not well developed in Oscan-Umbrian. There are also some gaps in the system of the Oscan-Umbrian verb, which may be accidental (e.g., the lack of a gerund category). Adjectives are inflected like nouns of the first three declensions, exactly as in Latin.

2.5.3. Syntax

Nearly all of the constructions common in Latin syntax are found in both Oscan and Umbrian. Very little variation in case usage occurs between the two subgroups, and though the syntactic evidence is on the whole scant, enough of it exists to recognize the general similarity to Latin. One interesting difference is that Umbrian has postpositions instead of the prepositions commonly found in Latin and Oscan: cf. Osc. *az hurtum* 'at the grove', Umbr. *asam-a* 'to the altar'.

2.6.   A Sample Oscan Text

The following brief text is from the Tabula Bantina (text and translation from Buck 1928:233–38).

Oscan:	Pr.,	suae	praefucus	pod	post	exac	Bansae	
Latin:	Praetor	sive	praefectus	(conj.)	post	hac	Bantiae	
English:	The Praetor	or	prefect		after	this	at Bantia	

fust,	suae	pis	op	eizois	com	atrud	ligud	acum
erit,	si	quis	apud	eos	cum	altero	lege	agere
will be	if	someone	before	them	with	another	to law	to conduct

herest,	auti	pru	medicatud	manim	aserum	eizazunc	egmazum
volet,	aut	pro	iudicato	manum	adserere	(de) eis	rebus
wishes,	or	for	judgment	the hand	to lay	on these	matters

pas	exaiscen		ligis	scriftas	set,	ne	phim
quae	hisce	in	legibus	scriptae	sunt,	ne	quem
which	these	in	laws	written	have been	not	which

pruhipid	mais	zicolois	x	nesimois.
prohibuerit	plus	diebus	x	proximis.
he shall prevent	more than	days	10	preceding

'The praetor, or if there shall be a prefect at Bantia after this, in case anyone wishes to go to law with another before them, or to make a forcible seizure, as if judgment had been rendered, on these matters which are written of in these laws, shall not prevent one for more than the ten preceding days.'

A Sample Umbrian Text   2.7.

The following brief text is from the Iguvine Tables, V A, 7–10 (text and translation from Buck 1928:260).

Umbrian:	Sakreu	perakneu	upetu,	revestu,	puře,
Latin:	Hostias	solemnis	deligito,	revisito,	cum
English:	Victims	sacrificial	let him select	let him inspect	when

teřte,	eru		emantur	herte,
datur,	(aliquae)	earum	accipiantur	oportetne,
they are given			they might be accepted	it is fitting or not

et	pihaklu	pune	tribřiçu	fuiest,	akrutu
et	piaculorum	cum	ternio	fiet	ex agro
and	of offerings	if	a triple	it should be	from the country

revestu	emantu	herte.
revisito	accipiantur	oportetne.
let him inspect	they might be accepted	it is fitting or not

'Let him select the sacrificial victims, and when they are given over let him inspect them to see if they are to be accepted, and in the case of a triple offering let him inspect them in the country to see if they are to be accepted.'

The Relationship of Oscan-Umbrian   2.8.
to Latin-Faliscan

How is Oscan-Umbrian related to Latin-Faliscan? This is a question of considerable controversy in Italic studies to which one can only provide the outlines of an argument. But it is sufficiently important in studies of Indo-European subgrouping (along with the issues of Indo-Iranian, Balto-Slavic, and Italo-Celtic) that it deserves some mention.

Since arguments based on ethnic and racial judgments are impossible to substantiate, for an assessment of the relationship we have little to depend on outside the linguistic correlations between Latin-Faliscan and Oscan-Umbrian. To be sure, the two groups are sufficiently similar to have long been considered different members of the same group, but they are also different enough to indicate that little or no mutual intelligibility occurred among speakers of the various dialects.

The traditional view of the relationship is that from a dialect of West Indo-European there split off a branch to be called Proto-Italic. From this branch, at a very early stage, Latin-Faliscan and Oscan-Umbrian split from each other. Thus, the similarities between the two groups are due to an early unity in Proto-Italic, and their differences are the result of the later linguistic divergence.

This view held for years, but in the 1940s a group of Italian linguists (neolinguists) proposed that the similarities between the two groups are not due to common origin, but rather to late linguistic and cultural interchange, and that the differences between the two are attributable to their separate origins in Indo-European. The neolinguistic position places a strong emphasis on the geographical component in language change, and this proposal is consistent with that view. But the larger issue is a more difficult one; that is, how does the historical linguist distinguish between common retention (archaism) and common innovation? This is a serious issue, and we shall see it recurring in other discussions of subgrouping below. In the case of Latin-Faliscan and Oscan-Umbrian, the view held by most is that the evidence is ambiguous and can be interpreted either way (cf. Beeler 1966). Sections 2.8.1 and 2.8.2 below constitute brief summaries of the major similarities and differences. (Note: Oscan-Umbrian forms are typically glossed by a Latin equivalent; I have supplied the English translations in these cases.)

2.8.1. Similarities

1. The spread of the ablative sg. in -*d* from -*o* stems to nouns of all five stem classes. Cf.

OLat. *eōd* 'him'	: Osc. *sakaraklúd*
	Lat. '*ā templō*' ('from the temple')
meritōd 'deservedly'	: Osc. *contrud*
	Lat. '*contrā*' ('against')
facilumēd 'easily'	
Falisc. *rected* 'rightly'	: Osc. *amprufid*
	Lat. '*improbē*' ('improperly')

OLat. *sententiād* 'opinion' : Osc. *toutad*
  (cf. Skt. *áśvād* 'horse')   Lat. *'ā populō'* ('by the people')

2. The organization of the nominal system into five inflectional categories, and the verb system into four.

3. The formation of the imperfect tense in **bhā-* (< PIE **bhuām* 'I was'), which stands alone in the Indo-European family. Cf. Osc. *fufans* 'they were' (**bh* > *f* in Osc.), Lat. *amābam* 'I was loving' (**bh* > *b* medially in Lat.). This is not universally accepted, however; *fufans* is the only example of this formation in Oscan-Umbrian, and it is a debated form. (The entire issue is recapitulated and discussed in Baldi 1976.)

4. The fusion of the aorist and perfect tenses—for example, Lat. *dīxī* (*dīc-s-ī*) 'I said': Umbr. *benust* Lat. *'venērit'* ('he will have come'). Cf. Gk. *epaídeusa* 'I taught'.

5. Fusion of the optative and subjunctive moods. In Latin the sole relic of the optative is *sim, sīs* (OLat. *siem, siēs*) 'be'.

6. The elimination of the PIE ablative in *-ās* in *-ā* stems, and its replacement with the *-d* from the *-o* stems. Cf. OLat. *sententiād* 'opinion', Osc. *dolud* Lat. *'dolō'* ('by deceit').

7. The specialized derivation of the relative pronoun from the interrogative. Cf. the following:

Lat. *quis, quid*   : Osc. *pis, pid* 'who, what' (interr.)
Lat. *quī, quae, quod* : Osc. *pui, pai, pud* 'who, which' (rel.)
Lat. *quisquis, quicquid* : Osc. *pispis, pitpid* 'whoever'

8. The formation of a gerundive in *-nd-*. Cf. Lat. *operandam*, Osc. *úpsannam* (*-nn-* < *-nd-*) 'must be carried out'.

9. The formation of an imperfect subjunctive in *-sē*. (Note: in Latin *VsV* > *VrV;* this is called *rhotacism*.) Cf. the following:

Lat. *foret* $\Big\}$ < **fusēd* 'he was' (subj.)
Osc. *fusíd*

10. The merger of the reflexes of **bh, *dh* as *f* in initial position. Cf. the following:

Lat. *frātrum* $\Big\}$
Umbr. *fratrum* $\Big\}$ 'brothers' (gen. pl.) < **bhrā́trōm*
Osc. *fratrum* $\Big\}$

Lat. *faciat* $\Big\}$
Osc. *fakiiad* $\Big\}$ 'will do' (< **dhə-*)
Umbr. *façia* $\Big\}$

11. General agreement of the verb 'to be': Lat. *sum,* Osc. *súm* (cf. Skt. *asmí*) 'I am'.

12. Dissimilation of the sequence *l . . . l* to *l . . . r.* Cf. Lat. *mīlit-āris* 'military' (cf. Lat. *cīv-īlis* 'civil', *mort-ālis* 'mortal'), Sab. *flusare* Lat. *'florali'* ('floral').

13. Agreement in the root **deik̄-* meaning 'say', which in other Indo-European languages means 'point out'. Cf. Gk. *deík-nūmi* 'show, point out': Lat. *dīcere,* Osc. *deíkum* 'say'.

14. Use of third-singular passive impersonally (but this also occurs in other Indo-European languages, notably Sanskrit and Celtic). Cf. Osc. *ferar* 'let one carry'; Lat. *ītur* 'one goes'.

2.8.2. Important Differences

1. Oscan-Umbrian retains the *-ās* of the nominal *-ā* stems in the nom. pl.; Latin replaces it with *-ae* (< *-āi*). Cf. Lat. *ārae:* Osc. *aasas* 'altar'.

2. Oscan-Umbrian retains the genitive in *-s* in *-o* stems, whereas Latin has *-ī.* Cf. Lat. *fīliī* 'son', Osc. *pukleis* 'son'.

3. Latin has a future tense formation from **bhū-* built on the analogy of the imperfect; Oscan-Umbrian has the future in *-s-.* Cf. Lat. *amābō* 'I will love', Umbr. *ferest* Lat. *'feret'* ('he will carry').

4. Latin has a future in *ā* (*ē*) in the third and fourth conjugation verbs (e.g., *regēs* 'you will rule'); Oscan-Umbrian lacks this formation.

5. Rhotacism (s > r/V__V), which occurs in Latin and Umbrian, does not occur in Oscan. Cf. the following:

> Lat. *amāre* (< **amā-se* 'love'; cf. *es-se*)
> Lat. *genus, generis* (< **genes-es*) 'race' (nom. and gen. sg.)
> Umbr. *erom* 'to be' ⎫
> Osc. *ezum* 'to be' ⎭ (< **es-om*)

6. The familiar Latin perfect in *-v-* (e.g., *amāvī* 'I have loved') is not found in Oscan-Umbrian, nor is the *-s-* perfect (e.g., *dīxī* 'I have said'). In Oscan-Umbrian a perfect in *-f-* is characteristic, though others are found as well. Cf. Osc. *aíkdafed* Lat. *'decrēvit'* ('it has decreased'), Umbr. *andirsafust* Lat. *'circum-tulerit'* ('he will have carried around').

7. The Latin infinitive in *-se* (cf. *es-se* 'to be') is matched in Oscan-Umbrian by a formation in *-om* (*-um*), unknown in Latin (Osc. *ez-um;* Umbr. *er-om* 'to be').

8. Treatment of PIE labiovelars:

(a) *k^w > Lat. *qu;* Oscan-Umbrian *p*
  Lat. *quanta* : Osc. *panta* 'how much'
     quis   :   *pis* 'who' (interr.)
     quī   :   *pui* 'who' (rel.)

(b) *g^w > Lat. *w* (initially): Oscan-Umbrian *b*
  Lat. *veniō* 'I come' : Osc. *benust* Lat. *'venērit'* ('he will have come')

9. Certain very important lexical differences:

(a) Osc. *toutā*   : Lat. *cīvitas* 'state, people'
    (cf. Goth. *þiuda*)

(b) Osc. *puklo-*   : Lat. *fīlius* 'son' (< *$dh\bar{e}$- 'nourish, suckle':
    (cf. Skt. *putrá-*)   cf. *fēmina* 'woman')

(c) Osc. *fuutreí*   : Lat. *fīlia* 'daughter' (cf. *fīlius* 'son')
    (cf. Skt. *duhitár-*)

(d) Umbr. *utur*   : Lat. *aqua* 'water' (cf. Goth. *ahwa*)
    (cf. Gk. *húdōr*)

The Romance Languages   2.9.

The Italic family continues in strength today, though in highly altered form. Now known collectively as the Romance languages (with its own field of comparative Romance), the modern descendents of Latin are French (first attested in mid-eighth century), Italian (tenth century), Provençal (eleventh century), Spanish, Catalan, and Portuguese (tenth and eleventh centuries), Rumanian (sixteenth century), plus the so-called minor Romance languages—Sardinian, Rhaeto-Romansch, and the now extinct Dalmatian. Since the information on the Romance languages is readily available, we shall not discuss them further.

References

I. Grammars and Historical Works

Buck 1928
Buck 1933
Conway 1967
Conway et al. 1933
Ernout 1961
Giacomelli 1963
Kent 1945
Kent 1946
Leumann 1977
Lindsay 1894
Meillet 1928
Meillet and Vendryes 1927
Palmer 1954
Pisani 1960–1964
Poultney 1959

Sommer 1914   Von Planta 1892–1897
Vetter 1953   Whatmough 1937

II. Dictionaries

Ernout and Meillet 1968
Hofmann 1930–1956
Thesaurus Linguae Latinae 1904–

III. Works Cited in the Text

Baldi 1976   Beeler 1966
Baldi 1977a   Buck 1928
Baldi 1977b   Ridgway 1981
Baldi 1978

Celtic   3

Introduction   3.0.

Relatively unknown until the modern period, the Celtic languages make up an important branch of the Indo-European family. The early Celts probably had their beginnings in Central Europe, and owing to their apparent restlessness and bellicosity, they spread out across the continent at an early stage. We have clear references to Celts as early as the fifth century B.C., and it is reasonably certain that they were firmly established in Italy at that time. When Caesar subjugated them in the Gallic Wars, the decline of their linguistic empire on the continent was begun; by the fourth century A.D., Celtic had been largely eliminated from the Roman area.

Those Celts who had made their way to Britain fared considerably better. They maintained themselves there well into the tenth century A.D., when their languages were largely displaced by the advancing Germanic tribes known as Angles, Jutes, and Saxons. But by this time the Celts were firmly enough entrenched in some of the outer reaches of Britain that some of the languages have survived to modern times.

It is customary to divide the Celtic languages into two groups based upon a typological bifurcation between those languages in which PIE *k^w developed as a velar (the so-called q-Celtic, or Goidelic) and those in which it was realized as a labial (p-Celtic, Brythonic, or Brittanic).

Goidelic (or Gaelic)   3.1.

The ancient people who spoke Goidelic called themselves Goídil, and their language Goídelg. It is not known at exactly what point in history the Goidelic-speaking Celts arrived in Ireland, and, interestingly, the language is never referred to as Irish. The most important sources of the ancient Goidelic (and of all

Celtic) are a variety of manuscripts written in Old Irish dating from the late seventh to early eighth century A.D. Older than these are the three hundred or so sepulchral inscriptions written in a special alphabet called the Ogam script, which have been dated to the fourth century A.D.

We generally speak of three distinct languages within Goidelic: Irish, Scots Gaelic, and Manx.

3.1.1. Irish

As mentioned, Old Irish provides our oldest records of Celtic. It is customary to divide Irish into three periods: Old Irish (up to about 850), Middle Irish (from 900 to about 1450), and Modern Irish (since about 1475). Our principal sources of information on Old Irish are many glosses in Latin manuscripts, where the Irish is interspersed within the Latin text. The most important of these are the Würzburg Glosses, which are glosses on a Latin text of the Epistles of St. Paul preserved at Würzburg. They are dated to approximately the eighth century A.D. In addition, there are the Milan Glosses, which are glosses on a Latin commentary on the Psalms and which stem from the ninth century. These glosses constitute the largest amount of information on Old Irish. The Turin Glosses and glosses from other locations round out the oldest data from Old Irish.

3.1.2. Scots Gaelic

The Celtic dialect Scots Gaelic was introduced into the Scottish Highlands by Irish settlers in the sixth century A.D.

3.1.3. Manx

Formerly spoken on the Isle of Man, Manx is now extinct, having been ousted by English from England.

3.2.   Brythonic (Brittanic)

Those Celts who settled in Britain, perhaps as early as the fifth century B.C., established a variety of Celtic known as Brythonic, or Brittanic. Like the Goidelic, it is divided into three language groups: Welsh, Cornish, and Breton.

3.2.1. Welsh

Probably our most important source for the Brythonic group, Welsh is the language of Wales. It is also known as Cymric, from the Welsh *Cymraeg*. The three commonly identified periods are Old Welsh (from the earliest records, about A.D. 800 to the twelfth century), Middle Welsh (twelfth to the sixteenth century), and Modern Welsh (from the sixteenth century to the present).

3.2.2. Cornish

Though Cornwall ceased to be an independent kingdom about A.D. 900, Cornish continued to be spoken until the late seventeenth century. When the last speaker died at the age of 102 in 1777, Cornish became extinct. Old Cornish dates to about the twelfth century A.D.

3.2.3. Breton

Introduced into the northwest corner of modern-day France by Celtic invaders from the fifth century onward, Breton is quite closely related to Cornish. Old Breton, which dates from about 800 B.C., is known only in glosses and early charters. Middle Breton (ca. A.D. 1100–1600) is represented in continuous texts only from about 1500. Modern Breton dates from about the seventeenth century and is maintained against the dominant French only by strong regional and nationalistic loyalties.

To these three we must add the poorly known Gaulish, which is a collective term used for the languages of the Celtic tribes in the two Gauls (*Gallia Cisalpīna* and *Gallia Transalpīna*), in the Iberian peninsula, in Galatia in Asia Minor, and in central Europe. (The Celtic monuments in the Iberian peninsula have motivated some scholars to propose an earlier "Celto-Iberian"; these have been augmented by some recent discoveries in Botorrita. "Celto-Iberian" is now a common, if imprecise, term in the Celtic literature.) Despite their wide geographical distribution, these languages are known only from fifty or so short inscriptions found chiefly in France. One of these languages, dating from the second century B.C., is often referred to as Lepontic; it is definitely Indo-European, but with questionable Celtic affinities. Also to be mentioned here is the poorly attested Pictish, which is known only from a few proper names found in the north of Britain.

The division of the two main Celtic groups into *q* and *p* Celtic is based, as already mentioned, on the development of the PIE labiovelar $*k^w$. In the Goidelic branch $*k^w$ is realized as a velar, whereas in Brythonic its reflex is a labial. Cf., for example, OIr. *cīa*, Welsh *pwy* (Lat. *quis*, Skt. *ká*- 'who'). This division has had a long-lasting effect on Celtic studies and has even been advanced as part of a wider hypothesis concerning the alleged special relationship between Italic and Celtic. (The issue will be taken up in 3.5.)

3.3.   A Brief Structural Sketch of Old Irish

3.3.1. Phonology

3.3.1.1. Vowels

Old Irish maintains in general the Indo-European system of vowels with a triangular system made up of long and short varieties:

One of the most important features of Old Irish phonology relative to the development of the vocalic system is the heavy expiratory stress on the first syllable of the word. This accent has caused a great deal of vocalic reduction in unstressed syllables, changing the quality of the unstressed vowels so that it is difficult to compare them with those of the other Indo-European languages. For comparative purposes the stressed Old Irish vowels correspond quite regularly to those of, say, Greek or Latin (cf. OIr. *māthir*, Lat. *māter* 'mother'; OIr. *ŏcht*, Lat. *octo* 'eight'; and so on). But unstressed vowels in all positions have undergone such radical changes (including general loss of final vowels) that their correspondences with the cognate languages are much more difficult to establish; cf. OIr. *fir* 'men' (nom. pl.), Lat. *virī* (both from *wirī*).

3.3.1.2. Consonants

Despite its differences from the postulated vowel system of Proto-Indo-European, especially in unstressed syllables, the vocalic system of Old Irish is very conservative indeed when compared to the system of the consonants. There are three major internal developments of Old Irish consonant phonology: lenition, nasalization, and gemination. Each of these marks the consonants of Old Irish as radically different from those of the proto-language.

a. Lenition. Lenition is the mutation of consonants in medial and initial positions caused by the preceding vowel. The mutations are realized in many different ways according to the sound affected and the exact phonetic environment of that sound. Lenition is best understood as a process of articulatory weakening as a result of which the articulation of a sound is laxer in certain phonetic environments.

Lenited forms are often very difficult to determine from the Old Irish texts because they are not always represented by special symbols. For example, the stops *p, t, k (c)* are marked orthographically by *ph, th, ch* in their lenited forms (representing the fricatives [f θ χ]). But while the stops *b, d, g* become the fricatives [β ð γ], they have no special written symbols.

Another difficulty is encountered in attempting to detect the historical origin of lenited forms. In the case of medial consonants, lenition was often conditioned by vowels, which were subsequently lost because of other changes and which can only be reconstituted on the basis of comparative and internal reconstruction. When we add to this the fact that, in the case of initial consonants, lenition is conditioned by the final sound of the preceding word (cf. *du·air-chēr* 'I have purchased', *crenaid* 'buys'), we see why lenition has provided a phonological riddle of considerable complexity in Indo-European and Celtic linguistics.

The Old Irish consonantal system contains eleven consonantal pairs, represented below in their lenited and unlenited form. (Note: unless a special symbol is available, a dot over a sound indicates its lenited form.)

k (ch)	t (th)	p (ph, f)
g (γ)	d (ð)	b (β)
	n (ṅ)	m (w̄)
	l (l̇)	
	r (ṙ)	
	s (h)	

b. Gemination. Yet another unusual feature of Old Irish consonantal phonology is gemination. As the name indicates, gemination refers to the doubling of consonants in certain phonetic environments in order to indicate that the consonant is not lenited (e.g., *ammann* for *amman* 'names', from the Würzburg Glosses). It occurs in specific lexical combinations (e.g., after certain pronouns, case-forms, verb-forms, and other disparate elements). There are also large numbers of geminated consonants that have been inherited from earlier patterns, which have in turn been assimilated (e.g., *attach* 'entreaty' < *ad-tech*).

A great deal of fluctuation and uncertainty is apparent in the attested Old Irish literature concerning the entire gemination process. The unpredictability of forms, when taken with the fact that Modern Irish has greatly simplified the geminates, strongly suggests that gemination was weakening as a phonological process even during the very early period of Old Irish.

c. Nasalization. The final phonological feature characteristic of Old Irish consonants is nasalization. Nasalization itself is a relatively common assimilatory phenomenon found in a wide variety of languages; its realization in Old Irish, however, is somewhat different from that of other languages, such as modern French, in which nasalization is very common. In Old Irish, initial sounds are modified by final nasal consonants from the preceding word. By this process such changes as *p, t, k* → *b, d, g* or *b, d, g* → *mb, nd, ŋg* (voiced stops preceded by the homorganic nasal) take place. The many restrictions and peculiarities associated with Old Irish nasalization are of interest only to the specialist, but the process is particularly interesting to the generalist in light of the frequent weakening of word boundaries so commonly associated with phonological change and abundantly clear in the Old Irish nasalization (cf. *inmain n·aim* 'dear the name': *ainm* 'name').

3.3.2. Morphology

Old Irish noun declension is in general representative of the early Indo-European system of nominal inflection. The three gender system of masculine, feminine, and neuter familiar from Greek, Latin, Sanskrit, and elsewhere is found in the language, though it is obvious from the time of the oldest texts in Old Irish that many phonological and analogical developments had served to reduce the overall number of discrete endings marking gender. Also represented are the three numbers of singular, plural, and dual. It is interesting to note that the dual number is always accompanied by some form of the numeral *dāu* 'two'.

Five cases can be distinguished for Old Irish: nominative, genitive, dative, accusative, and vocative, all with uses familiar from other Indo-European languages. But though the cases are modest in number, the number of distinguishable declensional groups is very large, with thirteen main classes of nouns and a fourteenth for irregulars and indeclinables. The classification of nouns is based on the final sound of the stem, with seven members in the vocalic group and seven in the consonantal group (including the irregulars). Adjectives are on the whole based on nouns of the vocalic group and are organized into five classes.

Verbs in Old Irish are classified according to so-called strong and weak categories. Strong verbs are primary (i.e., not derived from nouns or adjectives), whereas weak verbs are denominative or deadjectival. Weak verbs have a characteristic morphology that distinguishes them from the strong verbs.

The Old Irish verb contains fully developed active and passive voices. Within the active is also a so-called deponent category, characterized by the ending -r familiar from Latin verbs of the same name. But whereas in Latin the deponent is more closely associated with the passive and, to the extent that it survives, the middle voice, in Old Irish the deponent belongs with the active voice. The origin of the -r itself is a vexed question in Indo-European studies. Examples of deponents are OIr. *labrithir*, Lat. *loquitur* 'speaks'.

Three moods are distinguished in the Old Irish verb: the indicative, the imperative, and the subjunctive. In addition, there are five tenses: present, imperfect, preterite, future, and secondary future, or conditional. Not all of these tenses occur in all moods, however. Several of the tenses are characterized by different forms according to whether they are absolute (standing alone) or conjunct (compounded or prefixed). Cf. *lēicmi* (absolute), *-lecem* (conjunct) 'we leave'.

3.3.3. Syntax

Old Irish syntax is very complex, though such a statement is purely relative and evaluative. When it is compared with the syntactic patterns of other Indo-European languages, several distinguishing characteristics stand out. Chief among these is the syntax of the Old Irish pronominal system, where there is significant divergence from the structures found in the other languages. Most pronominal elements in Old Irish are found only in reduced form, and these typically function as proclitics or enclitics (i.e., they are attached directly to the verb). To these are frequently added enclitic particles of emphasis (e.g., *guid-mi-ni(pray-we-emph)* 'we pray'). Another distinguishing characteristic of pronominal syntax is the use of infixed pronouns, which are always unstressed and severely reduced in form. Cf. *ro-m·gab* 'he has taken me' (*m* < *mē* 'me').

Prepositions are used extensively in Old Irish and can be

piled up together to form multiple prepositions. Cf., for example, *comtherchomracc* 'assembly', from *com-to-er-com-ro* and *icc-*, lit. 'with-to-before-with-perfective-come'.

Still another feature of Old Irish syntax is its word order. Quite in contrast with the other Indo-European languages, Old Irish has the order Verb-Subject-Object (VSO) in unmarked constructions. Why this is so is not known; most of the older Indo-European languages have either SOV or SVO word order. It is possible that the VSO order found in early Celtic was brought about as the result of contact with people who spoke a VSO language, perhaps one of the Afro-Asiatic (Hamito-Semitic) family. In any case, the VSO order of Old Irish has the attendant harmonic structures characteristic of VSO languages (e.g., Noun + Adj. and Noun + Gen. orders).

Old Irish also uses large numbers of what are called verbal nouns. These are nouns in form but have the force of verbs and even take objects, usually in the genitive case. These structures correspond for the most part to infinitives in the other Indo-European languages.

3.4.   Sample Old Irish Texts

3.4.1. Glosses

Glosses play such an important role in the Old Irish tradition that a few should be presented here as examples. The three glosses below all appear in the Würzburg Glosses (from Strachan-Bergin 1970:103):

1. Würzburg 12^{c}29:

nī	ar	formut	frib-si	as-biur-sa	in so
not	because of	envy	to you	I say	this

'I say this not because of envy toward you.'

2. Würzburg 14^{d}26:

is	i	persin	Crīst	d-a-gnīu-sa	sin
(it) is	in	person	of Christ	I do it	that

'It is in the person of Christ that I do that.'

3. Würzburg 21^{a}8:

is	hed	in so	no	guidimm
(it) is	it	this	part.	I ask

'It is this which I ask.'

3.4.2. A Short Sample of Old Irish Prose

The following selection is from the TÁIN BÓ CÚALNGE, "The Cattle-Raid of Cooley." The TÁIN represents the heroic saga, which is one of the most important literary forms of ancient Irish. The TÁIN itself may be as old as the middle of the seventh century; it certainly existed by the first half of the eighth century. The manuscript in which it is found is from about 1100. In the passage below we find a description of a band of armed men (text and translation from O'Rahilly 1967: 5, 142, lines 161–64):

In   lorg   tánaise   berrtha   núa   léo.   Bruitt   forglassa   uli   impu.
The   band   second   shorn   new   of them   coats   grey   all   about them

Lēnti   glēgela   fria   cnessaib.   Claidib   co   muleltaib
shirts   pure white   against   their skins   swords   with   round guards

ōir   ⅂   co   n-imdurnib   argait   léo.   "Inn   ē   Cormac
of gold   and   with   handles   silver   on them.   interr.part.   he   Cormac

sūt?"   for   cāch.   "Nād   ē   omm,"   bar   Medb.
yonder   asked   each   not   he   indeed   said   Medb

'The second band had newly shorn heads of hair. They wore grey cloaks and pure white shirts next to their skins. They carried swords with round guards of gold and silver handles. "Is that Cormac yonder?" they all asked. "It is not indeed," said Medb.'

Italo-Celtic   3.5.

At an early period in comparative linguistics, it was proposed that there exists a special relationship between the Italic and Celtic languages. This special relationship, dubbed Italo-Celtic, is suggested by a series of features shared by the Italic and Celtic languages, frequently to the exclusion of the rest of the Indo-European stocks. Those who support the Italo-Celtic premise argue that these shared characteristics point to common innovations and, according to established procedure in the comparative method, are thus reflective of a period of unity. Those who oppose the notion of Italo-Celtic point to the paucity of data, as well as to the relative lack of importance of the shared features in the total language systems. Basically, we are faced here with difficult methodological questions: What conclusions can we draw when two related languages share a series of similar features? How do we judge the importance of these features? Does similarity always reflect common innovation? Can we always distinguish common innovations, which are extremely important, from common retentions, which imply nothing? What about 'negative innovations' (degree of divergence)?

The following is a somewhat selective list of similarities between the Italic and Celtic languages (from Meillet 1922 [1967: 49–58]):

1. The shift of the PIE sequence $*p \ldots k^w$ to $k^w \ldots k^w$ in Latin and Goidelic. Cf. Lat. *quīnque*, OIr. *cōic* ($< *pe\eta k^w e$ 'five'). Here we should expect Lat. *$*pīnque$* and OIr. *$*ōic$* (initial *$*p$* is lost in Celtic).

2. The parallel development of PIE $°r, °l$ as *ar, al* in both stocks (° stands for a 'half vowel') differing from their treatment of $\underset{.}{r}, \underset{.}{l}$ (syllabic *r* and *l*), which gave *or, ol* in Latin, *ri, li* in Celtic. Cf. OIr. *scaraim* 'I separate', Welsh *ysgar* 'separation', Lat. *cāro*, Umbr. *karu* 'flesh', Umbr. *kartu* Lat. *'distribūtio'* ('distribution').

3. Both represent the genitive singular of *o* stems as *-ī*, quite in contrast with the normal PIE *$*-osyo$*. Cf. here Lat. *virī* 'of the man', Ogam Ir. *magi* 'of the son', Gaul. *Segomari* (gen. of *Segomaros*). By contrast, cf. Skt. *áśvasya* 'of the horse'.

4. (a) They share the medio-passive ending in *-r*, which has taken the place of the normal primary endings *$*-mai$* (1st sg.), *$*tai$* (3rd sg.) (cf. Gk. *hépetai* 'he follows'). Note here Lat. *loquitur* (3rd sg.), *loquimur* (1st pl.), OIr. *labrithir* (3rd sg.), *labrimmir* (1st pl.) 'speak'. (b) They both use the *-r* for an impersonal passive. Cf. Lat. *ītur* 'one goes', Umbr. *ferar* 'let one carry', OIr. *berir* 'one carries', Welsh *gweler* 'one sees'.

5. Irish and Latin have two subjunctive forms in common: one in *ā* (cf. Lat. [1st sg.] *feram*, OIr. [1st sg.] *bera* 'carry', both with shortening of the final vowel); and one in *s*, OIr. (1st sg.) *tīasu*, (3rd sg.) *tēis* 'go', Lat. (1st sg.) *dīxim* 'say', (1st sg.) *faxim* 'do'.

6. The Italic future in *-b-* may correspond to the Irish future in *-b-* and *-f-*. Cf. Lat. *amābō* 'I will love', Falisc. *carefo* 'I will do without', OIr. *labrafammar* 'we shall speak'. This correspondence, however, is usually rejected (but see Bammesberger 1979).

7. There is a correspondence between the two in certain superlative formations in *$*-samo$*. Cf. Lat. *māximus* 'greatest', Osc. *nessimas* Lat. *'proximae'* ('closest'), OIr. *nessam*, Welsh *nesaf* 'nearest'.

8. They both make use of the nominal suffix *$*-tei(n)$*, as found in Lat. *nātio* (nom.), *nātiōnis* (gen.), Umbr. *natine* (abl.) 'nation', OIr. *toimtiu* (gen. *toimten*) 'thought'.

9. There is also a list of lexical correspondences, some of which are listed here:

Lat. *dē:* OIr. *dī,* Breton *di* 'from'
Lat. *cum:* OIr. *com-* 'with'
Lat. *īmus:* OIr. *ís,* Welsh *isel* 'below'
Lat. *pectus:* OIr. *ucht* 'chest'
Lat. *terra:* OIr. *tír* 'earth'
Lat. *veru:* Umbr. *berus* (abl. pl.): OIr. *bir,* Breton *ber* 'dart, spit'

Not included here are a few other similarities (the total is about eleven).

This outline of the evidence for Italo-Celtic provides a skeleton of the argument. The entire notion has been severely criticized, especially by Watkins (1966; but see Cowgill 1970). All things considered, the evidence seems rather meager and cannot be considered as secure as for other groups, for example, Indo-Iranian. The phonological evidence is surely the weakest, with the lexical correlations a close second. The morphological data are interesting and suggestive, but they must be placed in the perspective of the total language system.

One final word needs to be said before we leave Italo-Celtic, and that refers to the prehistories of these two stocks and the earlier dialect divisions. The careful reader may have noticed that there is a parallel development in Oscan-Umbrian and Brythonic in their treatment of PIE $*k^w$ ($> p$). A similar correlation can be made between Latin-Faliscan and Goidelic, where $*k^w > q(u)$. In the early twentieth century it was asserted that this distribution reflected an earlier unity for these two divisions and that Oscan-Umbrian-Brythonic and Latin-Faliscan-Goidelic should be treated as earlier historical entities. This position has won few adherents and is not widely followed.

References

I. Grammars and Historical Works

Evans 1964
Fleuriot 1964
Lehmann and
    Lehmann 1975
Lewis and Pedersen
    1937
Pedersen 1909–1913
Thurneysen 1946

II. Dictionaries

Holder 1961–1962   Marstrander et al.
Joynt et al. 1939–   1913–
                                      Vendryes 1959–1960

III. Italo-Celtic

Cowgill 1970
Meillet 1922 [1967:49–58]
Watkins 1966

IV. Celto-Iberian

Schmidt 1976

V. Works Cited in the Text

Bammesberger 1979   Strachan (-Bergin)
Cowgill 1970   1949 [1970]
Meillet 1922 [1967]   Watkins 1966
O'Rahilly 1967

Indo-Iranian (Indo-Aryan)   4

Introduction   4.0.

The Indo-Iranian group occupies a special position in the Indo-European family for several important reasons. First and foremost, it provides for us, in the form of Vedic Sanskrit and Avestan, some of the oldest and most extensive documents available in the Indo-European family. Second, it is the only group that directly attests to a period of common development between two branches of the Indo-European family, namely, Indic and Iranian. Because of this extensive documentation we are in an excellent position to claim detailed knowledge of the Indo-Iranian group, especially Sanskrit. And the elaborate structure of Sanskrit has formed the basis for a great deal of what we know about the Indo-European parent language.

The term 'Indo-Iranian' indicates the two main branches of the subgroup. The term 'Aryan' alone is often used to designate the Indic branch, and it is actually the word *Aryan* itself that provides the direct evidence of the prehistoric unity of the Indic and Iranian branches. In Sanskrit *ár(i)ya-* designates speakers of Vedic Sanskrit; in Avestan *airya-* was the name by which the speakers of Avestan designated themselves. In fact, the genitive plural of this name — 'of the Aryans' — is the name of the country of Iran. The Indic and Iranian branches split off from each other at a very early stage in prehistory, certainly before 1500 B.C.

Indic (Aryan)   4.1.

4.1.1. Old Indic

Following nineteenth-century tradition, we customarily divide the Indic languages into three periods: Old, Middle, and Modern. The oldest language in the Indic group, and indeed of all Indo-Iranian, is Vedic Sanskrit (*samskṛta* 'cultivated, polished').

The oldest Vedic material is the Ṛgveda, which is usually dated to 1200–1000 B.C. (though not in written form until much later). The Vedic literature is made up primarily of the four Vedas (*Ṛgveda, Sāmaveda, Yajurveda,* and *Atharvaveda*), though ample literature from other sources exists as well, especially the *Prātiśākhyas,* which are detailed and extremely accurate phonetic texts composed by grammarians to insure the correct pronunciation of the religious Vedas. The *Prātiśākhyas* are thus of great importance, not only in the Indian grammatical tradition, but also for the history of linguistics. Also included in the Vedic or preclassical period are the *Brāhmaṇas* and the *Sūtras,* both of which deal with matters of religion and ritual.

Classical Sanskrit is quite close to Vedic, principally because it was so closely regulated in the priestly tradition for religious purposes. Classical Sanskrit was codified in the fifth century B.C. by the grammarian Pāṇini in his monumental *Aṣṭādhyāyī* 'the eight chapters'. This highly abstract and algebraic grammar, which is based on earlier work that has not been preserved, is the object of enduring and serious scholarship both in India and in the West; in effect, the *Aṣṭādhyāyī* fixed the form of Sanskrit and prohibited further change. Most of the literature in the classical period was composed well after Pāṇini, with the exception of the two epics the *Mahābhārata* and the *Rāmāyana,* which are thought to have been composed around Pāṇini's time. These two are the main representatives of Epic Sanskrit and fit between the Vedas and the true classical literature, which comes possibly as late as A.D. 450. With such a considerable passage of time, certain changes made the classical language somewhat different from the Vedic. But these changes must be considered minor in the face of changes during comparable periods in the histories of other languages.

4.1.2. Prakrit

Sanskrit is distinguished from the speech of the masses, Prakrit (*Prākṛta* commonly glossed as 'unrefined'). Prakrit has the same remoter origins as Sanskrit, but whereas Sanskrit was fixed and codified, Prakrit evolved in a more normal way and eventually gave rise to the numerous later Indic dialects. The term 'Prakrit' is often used as a synonym for 'Middle Indic', but this designation is not technically correct.

4.1.3. Middle Indic (Pāli, Middle Prakrit, and Apabhramśa)

Middle Indic is frequently divided into three groups, Old, Middle, and Modern. The old period is represented chiefly by Pāli in a series of Buddhist religious documents. Other dialects are represented in the inscriptions of Aśoka (c. 250 B.C.). Middle Prakrit, which is sometimes referred to as Standard Literary Prakrit, is dated to the second century A.D. and is represented largely by Jainist religious writings in Jaina-Prakrit, and by some lyric and epic poetry in Mahārāṣṭrī. The late, or Modern, group is first represented in Apabhramśa from about the tenth century A.D.

4.1.4. Modern Indic

Nowhere else in the Indo-European family do we find such a bewildering display of modern languages that, though clearly related, often defy precise classification. This is largely due to the nature of the Indian subcontinent itself, with a predominantly rural and still largely illiterate population. Also to be considered is the significant influence on the local languages from the non-Indic languages of the region, particularly Persian, and the non-Indo-European Dravidian and Munda (Austro-Asiatic) languages. Since the precise classification of the Indic languages is of concern chiefly to the Indo-Iranian specialist, we shall proceed here with a simple partial listing: Sindhi, Lahnda, Panjabi, Gujarati, Rajasthani, Marathi, Hindi, Bihari, Oriya, Nepali, Bengali, Assamese, Sinhalese, Maldivian, Romany (Gypsy), and Urdu. Hindi and Urdu are essentially the same language, with the distinction that Hindi is spoken by Hindus and is written in the Nagari script, whereas Urdu is spoken chiefly by Muslims and is written in the Arabic script; there are also considerable lexical differences. The common language has been called Hindustani, though this name has fallen into disuse in recent years.

A Brief Structural Sketch of Sanskrit   4.2.

As mentioned above, evidence from the Indo-Iranian branch of Indo-European has had a considerable influence on our view of the proto-language. The reason for this, besides its great antiquity, lies chiefly in the fact that Sanskrit is far and away the most elaborately structured language of the entire family. In matters of phonology, word formation, and syntax, no other Indo-European language can lay claim to such richness of structure. Rightly or not (and many would say not), this richness had led many scholars to place particularly heavy emphasis on the Sanskrit evidence in the reconstruction of Proto-Indo-European. Such emphasis is based not only on the solid comparative evidence for a morphologically rich Proto-Indo-European available from the other stocks (especially Greek, Latin, Baltic, and Slavic), but also on the methodological principle that it is simpler to account for parallel losses in the less complex languages than it is to establish parallel innovations in the more elaborate ones. This constitutes a difficult issue, one that cannot be resolved in a volume such as this. But the reader should be alerted to the difficulties which inhere in argumentation of this sort. (See Polomé 1979 for a lucid discussion of the issues.)

4.2.1. Phonology

Sanskrit phonology is remarkably elaborate in comparison with that of most of the other stocks. It contains many functional distinctions lacking in the others, and it has lost some distinctions as well—for example, that between plain velar (k) and labiovelar (k^w), both realized as k. The innovations are due partly to internal phonological innovations—for example, the development of voiceless aspirates such as *ph*, *th*, and so on—and partly to language contact such as the development of a retroflex (retracted) series *ṭ*, *ḍ*, *ṇ*, and so on, under the influence of neighboring Dravidian languages.

4.2.1.1. Vowels

Vowels in Sanskrit are distinguished by the feature of length (long vs. short) as well as by the feature of diphthongization (simple vs. diphthongal). The vowels are as follows:

Simple Vowels	a	ā
	i	ī
	u	ū
	ṛ	ṝ
	ḷ	ḹ
Diphthongs	e	āi (ai)
	o	āu (au)

A crucial feature of many morphemes is root-vowel gradation, or ablaut. As we have noted, Proto-Indo-European made use
of two types of gradation, one based on vowel quality and one
based on vowel quantity. The qualitative ablaut was built primarily on the alternation $e : o : \phi$ in certain morphological environments (recall Gk. *pétomai* 'fly': *potḗ* 'flight', etc.). But in the
history of Sanskrit there occurred a change in the vowel system
that had a monumental effect on the overall structure of that system: in Sanskrit the Indo-European vowels *ĕ, *ŏ, *ă all merged
together as ă (phonetically this can be seen as a process of cen-
tralization, but I shall not attempt to describe it further). Thus
note the following correspondences:

Lat. *fert:* Gk. *phérei:* Skt. *bhárati* 'carries' (*e)
Lat. *mensis* (< *mēnsis): Gk. *mēn,* Skt. *mā́s-* 'month' (*ē)

Lat. *ovis:* Gk. *óis* (< *owis): Skt. *ávi-* 'sheep' (*o)
Lat. *ōcior:* Gk. *ōkús* 'swifter': Skt. *āśú-* 'swift' (*ō)

Lat. *ager:* Gk. *agrós* 'field': Skt. *ájra-* 'plain' (*a)
Lat. *māter:* Gk. (Dor.) *mā́tēr:* Skt. *mātár-* 'mother' (*ā)

This merger, of course, completely destroyed the Indo-European
qualitative ablaut system, though there is ample evidence that the
system was at one time operative. For example, the root *han-*
'slay' is related to the Gk. *phónos* 'murder', OIr. *geguin,* and reflects Indo-European $*g^wh$ (which merged with $*g^h$ in Sanskrit).
The normal development of $*g^h$, g^wh in Sanskrit is *h* before front
vowels and *gh* before back vowels. The presence of forms such as
the perfect participle *jaghanvā́ṅs* with *gh* reflects an earlier *o in
this form of the verb. That is, *han-* is from *ghen- and *(ja)ghan-* is
from *ghon- (*e : o*).

But, whereas the qualitative ablaut can only be recovered
through comparative and internal reconstruction, the system of
quantitative gradation is fully productive in the language. This
quantitative system, called by the native grammarians the *guṇa*
(full grade) and *vṛddhi* (lengthened grade), characterizes virtually
every word in the language, especially in derived forms. Different
derivational and inflectional forms are marked by different vowel
lengths dictated by the *guṇa* and *vṛddhi* increments. The system
appears in the language as follows. (Note: the Indian grammarians' description of this system differs organizationally from that
of traditional Indo-European scholarship, in which the *guṇa* form
is considered basic.)

Simple vowel	∅(a)	ā	i	ī	u	ū	ṛ	ḷ
guṇa ('secondary quality')	a	ā		e		o	ar	al
vṛddhi ('increment')		ā		āi(ai)		āu(au)	ār	—

The simplest characterization of this process is that the *guṇa* form is brought about by adding an *a* to the simple vowel; the *vṛddhi* form is made by adding *a* to the *guṇa* form. The following are a few examples:

> *pa-pt-imá* 'we fell': *pát-ati* 'he falls': *pāt-áyati* 'he causes to fall' (∅, a, ā)
> *díś-* 'direction, region': *deś-á-* 'place, region': *daiś-ika* 'local' (i, e, ai)
> *tul-ā́* 'scales': *tol-ana-* 'weighing': *taul-in-* 'weigher' (u, o, au)
> *kṛ-tá-* 'made'; *kar-tṛ́-* 'doer': *kār-yá* 'business' (ṛ, ar, ār)

As far as accent is concerned, the native grammarians note distinctions of tone or pitch, but make no mention of stress or emphatic accent. There are two primary accent pitches: acute and grave. A third type of accent is always of secondary origin according to combinations of acute and grave vowels in contraction.

4.2.1.2. Consonants

The consonantal system of Sanskrit is a typologically balanced, symmetrical system with a number of innovative distinctions not found in the other stocks. It takes the following shape:

	Voiceless	Voiceless Aspirated	Voiced	Voiced Aspirated	Nasal
Velar	k	kh	g	gh	ṅ
Palatal	c	ch	j	jh	ñ
Retroflex (Retracted)	ṭ	ṭh	ḍ	ḍh	ṇ
Dental	t	th	d	dh	n
Labial	p	ph	b	bh	m

There are in addition the semivowels *y, r, l,* and *v,* as well as the secondary sounds *ḥ* (visarga) and *ṅ* and *ṁ* (anusvāra).

The major points of interest in regard to the Indo-European are the voiceless aspirated series *kh, th,* and so on, which is not usually posited for Proto-Indo-European, and the retroflex series, which seems to be the result of Dravidian influence. Both have been the source of some controversy, not only in Indo-Iranian studies, but also in the wider Indo-European sphere.

4.2.1.3. Sandhi

Sanskrit phonology is of special interest even to the general phonologist because of the existence of a phenomenon known as *sandhi,* literally 'a putting-together'. Sandhi is a phonological process whereby sounds join together, both within words (internal sandhi) and across word boundaries (external sandhi), to produce other sounds. These combinatory, or euphonic, changes often have the result of making words very difficult to analyze, simply because they often destroy the transparency of the phonological form of the words. And in the case of sandhi across word boundaries, the rules often blur the word boundaries, making syntactic and morphological analysis difficult. A few examples will serve to illustrate:

1. Simple similar vowels coalesce to form the corresponding long vowel—for example, $\breve{a} + \breve{a} \rightarrow \bar{a}$: cf. *na + asti → nāsti* 'is not'; $\breve{u} + \breve{u} \rightarrow \bar{u}$: cf. *sādhu + uktam → sādhūktam* 'well spoken'.

2. Vowels *a* and *ā* merge with dissimilar simple vowels to produce their guṇa form—for example, *ca ihi → cehi* 'and here'; *sā uvāca → sovāca* 'she said'.

3. Vowels *a* and *ā* merge with dissimilar diphthongs to produce the vṛddhi form—for example, *ā eti → aiti* 'comes here'; *sā oṣadhiḥ → sauṣadhiḥ* 'the medicinal herb'.

Similar rules of combination exist for consonants. The following are a few examples:

1. Voiceless stops become voiced between vowels—for example, *pattanāt āgacchati → pattanād āgacchati* 'he comes from the city'.

2. Final *t* assimilates to following palatals, retroflexes, or *l*—for example, *tat ca → tac ca* 'and this'.

3. Final *n* changes to *ñ* before *j*—for example, *tān janān → tāñ janān* 'these people' (acc.).

4. Final *s* and *r* become *ḥ*—for example, *punar pratiṣṭhati → punaḥ pratiṣṭhati* 'he goes away again'.

5. Final *as* becomes *o* before voiced consonants and *a* (which disappears)—for example, *devas gacchati → devo gacchati* 'a god is coming'.

The preceding hardly exhaust the rules of sandhi for Sanskrit. Indeed, they barely scratch the surface. They are, nonetheless, representative of the many rules of phonological coalescence characteristic of Sanskrit phonology. A full explanation would very nearly require a book by itself.

4.2.2. Morphology

As was noted earlier, Sanskrit is prized by Indo-European scholars because of the richness of its overall structural system. This feature of the language is especially evident in its morphological patterns of nouns, verbs, adjectives, participles, and other formal classes.

Sanskrit has the three genders masculine, feminine, and neuter that characterize so many of the Indo-European languages. The language is quite strict concerning concord, and it marks each substantival form for one of these genders. In addition to the three genders, Sanskrit also marks three numbers: singular, plural, and dual. Though every noun has these three numbers, the dual is not a well-marked category in the sense that one form frequently fills the case role of two or three different cases, while this formal identity of case forms is somewhat less extensive in the plural and considerably less so for the singular.

Sanskrit marks eight cases, as many as are found in any Indo-European language. These are the nominative, genitive, dative, accusative, ablative, vocative, locative, and instrumental, all with familiar functions. Nouns are divided into two broad categories according to whether the stem ends in a vowel or a consonant. Each contains a number of subclasses, and there is considerable variation in endings among the various subgroups. Adjectives are declined in accordance with the different noun groups, with the majority conforming to the pattern of the vocalic stems in -*a*. The line between substantive and adjective in Sanskrit is often very difficult to establish. Pronominal forms in the language are for the most part unremarkable in comparison with those of the other stocks.

The verb in Sanskrit is exceedingly complex in the number of categories that it marks and the system of stems and endings by which the distinctions are expressed. There are three voices: active, middle, and passive. But, as in Greek, the passive is usually formally identical with the middle, differing only in the present tense. The middle voice definitely predominates in this language; in fact, the native grammarians did not even recognize a separate passive.

There are in Sanskrit a total of eight tenses (though I hasten to add that not all of these are found at all times throughout the history of the language and not all are found in all verbs): present, imperfect, perfect, pluperfect, aorist, future, conditional, and periphrastic perfect. The system is usually divided into four tense systems: the present system (present and imperfect), the perfect system (perfect and pluperfect), the aorist system (with three types of aorist), and the future system (with two different future types).

The verb has the same three numbers as the noun, namely, singular, plural, and dual, as well as the markers of first, second, and third person. A well-developed participial system and a less developed gerund and infinitive system also are found in the verb.

On the matter of mood, Vedic Sanskrit differs from the later language in the presence of a subjunctive mood. In Classical Sanskrit we can distinguish only an indicative, optative, and imperative mood. Another distinguishing feature of the Sanskrit verb is the large number of derivative verbal categories marked morphologically—for example, the causative, the desiderative, and the intensive.

4.2.3. Syntax

Sanskrit syntax is marked by a number of interesting characteristics, a few of which we will note here. The most interesting is the system of compounding (this could perhaps be considered morphological). Sanskrit makes elaborate use of nominal compounds formed according to three major classes. Compounds result from the combination of declinable stems with one another to form a unit that is treated as if simple in matters of accent and inflection. Compounds generally consist of two members, but they can themselves become members of a new compound. The lack of internal inflection often makes syntactic analysis difficult. The major types of compounds are the following:

1. *Copulative Compounds* (*Dvandva*). These involve two syntactically coordinate members, with the unit often inflected in the dual or plural—for example, *indrávárunāu* 'Indra and Varuna'; *kṛtākṛtám* 'done and undone'.

2. *Determinative Compounds* (*Tatpuruṣa*). In these the former member is syntactically dependent on the latter—for example, *pādodaka* 'water for the feet'; *hástakṛta* 'made with the hands'. Also in this group are descriptive compounds of the type *priyasakhi* 'dear friend', *nīlotpala* 'blue lotus'; these have the name *karmadhāraya* in the Indian tradition.

3. *Possessive Compounds* (*Bahuvrīhi*). These are determinative compounds in which adjective inflection is assigned to the

last substantive; the resulting meaning is 'having' or 'possessing' that which is specified by the determinative—for example, *ahastá* 'he who does not have a hand'; *bahuvrīhi* 'he who has much rice'.

There are other types of compounds, built on adjectival, participial, and adverbial bases, that will not be discussed here.

Another feature of Sanskrit syntax is its extreme freedom in matters of case selection of nouns. For example, the genitive case will often substitute for a dative, an instrumental, an ablative, or a locative; the same is true of the locative and instrumental, both of which substitute rather freely for genitives and datives. All of this is in marked contrast with other Indo-European stocks, especially Latin, where case-selection is fairly rigid and invariable.

The extensive use of participial constructions in place of full clauses is another feature of Sanskrit, but this is one it shares with a number of other stocks in the Indo-European family.

On matters of word order the language is generally SOV, though there are ample SVO structures in the language as well. Postpositions abound in Vedic, though prepositions dominate in the later language. One typically finds Adj. + Noun and Poss. + Noun constructions. Compounds are an extremely rich area in which to discover ancient word-order patterns in Sanskrit, as elsewhere. Many scholars have sought recently to uncover the syntactic principles of compounding as a means of approaching the entire syntax of the language (see most recently Tischler 1979 and Lehmann 1974).

4.3.   A Sample Sanskrit Text

The following selection is one familiar to anyone who has undertaken the serious study of Sanskrit. This brief excerpt comprises the first lines of the great story of Nala and Damayantī from the *Mahābhārata*. Nala was a prince of Nishadha, and Damayantī was the daughter of Bhīma, the king of Vidarbha; the two fall in love (text and transliteration from Lanman 1884:1):

| atha | | nalopākhyānam | | | |
| Here begins | | nala-episode | | | |

| bṛhadaśva | | | uvāca. | | |
| Brhadaśva (Great-Horse) | | | has spoken | | |

| āsīd | rājā | nalo nāma, | vīrasenasuto | balī, | upapanno |
| there was | king | nala by name | of Virasena the son | strong | possessing |

guṇair	iṣṭāi,	rūpavān,	aśvakovidaḥ.		atiṣṭhan	manujendrāṇām
qualities	desirous	handsome	in horses skilled	he stood	of princes

mūrdhni	devapatir	yathā,	upary	upari	sarveṣām	āditya	iva
at the head	Indra	as	above	above	of all	in splendor	as

tejasā;	brahmaṇyo,	vedavic,		chūro,	niṣadheṣu
in majesty	pious	Veda-knowing	mighty	among Nishadhesians

mahīpatiḥ,	akṣapriyaḥ,	satyavādī,	mahān	akṣāuhiṇīpatiḥ;
mighty earth-lord	lucky at gaming	truth-speaking	great	army-master

'Here begins the Nala-episode
Bṛhadaśva (Great-Horse) has spoken.'
'There was a king, Nala by name, Virasena's son, strong, endowed with desirous qualities, handsome, well skilled in horses. He stood at the head of princes as Indra is at the head of the gods, far above all in majesty as the sun is in splendor; pious, Veda-knowing, mighty earth-lord among the Nishadhesians, lucky at gaming, truth-speaking, great master of an army.'

Iranian   4.4.

With the Indo-Aryan migration into India in the second millenium B.C., the earlier Aryan community was split into the two distinct groups we now call Indic and Iranian. The Iranians themselves spread out quite early (approximately 1500 B.C.) over a wide area, reaching not only the Iranian plateau, but also parts of China and Southern Russia.

4.4.1. Old Iranian

The earliest records of Iranian are the Gāthās of Avestan (often called Gathic). These are ancient scriptures attributed to Zarathuštra that are usually dated to approximately 600 B.C., though some believe them to be much older. Gathic is structurally, almost mechanically, related to the language of the Vedas, and it is for this reason that some scholars have dated it earlier. Avestan is more important for comparative Indo-Iranian than for Indo-European studies, and is usually studied in conjunction with Vedic.

Old Persian, a southwestern Iranian dialect, is chiefly represented in inscriptions written in a special cuneiform script chronicling the Achaemenid Records, as well as in some other inscriptions dated to about 500–400 B.C. Old Persian, very close to Avestan, is known by the inscriptional texts found in Persis— at Persepolis, Naqš-i-Rustam, and Murghab—as well as in other locations in Elam (at Susa), in Media (at Hamadan), and elsewhere. Most of the inscriptions are those of Darius the Great (521–486 B.C.) and Xerxes (486–465 B.C.).

4.4.2. Middle Iranian

Middle Persian, or Pahlavi, is the most important language of the Middle Iranian period, which spans the years about 300 B.C. to A.D. 900. Also included in this grouping are Chorasmian, which survives only in a few hundred glosses, Sogdian, and Saka. Saka Iranians have been connected since the time of Herodotus with the ancient Scythians.

4.4.3. Modern Iranian

The most important languages of modern Iranian are Persian (Farsi), which is spoken in Iran; Pašto, the national language of Afghanistan; Baluchi; and Kurdish. There is also a host of other languages with less significant populations of speakers—for example, Tati, Gorani, Talishi, and others.

4.5.   Avestan: A Brief Overview

Since Old Persian and especially Avestan agree with Sanskrit in a general way, we shall omit here a detailed structural sketch of either of these two languages. Briefly, the phonology is generally comparable: vowels in Avestan, for example, are marked by a length distinction, though there are more diphthongs in Avestan, a nasal vowel *ą,* and phonemic *ə.* Word-internal sandhi of vowels is considerable, but not to the same degree as in Sanskrit. Liquids and semivowels are generally the same as in Sanskrit.

In consonants Avestan differs more widely from Sanskrit. There are no aspirated stops (*bh, ph,* etc.): where Sanskrit has voiceless aspirates, Avestan has voiceless fricatives (cf. Skt. *gáthā-,* Av. *gaθaō* 'song, verse'). Where Sanskrit has voiced aspirates, Avestan has plain voiced stops (cf. *bhrátar-,* Av. *brāta* 'brother'). Except for the presence of the phonemes *ţ* (a dental spirant) and the sibilant *ž* in Avestan, and the presence of the retroflex series in Sanskrit (*ţ, ḍ, ṇ,* etc.), the consonantal systems of the two languages are for the most part comparable.

In morphology Sanskrit and Avestan are very close to each other. Nouns are inflected in the same eight cases, three numbers, and three genders, with parallel functions and morphological distribution in form classes. The same is true of pronouns, numerals, adjectives, and other morphological classes.

Verbs are characterized by the active and the middle voices, and by the same tenses and moods we find in Vedic Sanskrit, including the subjunctive. Special participial, infinitive, and imperative forms generally parallel those found in Vedic.

In syntax, too, there is extreme similarity between Avestan and Sanskrit. Cases have the same general syntactic and semantic functions. Word order in Gathic is very unstable, however. SOV predominates, but there is also variable SVO, OSV, and OVS. Prepositions predominate, but postpositions are also found. The order of nouns and adjectives is highly variable. Avestan also has the same nominal compounding properties that Sanskrit has.

A Sample Avestan Text <br> with Its Sanskrit Equivalent   4.6.

The following short text (the first verse of Yasna IX; from Taraporewala 1962:315–16) from Avestan is given with its Sanskrit equivalent in order to illustrate the closeness of the two languages. (Note: words marked with an asterisk (*) are not actual Sanskrit words, but the formal phonetic equivalents of the Avestan words.)

Avestan:	hāvanīm	ā	ratūm	ā	Haomō	upāit̲
Sanskrit:	*sāvānim	ā	r̥tum	ā	Somaḥ	upait
English:	pressing	at	time	at	Soma	went up to

Zaraθuštrəm	Ātrəm	pairi-	yaoždaθəntəm	Gāθås-ca	
Jarathuṣṭram	Ātrim	*pari-	yoḥ-dadhantam	gāthāśca	[api]
Zarathuštra	altar	around	cleaning	Gāthās and	

srāvayntəm.	ā-dim	pərəsat̲ī	(Zaraθuštrō):	kō-narə,	ahī?	yim
śrāvayantam.	ā-*dim	pr̥cchat	(Jarathuṣṭraḥ)	ko nara	asi	yam
reciting	him	asked	Zarathuštra	who man	are	whom

azəm	vīspahe	aŋhəuš	astvatō	sraēštem	dādarəsa.
aham	vīśvasya	āsoḥ	asthivataḥ	śreṣṭham	dadarśa.
I	of world	whole	bonelike (material)	most exalted	saw

'At the time of pressing (the hour of early morning), Soma went up to Zarathuštra, who was cleaning the altar and reciting the Gāthās. Zarathuštra asked him: "Who are you, man, whom I have seen as the most exalted one of the whole world?" '

Indo-Iranian   4.7.

Since, as we have mentioned, the Indo-Iranian group is the only Indo-European stock with an indisputable claim to status as an intermediate subgroup, it is appropriate that we enumerate some of the evidence for this classification:

1. The common use of the term **Arya-* as a proper noun of self-designation by both groups.

2. The extensive use of quantitative gradation (ablaut) of the type *ă/ā* in both Indic and Iranian. This results from the historical Indo-Iranian merger of PIE **ĕ*, **ŏ*, and **ă* into *ă* that destroyed the more familiar qualitative gradation based on vowel alternation, chiefly between *e* and *o*, as found, for example, in Gk. *leípo* (*e*): *lé-loipa* (*o*) 'leave, left'; Lat. *tegō* (*e*): *toga* (*o*) 'cover, covering'. Although internal evidence for this type can be found in Sanskrit, the productive gradation was of the type Skt. *sádas* (*a*) 'seat'; *sādáyati* (*ā*) 'cause to sit'; *hásati* (*a*) 'laughs': *hāsa-* (*ā*) 'laughter'; OPers. *daraniya* (*a*) 'gold': *dāraniya-kara-* (*ā*) 'goldsmith'; OPers. *baga-* (*a*) 'god': *Bāga-yādi-* (*ā*) 'God-worship'. The *ĕ*, *ŏ*, *ă* merger is illustrated by Skt. *ábharam*, OPers. *abaram*, but Gk. *épheron* (*e*) 'I carried'; Skt. (acc.) *áśvam*, OPers. *asam*, OLat. *equom* (*o*) 'horse'; Skt. *ápa*, OPers. *apa-*, Gk. *ápo* (*a*) 'from'.

3. The passage of PIE **ə* to *i*, which is peculiar to Indo-Iranian. Cf. Skt. *pitár-*, Av. *pitar*, Lat. *pater*, Gk. *patḗr* 'father'.

4. The peculiar reduction and exchange of voiced aspirated stop + voiceless stop to voiced stop + voiced aspirated stop (Bartholomae's Law)—for example, *bh* + *t* > *bdh*. Cf. Skt. *labdhá-* < *labh* + *ta* 'taken'; *buddhá* < *budh* + *ta* 'awakened'; Av. *vərəzda*, Skt. *vṛddhá* < *vardh* + *ta* 'increased'; Av. *dərəwδa-*, Skt. *dṛbdhi* 'tufted'. But it should be noted that the Iranian evidence for Bartholomae's Law is far from overwhelming. This is primarily due to the fact that the aspiration of the etymological voiced aspirates was lost, and there are actually more instances of voiceless stops than voiced ones in the cases where one would expect voiced.

5. The use of the infix *-n-* in the genitive plural of stems ending in *-a*, *-ā*, *-i*, and *-u*, resulting in genitive plurals such as those in *-nam*: Skt. *vṛkāṇām*, Av. *vəhrkanąm* 'wolves' (cf. Lat. *lupōrum*).

6. The use of the ablative-genitive ending of the type Skt. *-āyāḥ*, OPers. *-āyā*, Av. *-āyå*.

7. The use of *-u* as a marker of third-person imperatives—for example, Skt. *bháratu*, Av. *báratu*, OPers. *baratuv* 'let him carry'.

8. The near complete agreement of certain inflectional groups—for example, first-person pronouns:

Singular 'I, me'

	Sanskrit	Avestan	Old Persian
Nom.	ahám	azəm	adam
Tonic Acc.	mā́m	mə̨m	mām
Atonic Acc.	mā	mā	
Tonic Gen./Dat.	mama	mana	manā
Atonic Gen./Dat.	me	me	maiy
Tonic Dat.	máhya(m)	maibyā	
		(Gathic)	
Abl.	mat	maṯ	ma

9. Lexical similarities more extensive than those between any other Indo-European groups— for example:

Sanskrit	*Avestan*	*Old Persian*	
híraṇya-	zaranya-		'gold'
sénā-	haēnā-	hainā-	'army'
ṛṣṭí-	aršti-	aršti-	'spear'
sóma-	haoma-		'the sacred drink soma'
átharvan-	aθaurvan-	āθravan-	'fire priest'
('a class of priest')			
yajñá-	yasna-		'sacrifice'

Dardic   4.8.

In addition to the major Indo-Iranian languages we must mention also a third group, whose Indo-Iranian and Indo-European affinities have been the subject of some controversy. These are the so-called Dardic languages. They offer us no ancient literature such as Sanskrit or Avestan that allows for an easy classification. They seem to be genetically close to the Indic branch, perhaps with an Iranian admixture, but here again we must admit the problem of identifying common innovation, common retention, or late influence. The basic vocabulary seems to be Indo-European (cf. Chowar *dirū,* participle of 'give', and Hindi *diyā*). The classification of the Dardic languages is further complicated by the Kafir languages (e.g., Kati, Prasun), which may or may not be part of the Dardic group. Among the Dardic languages the most important is Kashmiri. Whatever their remoter origins, these languages have no significance for the reconstruction of PIE, and their classification need not concern us further.

Also of note in the Indo-Iranian area are the many non-Indo-European languages that are present, many of them clearly predating the Indo-Aryan invasions. Among these are, in India, the Dravidian languages (especially Telugu, Kannada, Tamil, Malayalam, Gondi); the Munda languages (Santali, Mundari, Ho); and the Tibeto-Burman languages (Balti, Newari, Boro, and Garo). Also important are Khasi, Nahali, Burushaski, and Andamanese, which have not been securely classified. On the Iranian side the most important of the neighboring languages is Arabic, which has considerably influenced Persian and the other languages of that region.

References

I. Grammars and Historical Works

Back 1978
Bartholomae
    1895–1896
Bloch 1934
Brandenstein and
    Mayrhofer 1964
Burrow 1965
Delbrück 1888
Hoffmann et al. 1958
Kent 1953

Macdonell 1968
Meillet 1931
Pischel 1900
Reichelt 1967
Renou 1930
Thumb et al.
    1958–1959
Wackernagel et al.
    1896–1954
Whitney 1889

II. Dictionaries

Bartholomae 1904
Böhtlingk 1923–1925
Böhtlingk and Roth
    1966

Grassmann 1964
Mayrhofer 1953–

III. Indo-Iranian

Meillet 1922 [1967]

IV. Works Cited in the Text

Lanman 1884
Lehmann 1974
Polomé 1979

Taraporewala 1962
Tischler 1979

Hellenic (Greek)   5

Introduction   5.0.

Along with Indo-Iranian, Italic, and Anatolian (to be discussed later), the Hellenic, or Greek, branch stands out as a primary source of information concerning the parent language. It is
not known at exactly what point in prehistory the Greeks came
into Greece, but the evidence suggests that they arrived in the
country well before 1000 B.C. and found there a flourishing advanced civilization. This civilization was that of the Pelasgians,
who are frequently mentioned in ancient history. Other non-Indo-
European peoples were almost certainly in the land as well, but
the identification of these groups is very difficult because of the
sparseness of concrete evidence. Most of the evidence for non-
Indo-European settlers comes from place names—for example,
Mukênai 'Mycenae', *Athênai* 'Athens'—as well as from a few
cultural terms that have found their way into the Greek lexicon—
for example, *basileús* 'king'.

Whatever their exact origins, the Greeks had established
themselves and become dominant on the mainland, the coastal
islands, and the Aegean coast by about 1000 B.C. Our oldest literature from the Hellenic branch is Homer's *Iliad* and *Odyssey*,
which are thought to have been written down about 800 B.C.
Homeric Greek, as it is usually called, is a curious composite of
many Greek dialects. Fundamentally Ionic in character, the Homeric epic also contains an Aeolic layer, though some scholars
have detected an Achaean stratum that would link it remotely
with earlier Mycenaean elements (see below).

Because of their intellectual and cultural sophistication, the
Greeks stand out in the Western tradition as the most gifted and
accomplished thinkers and writers of their era. We have inherited
countless pieces of literature from Hellenic civilization on topics
in philosophy, grammar, mathematics, literature, medicine, and
nearly every other cultured intellectual activity. As a result, we

have extensive documentation, not only of the Greek civilization itself, but also of the early language. From the material provided by this literature, plus the thousands of inscriptions found in the Greek-speaking world, we know Greek as well as we know any ancient language and are even able to identify the major dialect divisions within the language (we have some help on this score from the native Greek grammarians as well).

5.1. The Greek Dialects

Greek is most frequently divided into two major dialect groups, each with subdivisions. The main dialect areas are East Greek and West Greek (see Buck 1955:9–14).

5.1.1. East Greek

5.1.1.1. Attic-Ionic

Attic-Ionic (A-I) is the most important literary dialect of ancient Greece, serving as the vehicle for all the most important Greek literature available today. It served as the official dialect of Greece in the Athenian empire from the mid-fifth century B.C. onward.

The Attic-Ionic group is characterized by certain significant differences from the other Greek dialects, the most noticeable being $\bar{e}$ instead of $\bar{a}$ (< *$\bar{a}$, cf. *mḗtēr,* Doric *mā́tēr* 'mother'); very early loss of *ϝ,* or digamma, which represents the sound *u* and is still identifiable metrically in Homeric texts; and others.

a. Attic. The principal dialect of Attic-Ionic is the Attic, which eventually evolved into the *koínē,* or common dialect, and attained official status in Athenian times. Attic also eventually provided the basis for a sort of international language, serving as the principal scriptural language of the early Christians. The Attic *koínē* eventually all but suffocated the non-Attic dialects by the end of the Hellenistic period in A.D. 330.

b. Ionic. The Ionic dialect is very closely related to the Attic dialect of Attic-Ionic; it is usually divided into East, Central, and West (Euboean) Ionic.

5.1.1.2. Aeolic

Closely connected with the Attic-Ionic group of East Greek is the Aeolic group, which includes Lesbian, Thessalian, and

Boeotian. The material from this group is fairly extensive, but as a rule is mostly from the later period.

5.1.1.3. Arcado-Cyprian

The third group listed under the East Greek heading is the Arcado-Cyprian group. In many classifications this group is seen to be somewhat intermediate between Aeolic and Attic-Ionic. It, too, is characterized by certain phonological and morphological peculiarities (e.g., *in* for A-I *en* 'in', *kás* for A-I *kaí* 'and', and others). It includes the two major dialects Arcadian and Cyprian, and by some classifications also includes the poorly known Pamphylian, which, however, also shares certain Doric, or West Greek, characteristics.

5.1.2. West Greek

The West Greek group remained in relative obscurity during the Homeric period and later, principally because of the cultural and political preeminence of Athens and hence the Attic dialect. This group includes a large number of dialects which, though fairly homogeneous linguistically, are geographically dispersed. The West Greek group is characterized by a number of significant innovations and retentions from the earlier parent speech—for example, retention of *ā* (A-I *ē*, cf. Doric *mátēr*, A-I *métēr*); retention of intervocalic *t* (instead of *s,* cf. Cretan *portí, protí,* Attic-Ionic *prós*); the articles *toí, taí* instead of *hoi, hai;* and a large number of others. West Greek is normally classified into two major subdivisions, Northwest Greek and Doric.

5.1.2.1. Northwest Greek

Providing mostly inscriptional material, the Northwest group is made up of Phocian (Delphian), Locrian, Elean, and the Northwest Greek *koínē,* which is a mixed dialect from Aetolia.

5.1.2.2. Doric

The Doric group of West Greek comprises a large number of dialects including Laconian, Heraclean, Messenian, Megarian, Corinthian, Argolic, Rhodian, Coan, Theran, Cyrenaean, Cretan (the best known), and Sicilian Doric. The famous Sparta was a Doric-speaking city state. Doric Greek was used in Greek literature for choral lyric, not in the form of a single dialect but as a literary composite in which many of the local peculiarities were

neutralized. In general, Doric Greek is prized by Indo-Europeanists because of its frequent archaisms and interesting regional
peculiarities.

The preceding classification of the Greek dialects, though it
is common, is not the only one available. Some scholars have
proposed a three-way classification made up of West Greek,
Achaean, and Attic-Ionic. The issues are far too complex to be
discussed here, but the very existence of differences of opinion
serves to illustrate the hazards of such classifications. In any case,
it should be emphasized that whatever division one adopts, the
differences among the various groups and dialects of Greek are
not nearly so extensive as those found in other branches of
Indo-European—for example, Italic or Indo-Iranian. Judged by
the standard of mutual comprehensibility, which is a frequently
employed criterion used in distinguishing dialect from language,
the Greek divisions can lay particular claim to the term 'dialect'
and in this respect are to be clearly distinguished from such
groups as Latin and Oscan, for example, which were clearly separate languages.

Greek has continued to the present day (Modern Greek),
though of course with basic changes that now make it completely
different from Classical Greek. By means of early expansion and
colonialism, Greek spread widely in the ancient period, but later
political and cultural conquests, especially by Romans, Turks,
and Arabs, have severely changed the earlier linguistic maps of
the Greek-speaking area. Greek is spoken today chiefly in Greece
proper, with enclaves of speakers in Albania, Cyprus, and southern Italy (Italot Greek).

5.3.   Mycenaean

Since the discovery of the Indo-European family through the
analytical techniques of the comparative method, several events
have altered our conceptions and shaken the basic foundations of
our discipline. One such event was the discovery and eventual
decipherment of Hittite (see chapter 12). Another, though less
significant, was the unearthing of Tocharian (see chapter 11). Still
another controversial development surrounded the decipherment
of the famed Knossos Tablets, when a young British architect

shocked the scholarly world with the startling claim that he had deciphered the script and that the language it contained was Greek in an earlier form.

The tablets in question had been unearthed in excavations at Knossos by the British archaeologist Sir Arthur Evans around the turn of this century. The excavations yielded over 3,000 pieces containing inscriptional material written in a system that came to be called Linear B. It was called Linear B to distinguish it from the very different Minoan, or Linear A, script that had been found, along with the celebrated Phaistos Disk, in the south of Crete.

The Linear B tablets found at Knossos contain principally numerical inventories of persons, animals, and commodities. Owing largely to Evans' reluctance to make the material available to the scholarly world, a great deal of confusion and misinformation surrounded Linear B and its relation to the Linear A. Despite their differences, the two systems were thought by many scholars to represent different stages of the same language, 'Minoan'. There were no convenient bilingual texts to aid in the decipherment of either script, and it must be said that, despite serious efforts by noted scholars, there was little progress in figuring them out for nearly fifty years.

In the meantime, discoveries made at other sites yielded more inscriptional information. Especially important was the discovery of about six hundred additional inscriptional tablets and fragments at Pylos written in Linear B script. By this time it had become quite certain that the Linear A and Linear B scripts did not represent the same language. Linear A, which still resists decipherment, almost certainly does not represent an Indo-European language.

It was in 1952 that Michael Ventris finally broke the code of Linear B. An architect and amateur philologist, Ventris suggested that the Knossos and Pylos tablets were written in Greek, a Greek at least five hundred years older than the language of Homer. Ventris had been in frequent contact with British archaeologists and philologists, and made his findings available to John Chadwick, a philologist with whom Ventris collaborated until his untimely death in an auto accident in 1956.

In breaking the script, Ventris produced a complete grid of phonetic renditions for the Linear B script; the phoneticizations of the Linear B that emerged showed very close correspondences with Classical Greek. Ventris received startling confirming evidence for his decipherment when Blegen, one of the excavators of Pylos, used Ventris' system to decode some of the new tablets. By using this system, Blegen found the roots *tri-* 'three', *qᵘetro-* 'four', *an-* prefix 'not', *mezoe-* 'small, mid', all with very close Greek equivalents. Other words such as *i-qo* 'horse' (Gk. *híppos,* but dialect *íkkos,* Lat. *equus*), *o-no* 'ass' (Gk. *ónos*) seemed to confirm the decipherment.

The demonstration that the Linear B tablets of Knossos and Pylos represented an early form of Greek came as startling news to classical archaeology and comparative linguistics. This new evidence extends our knowledge of Greek to perhaps the fifteenth century B.C. and now provides us with some of our oldest recorded documents of an Indo-European language.

The decipherment of Linear B as Mycenaean Greek, as it has come to be called, has not been without its critics. Though their numbers are dwindling, some modern scholars refuse to accept Ventris' decipherment. Unfortunately, however, the skills required for comparative grammar are quite different from those required for the decipherment of unknown scripts, and the two need not go hand in hand. It is clear in many cases that the philological and linguistic attacks on the identification of Linear B with Mycenaean are based on an incomplete understanding of the decipherment itself.

For Indo-European studies Mycenaean Greek has proved extremely valuable, showing some definite Indo-European features not found in later forms of attested Greek. (Note, for example, the word *qᵘetro-* 'four', which much more closely resembles the cognate Latin *quattuor,* Skt. *catvára-,* and so on, than does Classical Greek *téssares*). Our view of the Greek dialects has also been modified somewhat, with Mycenaean being considered by some to be close to Arcado-Cypriot (they share certain syntactic features such as the use of the dative for the older ablative function, whereas Attic-Ionic uses a genitive). Mycenaean also seems to have strong ties to Aeolic, with which it shares certain features of phonology and morphology.

Ventris did not live to defend his decipherment. But Chadwick has (see Chadwick 1970), and the evidence at this point seems to be strongly in their favor.

A Brief Structural Sketch of Greek　　5.4.

5.4.1. Phonology

5.4.1.1. Vowels

Of all the languages of the Indo-European family, none has played so prominent a role in the reconstruction of the proto-vowel system as has Greek. Though certain marked differences occur among the dialects, Greek has in general been spared the radical reorganization of the vowel system we have seen in some of the other languages, notably Latin and Old Irish, as well as Sanskrit and others. In both Italic and Celtic, a large part of the blame for these severe changes can be placed on the heavy expiratory stress systems characteristic of both languages, which tend to cause weakening of vowels in unstressed syllables. In Sanskrit a merger of the Proto-Indo-European vowels *$\ddot{a}$, *$\ddot{o}$, and *$\ddot{e}$ into $\ddot{a}$ played a significant role in the development of the vocalic system in that language, as well as in the loss of the earlier qualitative ablaut based on the alternation of $e : o : \phi$ (see below).

The Greek vowel system maintains the Indo-European distinctions of length. It is triangular in organization, though as with Latin it is certain that some qualitative differences existed between the long and the short varieties. Two of the Greek long vowels had their own special symbols; these are *ω omega*, which means 'big-*o*', contrasted with *o omicron* 'little-*o*', and *η eta*, which is the *ē*, contrasted with *ε epsilon* 'simple *e*'. The length of any given *i*, *a*, or *u* can be established by phonetic analysis alone. The vowels then are as follows:

In addition, Greek has a number of diphthongs formed by the union of an open vowel with a close vowel, namely, *ai, au, ei, eu, oi, ou, ēu,* and *ui*. Other diphthongs formed by contraction (so-called spurious diphthongs) yield further instances of *ei* and *ou* (e.g., *légein* for *légeen* 'read', etc.). There are, finally, the so-called improper diphthongs based on the long vowels *ā, ē,* and *ō* plus *i*, but the diphthongal pronunciation yielded to that of a monophthong after the first century B.C.

Accent in Greek is quite interesting. The existence of the accent marks in the writing system—acute (´), grave (`), and circumflex (ˆ)—as well as the descriptions provided by the native grammarians and other evidence, strongly suggests that the early accent was musical or tonal, and not expiratory as in Latin, Celtic, Germanic, and elsewhere. This fact above all others accounts for the relative stability of the vowels in the evolution of Greek from Proto-Indo-European. In the later language, however, the system shifted to the stress-accent type.

Vowel alternation, or ablaut, is a striking characteristic of Greek (morpho-) phonology. In fact, apart from Germanic, no Indo-European language provides so much systematic evidence of a productive ablaut system based both on the quality and the quantity of the vowels. Some examples follow:

1. *Qualitative* (based on differences in vowel quality, primarily *e, o, ∅*):

pét-o-mai 'fly' :	*pot-ḗ* 'flight'	: *e-pt-ómēn* 'flew'
ékh-ō 'have' :	*ókh-os* 'carriage'	: *é-skh-on* 'had'
peíth-ō 'trust' :	*pé-poith-a* 'trusted'	: *é-pith-on* 'trusted'

2. *Quantitative* (based on vowel length):

patḗr 'father' (nom. sg.) : *patéres* (nom. pl.) : *patrós* (gen. sg.) (*ē : e : ∅*)
kúōn 'dog' (nom. sg.) : *kunós* (gen. sg.) (*ō : ∅*)

5.4.1.2. Consonants

The consonantal system of Greek, relatively straightforward, is a well balanced and typologically secure system. It contains the following sounds:

p	t	k
b	d	b
ph	th	kh
m	n	(ŋ)
(ϝ)	s	ɾ (h)
	l	
	r	

Note: (a) Greek has special letters for the phonetic sequences *ps* (ψ), *ks* (ξ), and *dz* (ζ). (b) The [ŋ] listed above replaces the sound *g* occurring before *k, g, kh,* or *ks* (i.e., when there are two successive velars)—for example, *ággelos* (Lat. *angelus*) 'messenger'. (c) ϝ, or digamma, was a sound like *u* and is not included in the later Greek writing systems. Its presence in Homeric Greek is evident from metrical scansion only. Cf. Mycenaean *wa-na-ko,*

Iliad A7 (ϝ)ánax 'king'. (d) The ancient Greek aspirates *ph, th, kh* (φ, θ, χ) were aspirated stops, not the fricatives [f, θ, χ], as commonly pronounced today.

The most important feature of the Greek consonant system when considered in the light of reconstructed Proto-Indo-European is that it has systematically devoiced all the voiced aspirates of the parent language. That is, where Indo-European probably had a **bh*, Greek has *ph;* where we postulate **dh*, Greek has *th;* and so on. Cf. here Skt. *bhrātar- :* Gk. *phrāter* 'brother'; Skt. *dhā̆-*, Gk. *(tí)thē-mi* 'place'; Skt. *hám̐sa-*, Gk. *khḗn* 'goose' (< **gʰāns-*).

5.4.1.3. Breathings

In addition to the vowels and consonants, one further feature of Greek phonology deserves brief mention: the presence of the so-called breathings that obligatorily begin all words with initial vowels, diphthongs, or the consonant *r*. There are two such breathings, one 'smooth', one 'rough'. The smooth breathing is written as ' and has no phonetic realization; it is of disputed origin. The rough breathing, on the other hand, is usually written ' and has the phonetic effect of beginning the word with aspiration, namely, [h]. Most of the rough breathings in Greek derive from an earlier Indo-European **s:* cf. Lat. *sex,* Gk. *héks* 'six'; Lat. *sequor,* Gk. *hépomai* 'follow'.

5.4.2. Morphology

Greek has many morphological features characteristic of the early Indo-European languages. Nouns are declined in five cases (nominative, genitive, dative, accusative, and vocative). There are the typical three genders of masculine, feminine, and neuter based partly on a natural and partly on a grammatical classification. Greek also marks three numbers: singular, plural, and dual.

Nouns in Greek are divided into three declensions, which, incidentally, correspond historically to the first three declensions of Latin (the *ā-* declension, cf. *oikí-ā* 'house'; the *o-* declension, cf. *lóg-os* 'word'; and the consonantal declension, cf. *phúlak-s* 'watchman'). Each group has many subvarieties.

Adjectives in Greek are declined according to the pattern of the three noun groups, also with combinations and subgroups based on reanalyses within Greek and on new analogical formations. Pronouns and other morphological classes are generally unremarkable in comparison with the other stocks.

The Greek verb is extremely complex, with a full comple-
ment of tense, mood, and voice categories, and a number of
inflectional groups. There are three voices: active, passive, and a
well-developed middle that is in most forms identical with the
passive. There is also a deponent category, which has the same
peculiarities as those found in Latin—that is, passive/middle form
with active meaning. There are also four moods—indicative,
subjunctive, optative, and imperative—plus infinitives and a fully
developed participial system.

Tense is an important feature of the verb in Greek, with
seven in the indicative: present, imperfect, future, aorist, perfect,
pluperfect, and, in some verbs, the future perfect. Of these, the
imperfect and pluperfect are found only in the indicative, whereas
the future and future perfect are not found in the subjunctive or
imperative. The verb in the indicative denotes not only tense in
the strict sense, but also the aspectual distinction between *continued action* (present, perfect, future, and future perfect) and
completed action (imperfect, aorist, and pluperfect). From a formal point of view, it is sometimes convenient to divide the Greek
verbs into eight inflectional classes based on the tense stems and
their internal relations.

5.4.3. Syntax

Greek syntax is in general unremarkable when compared
with the syntactic systems of the other older languages. Several
distinguishing features stand out, however. One is the relative
flexibility that the language allows, especially in verbal constructions. The tense, mood, and voice systems are so rich that a wide
range of options is available for expression of certain notions
(e.g., the middle voice or the active voice plus the reflexive pronoun can interchangeably denote reflexivity). Another characteristic of Greek syntax is its heavy dependence on participial
constructions where some other Indo-European languages use
either complete sentences or infinitive constructions, especially in
the so-called indirect statements. Here we find the participle used
to represent a finite verb in a subordinate sentence—for example,
ékouse Kûron en Kilikíai ónta (Xenophon) 'he heard that Cyrus
was in Cilicia' (lit. 'he heard Cyrus in Cilicia being'). In this respect Greek far outdoes the cognate stocks in the use of the participles, though both Sanskrit and especially Lithuanian are also
known for the richness of their participial uses. The syntax of the

Greek moods is also extremely complex, with complicated requirements for mood and tense in subordinate sentences.

Case selection is relatively straightforward; it is not as rigid as in Latin, but not as variable as in Sanskrit. In most respects the constructions found in Greek cases reflect those of the other languages (e.g., partitive genitive, dative of agent, accusative of extent of space). Prepositions are common and very important. Some occur with only one case, whereas many occur with two or three.

As in Latin and many other stocks, there is a close connection between the prepositions and the preverbs (cf. *pros-ágō* 'bring to', *prós* 'at, by'). There is ample evidence that these prepositions were at one time postpositions (cf. *Ithákēn katá* 'down toward Ithaca' [Homer]). Word order is generally SVO with Adj. + Noun and Gen. + Noun constructions predominating.

A Sample Greek Text   5.5.

The following text is from the *Odyssey* (4:26–29) of Homer, one of the most important pieces of literature in the history of Western civilization. This brief passage recounts the announcement of the arrival of Telemachus and Nestor at the palace of Menelaus:

Kseínō	dē	tine	tóde,	diotrephès	ô	Menélae,	ándre	dúō,
Strangers	(prt.)	here	these	Zeus-fostered	o	Menelaus	men	two

geneêî	dè	Diòs	megáloio	éikton.	all'eíp',	ē	sphôin
to the family	(prt.) of	Zeus	great	similar	but tell	either	for them

katalúsomen	ōkéas	híppous,	ê	állon	pémpōmen	hikanémen
we shall unyoke	swift	horses	or	another	we shall send	to seek

hós	ke	philésēi
who	(prt.)	will welcome

'Here are two strangers, Menelaus, fostered by Zeus, two men who are like the family of great Zeus. But tell me, shall we unyoke their swift horses, or send them on their way to another host, who will welcome them?'

References

I. Grammars and Historical Works

Bechtel 1921–1924   Buck 1933
Brugmann 1913   Buck 1955

Chantraine 1942–1953
Heilmann 1963
Hirt 1912
Meillet and Vendryes
    1927

Schwyzer and
    Debrunner
    1934–1950
Thumb et al.
    1909–1959

II. Dictionaries

Boisacq 1938
Chantraine 1968–1977

Frisk 1954–1972
Lejeune 1964

III. Mycenaean

Chadwick 1970
Levin 1964
Vilborg 1960

IV. Works Cited in the Text

Buck 1955
Chadwick 1970

Armenian   6

Introduction   6.0.

The language we now call Armenian has a long and involved history in Indo-European studies. It has changed and evolved so radically in its structure, phonology, and lexicon that it was thought to be a non-Indo-European language in the early period of comparative grammar. Once it was definitively classified as Indo-European, it was incorrectly grouped with Iranian because of the strong similarity in the lexicons of the two stocks.

The pre-Armenians are thought by many specialists to have been one group of Thraco-Phrygian invaders who moved across the Hellespont and into Asia Minor about 1200 B.C. Although many comparativists have listed Armenian as a member of the Thraco-Phrygian group, this highly speculative classification is not well substantiated by the Thraco-Phrygian data. Indeed, Armenian holds a special, though not unique, position among the Indo-European languages in that it has no close ties with the cognate stocks. To point to some connections with Greek and Indo-Iranian is the closest one can get to even shaky conjecture.

The Armenians probably did not establish themselves as a separate ethnic group in Asia Minor until sometime around the sixth century B.C., and it is certain that they assimilated large numbers of non-Indo-European peoples in the process. The assimilation of foreign peoples and the substantial influence of other cultures on Armenian are evident from the abundant lexical borrowings from Greek, Arabic, Syriac, and especially Persian. This massive lexical importation contributes to the hazardous business of classification. Armenian has a "core" vocabulary that strongly indicates Thraco-Phrygian connections, but the foreign influences blur the picture beyond this tenuous link. It was not until the famous Armenianist Hübschmann was able to sort out the Iranian loanwords that Armenian was no longer thought to be a radical Iranian dialect.

The large number of loanwords in Armenian is in fact one of its most distinctive characteristics. Most of the loans from Greek and Syriac are late and reflect the process of christianization. But besides these there are several other strata of loans that render the etymological basis of much of the Armenian vocabulary somewhat opaque. First are the many words of unclear origin that are apparently borrowed from ancient Caucasian and Anatolian languages; but these are highly speculative suggestions. The second, and numerically the most significant, are the loans into Armenian from Middle Persian. The borrowing of these words from Iranian apparently began during the period of the New Iranian empire (247 B.C. to A.D. 226). The phonological evidence suggests Parthian as a likely source, with most words coming from the social, religious, and legal vocabularies, but with others coming from across the lexicon. Among them are the following: Arm. *ašxarh* 'world': cf. OPers. *xšaθʳa-* 'rule'; Arm. *bag-* 'God': cf. OPers. *baga-* 'God'. And it seems that the Iranian influence on Armenian at this time was sufficiently strong that even native words that would have already been inherited from Proto-Indo-European were replaced in some cases by words borrowed from Parthian; an example of this phenomenon is *ma(r)h* 'death', from Old Iranian **mr̥θyu-*, PIE **mr̥tyu-*.

To say that Armenian is well known in the Indo-European tradition would be misleading; in fact, many Indo-European scholars are ignorant of this language, save for a few specialists and experts. Part of the reason for this relative neglect is the highly complex alphabet in which the language is written. Developed in A.D. 406–7 by St. Mesrop, the script is apparently based on Aramaic and shows some Greek influence, especially in the vowel symbols, angularity, and direction. But the link with Greek is of only marginal substance, and the alphabet remains an obstacle for many scholars who wish to pursue studies in the language.

Our first literature in Armenian stems from the fifth century A.D. in the form of biblical translations; the language is commonly called Old Armenian. Even at this quite early date Armenian phonology had diverged so far from the proto-language that it is easy, in retrospect, to see how our predecessors could misclassify it; cf. *erku* 'two' (Lat. *duo*, Gk. *dúo*); *erekh* 'three' (Lat. *trēs*, Gk. *trêis*); also Arm. *hayr* 'father' alongside Gk. *patḗr*, or Arm. *hur* 'fire' beside Gk. *pûr* (PIE **p-* > Arm. *h-*). On the other hand, the inflectional system of Old Armenian is more conservative than that of many other Indo-European languages (and by some recent accounts the phonology of Armenian is also very conservative, especially its system of consonants; see Hopper 1973:161–64). One outstanding characteristic of Armenian phonology is the fact that it underwent a consonantal shift similar to that of the Germanic languages (see 10.4).

Middle Armenian is dated from the tenth to the fifteenth century A.D. and offers a rich literature from the kingdom of Cilicia (1198–1375). In the modern period we find most of the speakers of Armenian in the Armenian Soviet republic, with others scattered throughout Turkey, Greece, Iran, and other adjacent lands. Of the two main dialects of Armenian, Eastern and Western, Eastern is the official dialect of Armenia.

A Brief Structural Sketch of Old Armenian   6.1.

6.1.1. Phonology

6.1.1.1. Vowels

Old Armenian has a vowel system of the triangular type, containing the following vowel phonemes:

i		u
ē		o
e	ə	
	a	

Note: *ē* represents a close vowel, not a long one; the vowel system of Old Armenian has lost the length distinction found in many of the other languages.

A stress accent in Old Armenian falls uniformly on the last syllable of the word. However, the accent on this syllable results from stress placement in Proto-Armenian on the penultimate syllable, with concomitant reduction and loss of final vowels and consonants, if any. In this way the stress in Old Armenian was settled on the last syllable.

6.1.1.2. Consonants

The Old Armenian consonant system is a highly structured and systematic one. It includes the following sounds:

	Voiceless	Voiceless Aspirated	Voiced	Nasals
Stops	p	ph (= p‘)	b	m
	t	th (= t‘)	d	n
	k	kh (= k‘)	g	
Affricates	ts	tsh (= ts‘)		
	č	čh (= č‘)		
Fricatives	s		z	
	š		ž	
	x			
	h			
Resonants	l, r, v(w), y, ł, ṙ			

This consonantal system is built primarily on a typological base of voiceless–voiceless-aspirated–voiced distinctions among stops, as well as distinctions relating to place and manner features.

In Old Armenian, the Indo-European ablaut pattern *e : o : φ* can be recovered, but only with some difficulty. The best reflexes of the qualitative system are preserved in the *n-* stem nouns, where stems vary between *-in* (< *-en*), *-un* (< *-on*), and *-an* (< *-ņ*); cf. nom. sg. *jern*, gen., dat., loc. *jeṙin*, abl. *jeṙan-ē* 'hand'. Interestingly, new ablaut patterns have developed in Old Armenian as a result of purely phonological developments related to the fixing of accent and the treatment of certain vowels and diphthongs in unstressed vowels. Cf. *gir* 'letter', *groy* (gen., dat., abl.), *grem* 'I write'.

6.1.2. Morphology

As was noted earlier, the Old Armenian system of nominal inflections seems to be very conservative. Every noun, adjective, and pronoun must be inflected in one of the seven cases, namely, nominative, genitive, dative, accusative, ablative, locative, and instrumental. Interestingly, the masculine-feminine-neuter gender distinction evident in the other languages is totally lacking in Old Armenian. The dual number has also been eliminated.

It is customary to speak of Old Armenian as a seven-case system, but it is very difficult to find clear examples of all seven cases within a single paradigm. That is, if we say that the Indo-European system was like the Sanskrit eight-case system, then Old Armenian underwent a large amount of case syncretism, where the forms and functions of previously distinct cases have fallen together. In Old Armenian nouns, for example, the singular genitive, dative, and ablative cases are frequently identical, as are the nominative and accusative; similar patterns are found in the plural. And even in the pronouns, where the purported original system is best preserved, we find case syncretism of forms such as the accusative-locative (cf. *is* 'me') or accusative-locative-dative (cf. *k'ez* 'you' sg.). The syntactic and semantic distinctions that would otherwise be obliterated by this syncretism are carried by the prepositions *z-* and *i-(y-)*, which in some instances have actually been attached to the following pronoun with complete morphological restructuring. Cf. *zi, zinč* (nom., acc.) 'what?'.

Thus the *composite* system of Old Armenian cases points to a system with seven cases in the singular and plural, even though no single form has all fourteen distinctions. (In fact, overlap of this sort occurs in all the Indo-European languages.) Our analysis of the system thus reflects our analytical tendency to postulate large systems that we collapse rather than small systems with uneven growth patterns.

Quite unlike many other Indo-European languages, Old Armenian has a considerable amount of stem variation in nouns reflecting the older ablaut grades of $e : o : \phi$ (most other languages leveled these out). Thus it is not uncommon to find a word that will show three different stems according to case forms, as in the following examples:

	Nom., Acc. Sg.	Oblique	Nom., Acc., Loc. Pl.
'source'	akn	akan-	akun-
'child'	manuk	mankan-	mankun-

In sum, there are many declensional patterns in the Old Armenian noun and adjective (which is exactly like the noun), each reflecting a range of different endings. The most convenient typology of the noun system divides it into two major groups, those with variable stems, such as those just mentioned above, and those with invariable stems, where such alternation is not found.

The Old Armenian verb is divided into two stem groups, the present stem and the aorist stem; each group is marked by a particular vowel and perhaps also by a suffix in several different patterns (e.g., *p'orj-em* 'I tempt': aor. *p'orj-ec'-i; pag-an-em* 'I kiss': aor. *pag-i; mor-an-am* 'I forget': aor. *mor-ac'-ay*). There are in general two major groups of verbs, rather blandly labeled *regular* and *irregular* according to predictability of inflection.

There are in Old Armenian three moods—indicative, subjunctive, and imperative (with a negative counterpart called the 'prohibitive')—as well as an infinitive, a participle, and some verbal adjectives. The tenses, which are not evenly represented in the different stem or mood groups, are present, imperfect, and aorist. There is no future tense in Old Armenian, with the subjunctive present filling this role. The verb *em* 'be' is also used with certain verbal adjectives to form periphrastic forms denoting result—for example, *zarmac'eal ein* 'they were in a state of amazement'.

The highly developed morphological distinction between active and middle (and passive) found in many of the older Indo-European languages is for the most part lacking in Old Armenian. Most verbs have what is called a 'common' inflection, where the distinction between active and passive is marked not by morphological patterns, but by syntactic environment. For example, the verb form *banam* could mean either 'I open' or 'I am opened'; the same is true, for example, of *hamarim* 'I regard, am regarded', *moṙanam* 'I forget, am forgotten'.

6.1.3. Syntax

Old Armenian syntax is distinguished by several features that, though not uncommon, are not the rule in the other languages. One is that the case of the sentence subject varies according to the verb form with which it occurs. For example, the unmarked form of the subject is nominative; but when the verb is a transitive aorist participle, the case of the subject is the genitive. Another curiosity occurs in the case concord between adjectives and nouns. When adjectives follow the noun they modify, they must agree in case and number; but when they precede, this rule of concord does not always hold. Similar patterns hold for participles.

The derivational patterns of Old Armenian are another distinctive feature of the grammatical makeup of the language. In some instances derivations are obtained from whole phrases—for example, *erkrpag-u* 'worshipper', from *erkir paganem* 'I kiss the earth'; *noynžam-ayn* 'presently', from *noynžam* 'the same hour'. Most frequently, however, derivatives take the form of compounds of two or more members—for example, *č'ar-a-xaws* 'slanderer', from *č'ar* 'malicious' and *xawsim* 'I speak'; *leṙn-a-kołmn* 'hill country', from *leaṙn* 'mountain' and *kołmn* 'country'.

Old Armenian is generally SVO with prepositions. But while prepositions play a meaningful role in the language, there is none of the interesting interplay between prepositions and preverbs that we find in so many of the other stocks, where very often a perfectly transparent relationship will exist between a prepositional form and a verbal prefix (cf. Lat. *Caesar milites transduxit trans Rhenum* 'Caesar led across the soldiers across the Rhine'). In Greek, for example, we can sometimes find the same form used adverbially, prepositionally, and as a preverb (e.g., *pró*). In Old Armenian, in fact, very little verbal prefixing occurs at all, with either directional or locative significance, as in the Latin example above, or with temporal-aspectual significance, as in the Slavic languages. In addition to its having the dominant SVO pattern with prepositions, Old Armenian is generally Adj. + Noun and Noun + Poss.

A Sample Old Armenian Text   6.2.

As mentioned above, the oldest Armenian literature is from the fifth century A.D.; most is in the form of translations from Greek or Syriac by Armenian clerics. But the surviving manuscripts were copied much later, the oldest one having been copied in 887. Thus the reliability of the texts of Old Armenian is somewhat in doubt. The following brief passage is from the Gospel according to St. Matthew 6:9–13 (text and transliteration from Jensen 1964:21):

Hayr   mer   or   yerkins,   surb ełiçi   anun k'o.   Ekesçē
Father our   who   in heaven   holy become   name of you come

ark'ayut'iwn k'o;   ełiçin   kamk' k'o   orpēs yerkins,   ew
kingdom   of you become   will   of you as   in heaven and

yerkri.   Zhaç mer   hanapazord tur   mez   aysōr.   Ew   t'oł
on earth   bread of us daily   give to us this day and   forgive

mez   zpartis mer,   orpēs ew   mek' t'ołumk' meroç   partapanaç.
to us debts   of us as   and   we   forgive   our   debtors

Ew   mi   tanir zmez i   p'orjut'iwn, ayl p'rkea zmez i   çarē;
and   not lead us   into temptation   but deliver us   from   evil

zi   k'o   ē   ark'ayut'iwn ew   zōrut'iwn ew   p'aŕk' yawiteans amēn.
for   of you is kingdom   and power   and glory   forever   amen

References

I. Grammars and Historical Works

Godel 1975

Hübschmann 1875

Hübschmann 1962

Jensen 1959

Meillet 1913

Meillet 1936

Solta 1960

Winter 1966

II. Works Cited in the Text

Hopper 1973

Jensen 1964

Albanian   7

Introduction   7.0.

We move now to Albanian, the remote history of which, like that of Armenian, is cloaked in mystery. Although the Albanians are mentioned in historical documents from Greece in the first century A.D. (by Ptolemy), no physical record of the language predates the fifteenth century, and it is not considerable at that (e.g., baptismal formulae). And, just as with Armenian, the historical connections between the speakers of Albanian and those of adjacent languages have contributed to rather severe changes in the structure, phonology, and especially the lexicon of the language. The main foreign influences on Albanian are Latin (cf. Lat. [acc.] *palūdem* 'swamp', Alb. *pyll* 'forest', through Rumanian *pădure* 'forest'), Italian, Turkish, modern Greek, and Slavic, which reflect cultural contacts with speakers of these languages after the fifth century A.D. in the form of loanwords into Albanian.

A disputed question is whether the Albanians are the modern-day descendents of the mysterious ancient Illyrians, who seem to appear everywhere across the Indo-European speaking area, or whether they are another group of descendents from the Thracians (some scholars have noted certain Albanian-Armenian parallels). As the evidence is extremely poor and difficult to interpret, it is best here not to comment on this issue directly. Suffice it to say that, in the absence of strong evidence, the postulation of such distant affinities is very often based on wishful thinking rather than on scientific fact (see 13.5 on Thracian and 13.6 on Illyrian).

Since written documents in Albanian did not appear until the fifteenth century, it is very difficult to make systematic use of this language in comparative Indo-European work. By the time a sufficient quantity of texts appear, the language has changed drastically from reconstructed PIE. In fact, Albanian was not established definitely as Indo-European until the latter part of the nineteenth century, when certain structural and lexical correspondences that demonstrated the Indo-European character of the language were noted (especially by Gustav Meyer). Cf. Alb. *natë* 'night', Lat. acc. sg. *noctem*, Gk. gen. sg. *nuktós* (< *nok^wt-); *bjer* 'bring', Lat. *ferō*, Skt. *bhárāmi* (< *$bher$-); *pjek* 'I roast', Lat. *coquō*, Skt. *pácati* 'cook' (< *pek^w-); Alb. *ulk-u* 'wolf', OIc. *ylgr* 'she-wolf' (< *$w̥lk^w$-); and a host of others.

Just as Armenian had been classified with Iranian in the early period of comparative linguistics, so Albanian was grouped with Latin and Greek because of the large number of loanwords from these two languages. It was later shown, through careful analysis of the vocabulary and the sound correspondences, that in fact Albanian had no special relationship with either Greek or Latin beyond heavy lexical indebtedness. Albanian still today is thought to stand in no close genealogical relationship with any other Indo-European language group.

7.1.   Albanian Dialects

Modern Albanian dialectology is quite complicated, owing principally to the continuous movements of the Albanian-speaking people under foreign domination. Two main dialects are recognized: the Gheg, spoken in the north and in Yugoslavia, and the Tosk, spoken in the south and in various colonies in Greece, Italy, and elsewhere. The dialects are reasonably close in most respects and are mutually intelligible in forms that have not undergone extreme changes. But because of the geographical, political, and cultural differences among the speakers of Gheg and Tosk, both varieties exist as national media.

Since the distinction between the Gheg and the Tosk dialects is so important geographically and politically in Albania and the Albanian-speaking area, it is useful to list at least the most important differences between the two varieties:

1. The presence of nasal vowels in Gheg and their absence in Tosk. Cf. Gheg *pę:* Tosk *pe* 'thread'.
2. Intervocalic *n* is retained in Gheg, whereas in Tosk it is rhotacized (changes to *r*). Cf. Gheg *vena:* Tosk *vera* 'wine'.
3. Initial *vo* in Gheg corresponds consistently to *va* in Tosk. Cf. Gheg *votër:* Tosk *vatër* 'hearth'.
4. Certain morphological differences, among them the use

of different auxiliary verbs in periphrastic tenses—for example, Gheg *kam me shkue* 'I will go' (auxiliary verb 'to have' plus the infinitive): Tosk *do të shkoj* (auxiliary verb 'will' plus the conjunctive).

A Brief Structural Sketch of Albanian   7.2.

7.2.1. Phonology

Albanian phonology is relatively straightforward, with little of the internal sandhi, lenition, or other complex phonological processes that occur in some of the other stocks. Although the consonantal inventories of both Gheg and Tosk are essentially the same, the two dialects differ considerably in matters of vowel phonology, as we have seen in our brief review of the differences between the two dialects. We turn now to some of the specifics.

7.2.1.1. Vowels

a. Gheg. In Gheg there are twelve vowel phonemes in a triangular system. As is typical of vowel systems with a nasal-oral contrast (e.g., French), the system is not perfectly symmetrical; that is, there is not a nasal and an oral vowel for every value in the system. The Gheg vowels are the following:

$$
\begin{array}{cccccc}
i & \underset{\textstyle .}{i} & & & u & \underset{\textstyle .}{u} \\
\ddot{u} & \underset{\textstyle .}{\ddot{u}} & & & & \\
e & \underset{\textstyle .}{e} & \text{ə} & & o & \\
& & a & \underset{\textstyle .}{a} & &
\end{array}
$$

Note: /ə/ is usually written as *ë*.

By some accounts Gheg also contains distinctive vowel length for all the oral vowels but *ə*, and indeed some minimal pairs are available to support this; cf. *dhē* 'earth': *dhe* 'and'; *lē* 'born': *le* 'let'; *drōn* 'they feared': *dron* 'he feared'. No such analysis is possible for Tosk, however, and we will not mark vowel length in any of our texts or examples.

b. Tosk. In Tosk there are no nasal vowels and no distinctive vowel length. We find here also a triangular system, as follows:

$$
\begin{array}{cccccc}
i & & \ddot{u} & & u & \\
e & & & & o & \\
& & \text{ə} & & & \\
& & a & & &
\end{array}
$$

In addition to the simple vowels, numerous diphthongs appear in both dialects, namely, *ai, ei, oi, ui, üi,* and *ie, üe, ua,* and *ue.*

Stress is of the expiratory type and falls always on either the penultimate or the final syllable. It is for the most part noncontrastive, though a few forms are distinguished only by stress placement—for example, *bári* 'the grass': *barí* 'herdsman'; *móri* 'took': *morí* 'crowd'.

7.2.1.2. Consonants

The consonantal inventories of Gheg and Tosk are quite similar. Most of the familiar distinctions based on place and manner of articulation are found in Albanian (nasal, lateral, stop, fricative, affricate), as well as a distinction based on palatalization. There are in all twenty-nine consonantal phonemes:

p	t	k	k'	ts	tš	s	š	f	θ
b	d	g	g'	dz	dž	z	ž	v	ð
n	l	r	m	h	j				
n'	l'	r'							

7.2.2. Morphology

Albanian morphology is different in many ways from the reconstructed morphological system of Proto-Indo-European. Three genders are typically recognized, though the masculine and feminine are by far the most important, with the neuter falling out of use. Not counting the vocative, which is identical to the nominative, there are only five cases (nominative, genitive, dative, accusative, and ablative), each with functions familiar from the other languages and in no way special. But, from a morphological point of view, the assignment of even five cases to the Albanian noun is problematical. As with Armenian and other languages that preserve part of the Indo-European case system, no forms are distinguished in every case and number by a distinctive case ending. Thus the five-case system is really a composite system, not an absolute one.

Albanian makes an obligatory distinction in nouns and adjectives between the definite and the indefinite forms by suffixing the definite article to the noun. Thus every noun is declined in the singular and plural (there is no dual), as well as in the definite and indefinite, in the five cases. But note the overlap in endings in the following sample paradigms:

Singular

	Indef.	*Def.*
Nom.	(nji) mal '(one) mountain'	mali 'the mountain'
Gen.	i (nji) mali	i malit
Dat.	(nji) mali	malit
Acc.	(nji) mal	malin
Abl.	(nji) mali	malit

Plural

	Indef.	*Def.*
Nom.	(disa) male '(some) mountains'	malet 'the mountains'
Gen.	i (disa) maleve	i malevet
Dat.	maleve	malevet
Acc.	male	malet
Abl.	malesh	malevet

Similar patterns of a declined suffixed definite article can be found throughout the substantival system, showing up in all the other noun classes.

Adjectives, which, as mentioned above, follow the pattern of nouns in Albanian, are curious in interesting ways. The most important is that they follow the noun and its postposed article—for example, *burrë i mirë* 'the good man'; *grue e mirë* 'the good woman'. When in this position they do not inflect for case.

Pronouns are heavily used in Albanian and have some interesting peculiarities that set them off from those of most of the other stocks. There are three persons in both singular and plural; these inflect in the five cases (with gaps in the genitive forms of *unë* 'I', *na* 'we', *ti* 'you-sg.', and *ju* 'you-pl.'). Possessives, like adjectives, usually follow the noun they modify (e.g., *libri im* 'my book'), though this rule does not hold with words marking family relationships (e.g., *im vëlla* 'my brother'). Some of the pronouns have two forms, one independent and one that occurs with prepositions.

When there is both a direct and an indirect object, the pronominal forms of both are joined together in a single form, and the nominal object remains—for example, *Zefi ma dha librin* 'Joseph gave *it to me* the book'; the form *ma* results from the union of *më* (dat. 1st pers.) and *e* (acc. 3rd pers.): *më + e → ma*. Similar patterns are found for other pronouns.

The verb in Albanian matches the noun in inflectional complexity, but is by all accounts far more complex organizationally, with many moods, tenses, and other forms. To begin with, there is a distinction of aspect between perfective, or completed action, and imperfective, or noncompleted action. There are eight tenses: present, imperfect, aorist, perfect, pluperfect I, pluperfect II, future, and exact future. In addition, there are six moods—indicative, conjunctive, conditional, optative, admirative, and imperative—as well as separate forms for the infinitive, participle, and gerund. Verbs are inflected in two voices, active and passive, as well as in a reflexive construction.

Despite the complexity of the Albanian verb, only part of it can be traced back to secure Indo-European origins. By some accounts the Albanian verb clearly reflects active and mediopassive verb morphology, *e : o* ablaut, and inherited stem suffixes. But the changes that have taken place in this language make such continuities extremely difficult to establish.

7.2.3. Syntax

Albanian syntax is in general quite manageable when compared with the patterns of the other Indo-European languages. With such a rich and detailed inflectional system, much of what we might call 'syntax' is in fact served by the morphology. Higher-order syntactic structures such as complements and relative clauses generally follow the patterns found in the other languages. Prepositions are quite common; as already mentioned, adjectives usually follow the noun, as do genitives and relatives. The dominant word order in the sentence is SVO.

7.3.   A Sample Albanian Text

The following brief sample of Albanian is from the Gospel according to St. Matthew 6:9–13. It is chosen primarily for ease of comparison with the Armenian biblical passage in the preceding chapter. It is in the Tosk dialect.

Ati	ynë	që	je	në	qiell	u	shënjtëroftë	emri	yt.
Father-def.	our	who	is	in	heaven	be	holy	name-def.	your

Arthtë	mbretëria	jote.	U	bëftë	dëshira	jote,	si	në	qiell,	edhe
come	kingdom-def.	your	be	done	will-def.	your	as	in	heaven	and

mbi	dhe.	Bukën	tonë	të	përditëshme	jepna	neve	sot.
on	earth	bread-def.	our	the	daily	give to us	to us	today

Edhe	falna	fajet	tona,	sikundër	edhe	ne	ua
and	forgive to us	debts-def.	our	as	and	we	to them-it

falim   fajtorëvet   tanë. Edhe mos na shtjerë në   ngasje,   po
forgive   debtors-def.   our   and   not us   lead   into temptation but

shpëtona   nga   i   ligu.   Sepse jotja   është mbretëria   e
deliver-us from the evil-def. for   yours   is   kingdom-def.   and

fuqia   e   lavdia   në jetët   të   jetëvet.
power-def. and   glory-def. in age-def. the ages-def.

References

I. Grammars and Historical Works

Camaj 1969   Meyer 1888
Haebler 1965   Meyer 1891
Hamp 1966   Newmark 1957
Meyer 1883–1892   Pipa (n.d.)

8   Baltic

8.0.   Introduction

The Baltic subgroup of Indo-European has played a significant role in comparative Indo-European linguistics from the beginning. Despite the relatively late date at which Baltic is first
recorded (fourteenth century A.D.), the languages of this group
are remarkably archaic in comparison with other Indo-European
stocks, and for this reason they must be considered carefully in
discussions of the proto-language. The conservative and archaic
character of Lithuanian in particular has even been the source
of popular fantasy, with some accounts maintaining that native
speakers of Lithuanian were capable of conversing with Brahmin
speakers of Sanskrit, each in his own language, with almost complete mutual intelligibility. Such an assertion is, of course, wildly
untrue, but it does underscore the conservative nature of the Baltic languages.

The reputation for conservatism that the Baltic languages
enjoy is well deserved, and indeed in many instances it can be
shown that they reflect the Indo-European system more closely
than do Greek, Latin, or Sanskrit, the three languages on which
much of reconstructed Proto-Indo-European is based. The case
system of Lithuanian, for example, preserves seven cases, a
number exceeded only by Sanskrit with eight (cf. Greek with five,
Latin with six). Lithuanian also maintains a productive dual number in some dialects, a feature absent in Latin. Other conservative
tendencies can be recognized throughout the morphological and
syntactic systems. Baltic phonology is generally considered less
conservative than its morphology, especially in its consonants.
But, even in the phonology, there has not been the same degree of
radical change that occurred in some of the other stocks, even
older ones. For illustration, compare the following words for
'alive' in several Indo-European languages and note how close the

Lithuanian form is to the reconstructed form: Lat. *vīvus,* OCS *živŭ,* Skt. *jīvás,* Goth. *qius,* OIr. *biu,* Gk. *bíos,* Lith. *gývas*—all from **gʷīwos.*

Very little is known about the prehistory of the Balts, though hydronymic evidence places them in a wider area than they currently occupy. The Balts were probably established as an independent linguistic group by about 2000 B.C. At this time they came into contact with the Baltic Finns, as evident from the early loanwords in each group. In this respect, Baltic, especially Latvian, has some early loanwords from the West Finnish languages, but the Finnish languages have more loans from Baltic—for example, Estonian *tagiyas* 'thistle' (cf. Lith. *dagỹs*); Finnish *taivas* 'sky' (cf. Lith. *diẽvas* 'god'); and others.

The Baltic languages have also been in close contact with the Slavic and Germanic languages, which have left a number of loanwords in Baltic—for example, Lith. *kùrtas,* Latv. *kur̃ts,* OPruss. *curtis* 'hunting dog' (cf. Pol. *chart*); also Lith. *muĩlas* 'soap' (cf. Russ. *mylo*). On the Germanic side, note, for example, OPruss. *ylo,* Lith. *ýla,* Latv. *īlens* 'awl' (cf. OIc. *alr*).

Only two languages from the Baltic family are spoken today: Lithuanian and Latvian, or Lettish. Lithuanian is spoken primarily in Lithuania, and its speakers number about two and one-half million. Enclaves of speakers in Poland, Belorussia, and elsewhere abroad (mostly in the United States and Canada) add about another half-million speakers to the total. Counting speakers abroad, Latvian has about one and three-quarter million speakers; most are in Latvia. Both Lithuanian and Latvian have a number of geographically determined dialects across Lithuania and Latvia.

Besides the two surviving languages, Lithuanian and Latvian, there are many extinct languages in the Baltic group. These include Selonian, Semigallian, Curonian, and Yotvingian. The speakers of these languages were assimilated by Lithuanians, by Latvians, and, in the case of the Yotvingians, by Slavs before they could leave any written traces of their languages. The only remaining evidence of these extinct languages is place names. Another extinct language in the Baltic group, Old Prussian, provides our oldest documentation from the Baltic family (see 8.1.1 below). The Baltic languages are divided into two main groups, East and West Baltic. We turn now to a discussion of these two.

8.1.   West Baltic

8.1.1. Old Prussian

Old Prussian is the name given to the language spoken by Balts in certain coastal regions of the Baltic Sea. The Prussians are first mentioned in the first century A.D. by the Roman historian Tacitus, who called them Aistians. They are called Prussians for the first time in the ninth century. Old Prussian is the only language of the West Baltic group of which records have survived. Yotvingian is another member of West Baltic, but no records of this language are extant.

As mentioned above, Old Prussian provides us with the oldest written documentation of the Baltic languages. There are five major Old Prussian documents: the first is the Elbing Vocabulary, which is dated to about A.D. 1400 and which contains some eight hundred words; next is Simon Grunau's Vocabulary, containing about one hundred words and dated to somewhere between 1517 and 1526; there are also three catechisms, two published in 1545 and one in 1561. This meager inventory was increased slightly (by two lines) with the recent discovery of the Basel Epigram and its identification as Old Prussian by McCluskey, Schmalstieg, and Zeps (1975). Old Prussian's apparent early and rather extreme influence from German indicates considerable bilingualism. The language was eventually displaced by German, its last speakers dying out in the early 1700s.

8.2.   East Baltic

The East Baltic group comprises Lithuanian, Latvian, Selonian, Semigallian, and Curonian. Of these, of course, only Lithuanian and Latvian have survived, and only these will be discussed further in this survey.

8.2.1. Lithuanian

Lithuanian is the principal modern representative of the Baltic group of Indo-European. It is first attested in a manuscript text of the Pater Noster known as the Dzukish Prayers, written at the very beginning of the sixteenth century. Perhaps older than this is the very distorted and perhaps falsified few words of the Oath of Kęstutis from 1351, which, because of its doubtful validity, has practically no significance for Lithuanian historical grammar.

The first Lithuanian book to have appeared is a translation of Luther's catechism by M. Mažvydas in 1547. Mažvydas' Catechism is usually cited as the oldest surviving Lithuanian document, and it is certainly the oldest that is systematically helpful. A wealth of documents date from the sixteenth to eighteenth centuries, including a grammar of Lithuanian by D. Kleinas from 1653–1654 and a dictionary by K. Sirvydas from 1629.

As was noted earlier, Lithuanian is generally held to be the most archaic living Indo-European language. It has changed little since the time of the Mažvydas Catechism, though some demonstrably older forms are often referred to as Old Lithuanian. Among the modern languages it stands out as the most important source of information concerning the proto-language. The obvious conservatism of Lithuanian is due in part to its central geographical position within the Baltic region.

Although the Old Prussian monuments are older than the Lithuanian ones, Lithuanian is far more reliable and useful as a source of historical information. Part of its value in this respect is due to the fact that Lithuanian is so conservative, and part is due to the fact that the interpretation of the Old Prussian documents is extremely hazardous and speculative.

8.2.2. Latvian

In comparative Baltic studies, Latvian is the language typically cast in the role of innovator. Extensive simplifications in phonology and word formation make it possible in many cases to establish the modern written Lithuanian forms as proto-forms for their modern Latvian counterparts. Of course, in some areas Latvian appears to be more conservative (e.g., in the intonational system), and in many areas of the grammar there are simply matched features in the two languages. But, on the whole, Latvian is less conservative and more seriously altered in its structure than is Lithuanian. This state of affairs is probably due to the persistent influence on Latvian of Livonian, Estonian, and German.

The oldest Latvian material is a biblical translation, dated to 1585. A fairly substantial literature is from the seventeenth century, including a Latvian-German dictionary by G. Mancelius (1638) and a grammar by J. G. Rehehausen (1644). Like Lithuanian, Latvian is now being influenced by Russian, with which it shares the status of the official language of Latvia.

8.3.   A Brief Structural Sketch of Lithuanian

8.3.1. Phonology

8.3.1.1. Vowels

Lithuanian has a triangular vowel system in which the feature of length plays a distinctive role. The symmetry in the vowel system is disturbed only by the presence of the vowel *ė*, which is a tense mid-front vowel roughly equivalent to English /ey/, but without the glide. This vowel is always long.

Each vowel in the system except *ė* is found in both the long and the short categories, though there are certain qualitative differences between the long and the short varieties that we shall ignore in this survey. The vowels are as follows:

Note: (a) Lithuanian long vowels are often written with a subscript diacritic—for example, *ų* (= *ū*), *į* (= *ī*)—which signals the existence of a previous nasalization. (b) Like *į*, the letter *y* denotes a long vowel, but without etymological nasalization. The letter *ī* is never used in standard orthography.

In addition to these simple vowels, Lithuanian also has a number of diphthongs, namely, *ai, au, ei, ie, ui,* and *uo*.

Lithuanian orthography uses three accent marks: grave (`), acute (´), and circumflex (˜). Grave denotes accented short vowels; acute, or falling, accent occurs on long vowels or diphthongs; and, finally, the circumflex accent denotes long vowels or diphthongs in which the second part is more heavily stressed than the first. Accent in Lithuanian is free, in the sense that it can, under the proper phonetic conditions, fall on any syllable of a word. This sets Lithuanian apart from, say, Greek, Latin, or Celtic, where strict rules govern the syllables on which accent can fall. Accentually, Lithuanian is much closer to Sanskrit, which also has a free-accent system.

Inherited ablaut patterns are fairly well maintained in modern Lithuanian. Several alternation patterns are found. The first of these is the *i*-series, in which *i* alternates with *ī:* cf. Lith. *likti* 'to remain': *lỹkius* 'remnant, remains'. The next group is called the *u*-series; this is represented, for example, by Lith. pres. and inf. *bùria, bùrti*, pret. *bū́rė* 'to charm', with alternation between *u* and *ū*. The familiar Indo-European ablaut pattern of *e : o* is realized in Lithuanian primarily as *e : a*, since **o > a* in Baltic. To illustrate this ablaut pattern we have, for example, Lith. *vèsti* 'to lead' (from root *ved-* + inf. ending *-ti*): *vadžióti* 'to lead about'; also Lith. *velkù* 'I drag': *válkioti* 'to drag about'. There is also evidence in Lithuanian for ablaut patterns based on *ē : ō* and *i : e*, but the examples can only be justified after considerable internal reconstruction.

8.3.1.2. Consonants

Lithuanian consonantal phonology is relatively straightforward when compared with that of the other Indo-European stocks and the reconstructed Proto-Indo-European system. Among the most visible changes are the loss of the aspiration in the voiced aspirates **bh, *dh, *gh*, as well as the loss of the labial element in the labiovelars such as **kʷ, *gʷ*, and so on. The other remarkable feature is the generalization of palatalization as a distinctive feature of the entire system. The segments are as follows:

p	p'	t	t'	k	k'	f	f'	s	s'	š	š'	x(ch)	x'	h h'
b	b'	d	d'	g	g'	v	v'	z	z'	ž	ž'			
				c(ts)		c'		č	č'					
m	m'	n	n'	dz		dz'		dž	dž'	r	r'	l	l'	j

As can be seen from the preceding inventory, all consonants except *j* exist in both palatalized and nonpalatalized forms. Consonants are always palatalized before front vowels, but palatalization in Lithuanian is not predictable and is therefore a phonemically distinctive feature of the consonantal system. Palatalized consonants before nonfront vowels are signaled orthographically by an *i* (e.g., *brólio* 'brother's', which is equivalent to /bról'o/).

Lithuanian segmental sandhi is far less complicated than that of Sanskrit or Old Irish, and Lithuanian phonological rules do not usually interfere with the morphological transparency of roots in derived forms. We have seen examples in Sanskrit and Old Irish of internal changes that alter the shape of root forms; we do not find such changes in Lithuanian. This is not to suggest that historical Baltic phonology is simple; in fact, the Proto-Indo-European patterns have been substantially altered in all the Baltic languages, with many losses, mergers, and restructurings. In general, however, Baltic historical phonology is manageable and relatively well understood.

8.3.2. Morphology

When we speak of Lithuanian as the most conservative living language of the Indo-European family, it is the noun morphology that provides the main impetus for our claim. There are, as already mentioned, seven cases in Lithuanian: nominative, genitive, dative, accusative, instrumental, vocative, and locative. All nouns are inflected in both singular and plural numbers, and, though the dual has been lost in standard Lithuanian, it remains in some of the other dialects. Only the masculine and feminine genders survive productively in modern Lithuanian; the older neuters have for the most part been absorbed by the masculines. Nouns are divided into five large declensional groups, each with its own subgroups determined by the ending of the stem.

The efficiency and the longevity of an inflectional system are determined by a number of complex factors. We have seen throughout this volume examples of inflectional systems where large amounts of case syncretism had occurred, rendering the systems inefficient by virtue of the morphological identity of many of the different cases. Albanian and Armenian are particularly good illustrations of this phenomenon, though evidence is plentiful among the other stocks as well. When a case system becomes inefficient—that is, when there is insufficient formal distinction among endings because of phonological change or reduction—it is in effect doomed. Other grammatical devices will be called into play in the language, among them fixed word order (e.g., English) and increased use of pre- and postpositions (e.g., Latin). Lithuanian is rather remarkable among the languages of the Indo-European family in the relative amount of morphological discreteness evident in the nominal system. There are simply not very many cases marked by the same ending. Note the following two paradigms:

Tévas 'Father' (1st Dec. Masc.)

	Sg.	Pl.
Nom.	tévas	tévai
Gen.	tévo	tévų
Dat.	tévui	tévams
Acc.	tévą	tévus

Inst.	tévu	tévais
Loc.	téve	tévuose
Voc.	téve	tévai

Akìs 'Eye' (3rd Dec. Fem.)

	Sg.	Pl.
Nom.	akìs	ãkys
Gen.	akiēs	akių̃
Dat.	ãkiai	akìms
Acc.	ãkį	akìs
Inst.	akià, akimì	akimìs
Loc.	akyjè, akýj, aký	akysè
Voc.	akiē	ãkys

Adjectives in Lithuanian are noteworthy in that they are declined in two forms, the definite and the indefinite (they share this feature with the adjectives of the early Slavic languages). There are three principal adjectival declensions, and they follow the pattern of the corresponding noun class in all the cases but the dative and locative in the singular and the nominative and dative in the plural. These cases have been supplied by the endings of the demonstrative pronouns (a similar process took place in Germanic). The definite adjectives are formed by adding the appropriate case of the third-person pronoun to the indefinite adjective, namely, nom. sg. masc. mãžas 'small': mažàsis 'small' (def.)— that is, mãžas-jìs 'small-he'; gen. pl. masc. and fem. mažų̃jų— that is, mazų̃-jų̃ 'small-them'.

Pronouns are in general unremarkable in Lithuanian, being inflected in the same cases as the noun except the vocative.

The Lithuanian verb cannot lay claim to the same high degree of conservatism present in the noun system. Of course, since the factors influencing the maintenance or loss of a case system are in many ways different from those affecting a verbal system, there is really no reason why the two systems should develop in parallel fashion. One of the distinctive features of the Lithuanian verb is the lack of differentiation between the third-person singular, dual, and plural verb forms—for example, dìrba 'he works, they work', which was most likely an earlier singular.

Lithuanian has two voices, active and passive. The passive, however, is not an inherited category. It is, rather, a fairly recent development in the language, formed by the periphrasis of the verb bū́ti 'to be' and certain participial forms. The middle voice has been totally lost in Lithuanian as in all the other Baltic languages.

The number of separate verb tenses in Lithuanian is quite large, but only the present and future tense forms have clear Indo-European origins. There is a simple past tense and a frequentative past; the origin of both is not completely clear. In addition, there is a present and a future; periphrastic perfects, pluperfects, and future perfects all formed with different forms of *búti* 'to be' and past active participles; and a whole series of progressives that are also periphrastic in formation—for example, prog. pret. *bùvo bedirbą̃s* 'he was still working'.

There are two principal moods, indicative and subjunctive, and there are separate forms for both the imperative and the various infinitives. Lithuanian also has gerunds and supines, both of which are very ancient categories and are quite rare among the Indo-European languages (especially the supine, which is an old verbal form used as the object of a verb of motion—for example, *aš einù gul̃tų* 'I am going to sleep'). Such forms, however, are confined to certain dialects of the modern language.

Lithuanian is rich in participles, with a full set of active and passive forms. There are two varieties of present active participle, a future active participle, a past active participle, and a frequentative past active participle, as well as a present passive participle, a future passive, and a past passive. In addition, participles may be formed from reflexive verbs. Participles follow adjective declensions, and their function in Lithuanian is one of the most striking characteristics of the language (see 8.3.3 below).

8.3.3. Syntax

As is typical with richly inflected languages, the boundary between morphology and syntax in Lithuanian is often difficult to establish. Word order in Lithuanian is variable, but SVO order and accompanying Adj. + Noun predominates. Prepositions are plentiful and occur with four cases: the genitive, which is the most common, the dative, which is rare, the accusative, and the instrumental. There is some evidence for earlier postpositions—for example, Lith. *dė̃l* 'for, because of', which can follow the noun it governs.

By far the most distinctive feature of Lithuanian syntax is the heavy reliance on participial constructions. They can be used as simple adjectival modifiers—for example, *bė́gą̃s vanduõ* 'running water'. Participles are also used extensively in the various compound tenses—for example, *esù dìrbęs* 'I have worked' (past active part.), *buvaũ mùšamas* 'I was being beaten' (pres. passive part.), and so on. A third use of the participle in Lithuanian is in the so-called separate participial phrases such as *Aš mačiaũ žmõgų atnešusį̃ jám tą̃ knỹgą* 'I saw the man who brought him that book', lit. 'I saw the man having brought him that book'. Such uses of the participle are in effect reduced relative clauses, where instead of the full finite verb form with the relative pronoun (e.g., *kurìs àtnešė* 'who brought'), we find instead the appropriate participial form. Such participial uses are very much like those of Greek, Latin, and Sanskrit. The final participial usage of Lithuanian recalls the parallel usage in Greek, where the participle is used in indirect statement in place of a finite verb—for example, *Jõnas sãkosi daũg žiną̃s* 'John says that he knows a lot', lit. 'John says (himself) knowing a lot'.

A Sample Lithuanian Text   **8.4.**

The following brief text from the *Lithuanian Reader for Self-Instruction* by W. R. Schmalstieg and A. Klimas (1967:9–12) is called "The First Lithuanian Book":

Pirmoji	Lietuviška	Knyga				
The first	Lithuanian	Book				

Relìginių kovų̃	įtakoje		1547 m.	iř	pasiródė	pirmóji
Religious struggles	under the influence of	in 1547	even	appeared	first

lietùviška	knygà -	Martýno	Mãžvydo	"Katekìsmo	prastì	žõdžiai,
Lithuanian	book	of Martin	Mosvid	of the Catechism	simple	words

mókslas	skaĩtymo	rãšto	iř	gíesmės."	Šìta knygà	bùvo grynaĩ
skill	of reading	of writing	and	hymns	this book	was purely

relìginio	tùrinio,	jì	turéjo	supažìndinti	liáudį sù	grynaĩ
of religious	contents	it	was to	acquaint	people with	purely

relìginiais	kláusimais.
religious	questions

'In 1547 under the influence of the religious struggles there appeared the first Lithuanian book, Martin Mosvid's "Simple Words of the Catechism, the Art of Reading, and of Writing and Hymns." The book was of purely religious contents, it was supposed to acquaint people with purely religious questions.'

References

I. Grammars and Historical Works

Dambriūnas, Klimas
  and Schmalstieg
  1966
Endzelīns 1923
Endzelīns 1944
Endzelīns 1971

Leskien 1919
Schmalstieg 1974a
Schmalstieg 1976a
Senn 1966a
Stang 1966
Trautmann 1910

II. Dictionary

Fraenkel 1955

III. Works Cited in the Text

McCluskey et al. 1975
Schmalstieg and Klimas 1967

Slavic 9

Introduction 9.0.

Because they are highly conservative in character, the Slavic languages occupy a prominent position in Indo-European linguistics. As with the Baltic group, records of the Slavic languages are not particularly old, the oldest material dating from the tenth century. It is not known exactly when the proto-Slavs came into their historic homelands, nor is it clear where they came from or precisely where they originally settled. Botanical and archaeological evidence suggests a home somewhere between the Vistula and the Dnieper, and between the Carpathians and the Narew. The area of modern eastern Poland is another possibility, as is an even more westward location as far as the Oder.

Although the original homeland of the Slavs is uncertain, certain aspects of their sociocultural makeup seem securely established. To begin with, the proto-Slavs were forest-agricultural people whose largest political unit seems to have been the village; words implying higher levels of political organization are all loanwords (e.g., 'king', 'prince', 'emperor'). The wealth of lexical evidence from the Slavic languages shows a loose confederation of villages operating in a pastoral, though mobile, society with domesticated animals and advanced methods of agriculture.

The current wide area dominated by the Slavic languages, comprising most of eastern Europe between Germany and the Ural mountains, is the result of continued expansion by the Slavic people in every direction since the fifth century A.D. The Slavic languages have made their greatest advances against Baltic and Finnish, with whom they have long shared common borders.

The Slavic languages are divided into three main groups: Southern, Western, and Eastern, each further divided into several subgroups (see 9.1, 9.2, and 9.3 below). There have been some interesting attempts to redesign the classification of the Slavic languages as based on analyses of the relevant isoglosses (e.g., Birnbaum 1966), but we shall adhere to the traditional divisions in this section.

As mentioned earlier, the Slavic languages are extremely important for the reconstruction of Proto-Indo-European. This is especially true for OCS, the oldest attested Slavic language, but it holds for most of the remaining Slavic languages as well. In fact, it is safe to say that of all the larger Indo-European stocks with many internal divisions (e.g., Italic, Germanic, Indic), none is so coherent as the Slavic group.

Among the many reasons why the Slavic languages are important for historical Indo-European studies, several stand out: (1) a high degree of inflectional complexity in nouns, pronouns, adjectives, and verbs that is in some ways more elaborate than that found in Latin (e.g., Latin preserves six cases, OCS preserves seven; OCS maintains the dual number, which survives only in a few traces in Latin); (2) the presence of a productive functional aspectual distinction in the verbal system that marks the action identified by the verb as either completed (perfective) or noncompleted (imperfective), or else as a single action or a habitual action; (3) as a consequence of the rich inflectional system, a relatively free word order that provides valuable insight into the interplay between syntax and morphology in inflectionally complex languages such as Proto-Indo-European.

Phonologically, the Slavic languages are considerably less archaic, having eliminated many of the distinctions we assume for Proto-Indo-European (e.g., aspiration in consonants), and having introduced or elaborated some others (e.g., the palatalization of consonants by yod, which characterizes all Slavic languages, and palatalization by front vowels, which is found in many languages of this group). Other phonological features characteristic of the Slavic group are the extensive use of sibilants and affricates, and complex consonant clusters.

9.1.   South Slavic

The South Slavic languages are Old Church Slavic, Slovenian (or Slovene), Serbian and Croatian (Serbocroatian), Bulgarian, and Macedonian.

9.1.1. Old Church Slavic (Old Bulgarian)

The oldest recorded Slavic language is Old Church Slavic (OCS), or Old Bulgarian (so called because it is thought to be a much earlier form of Bulgarian). OCS is securely dated to the mid-ninth century, though the actual documents that have survived are from the tenth and primarily the eleventh centuries.

OCS must be kept distinct from Church Slavic. Church Slavic is a language that serves as a liturgical medium in the Russian, Bulgarian, Serbian, and Ukrainian Orthodox churches. Since the various national languages have all exerted great local influence on Church Slavic, it exists in many different varieties. In addition to its liturgical function, Church Slavic also served as a standard literary medium in many of these languages, in some cases until quite recently.

When we speak of OCS as a historical unity, we are referring to a small group of South Slavic manuscripts dating from the tenth and eleventh centuries. The principal texts on which they are based are religious translations made during the years 863–865 by the Slavic apostles Constantine (Cyril) and Methodius, and later copied by their disciples. The OCS manuscripts generally thought to be the most archaic are the Slavic versions of the Four Gospels called the Codex Zographensis (considered the most reliable) and the Codex Marianus. The oldest dated text in OCS is a grave inscription from 993.

OCS flourished as a literary language in eastern Bulgaria for more than three quarters of a century (893–969). It was written in two alphabets, the Cyrillic and the Glagolitic, which are both ultimately based on the Greek alphabet. The Glagolitic alphabet was probably invented by St. Cyril, whereas the Cyrillic was probably invented by St. Clement. The Glagolitic was eventually superseded by the Cyrillic script, though the majority of the older Slavic manuscripts are written in Glagolitic. There was probably a considerable nonecclesiastical literature in OCS, but none of it has survived.

From the Indo-European standpoint, OCS is by far the most important of the Slavic languages. It preserves many older features such as the elaborate case system, the dual number, the three-gender noun classification, and a complex participial system. (More will be said about the linguistic features of OCS in 9.4.)

9.1.2. Slovenian

Currently spoken in Slovenia in the mountainous northwest part of Yugoslavia, Slovenian has only about one and one-half million to two million speakers. It is first recorded in an interesting text called the Freising Leaves, dated to about the eleventh century, which contains prayers, confessions, and homilies written in the Latin alphabet. Slovenian has certain archaisms that make it interesting from the Indo-European point of view—for example, the maintenance of the dual number in both the noun and the verb, and an archaic accentual and intonational system. It has a fairly large number of major dialects (about seven), and perhaps as many as forty minor dialect areas, all of which are determined largely by the mountainous terrain of the area of Slovenia.

9.1.3. Serbian and Croatian

Spoken in Yugoslavia on the western part of the Balkan peninsula, the Serbian and Croatian languages enjoy separate allegiances and boast separate literatures. The two are most commonly referred to as a composite language, Serbocroatian (or Serbo-Croatian), but the political and regional differences among Serbs and Croats make the distinction one worth maintaining, even though the two are mutually intelligible. That Serbian and Croatian share several important features with Slovenian prompts some to classify the three as West South Slavic, with Bulgarian and Macedonian as East South Slavic.

Like Slovenian, Serbian and Croatian have a musical accent (as opposed to an expiratory one); they also maintain traces of the Indo-European ablaut patterns, seven cases in the noun, and the imperfect and aorist verb tenses in the written language. Three different dialects of the composite Serbocroatian are typically recognized: the *što, kaj,* and *ča* dialects, based on the word for 'what' in each. Subvarieties of each dialect occur as well.

9.1.4. Bulgarian

Though its history is, of course, tied closely with that of Old Church Slavic (Old Bulgarian), the language we now call Bulgarian has literature beginning only from the eighteenth century. The linguistic structure and history of Bulgarian are extremely complex; the language has been subjected to a great deal of foreign influence, especially from Turkish. This fact and certain internal developments mark Bulgarian as quite unlike all the other Slavic languages except Macedonian, with which it is closely grouped. Accentually it has a free heavy-stress accent rather than a musical or pitch accent, and there is a great deal of reduction of unstressed vowels. Indo-European ablaut is preserved, but certain other features make Bulgarian (and Macedonian) special among the Slavic languages. Chief among these characteristics are the near complete loss of nominal declensions and a number of other morphological innovations relating to articles, infinitives, adjectival comparison, and verb tenses. Interestingly, though the nominal inflections have been lost, the three common Slavic genders of masculine, feminine, and neuter have been preserved. Bulgarian and Macedonian also preserve the old aorist and imperfect tenses.

Though dialect classification is hazardous because of the many transitional regions shared with Macedonian, three main groups are typically recognized: Western, Northeastern, and Southeastern.

9.1.5. Macedonian

Macedonian is spoken by about one million people in various enclaves in Yugoslavia (Serbia), Greece, and Bulgaria. Macedonian is considered by most specialists to constitute a separate South Slavic language, but its closeness to Bulgarian in crucial features has prompted some to consider Macedonian a variety of Bulgarian. Of these shared features the most important are the loss of nominal inflections and certain features relating to verb morphology, tense formation, and a few others, including the stress accent on the third syllable from the end in the literary language. There are at least six different Macedonian dialects.

West Slavic 9.2.

The West Slavic languages are numerically the largest group in the Slavic branch of Indo-European. They include Polish, Czech, Slovak, Kashubian, Wendish, and the extinct Polabian.

9.2.1. Polish

Spoken by a total of about twenty-five million people, Polish is one of the most important of the Slavic languages. It is not documented until a fairly late date (1270), and then only by a single sentence translating a quotation. The first continuous documents to have survived date from the fourteenth century in the form of sermons and other religious writings. The reason for the late attestation of the language is that Latin predominated as a literary medium in Poland until the fourteenth century. Polish shows some moderate influence from Czech and German.

Polish is a characteristic West Slavic language. It has a moderate-stress accent fixed on the penultimate syllable, extensive palatalization of consonants, and evidence of inherited ablaut. It has lost the dual number, but maintains the three-gender system, and has nasal vowels. It has seven cases and a tense-aspect system characteristic of other West Slavic languages. As in all other Slavic languages, the inherited mediopassive has been lost (though passive participles are common, as in all Slavic languages).

There are at least four major dialect groups of Polish (the fifth, Kashubian, is considered a separate language in this book): the dialects of Wielkopolska and Kujawy, the dialects of Małopolska, the dialects of Polish Silesia, and the dialects of Mazovia.

9.2.2. Wendish

Also known as Sorbian or Lusatian, Wendish is one of the lesser-known Slavic languages. There are at present only about 75,000 speakers of this language in its two varieties, Upper and Lower Wendish, living in an area of East Germany that borders on northwest Czechoslovakia and southwest Poland. The number of speakers of Wendish has been steadily dwindling in the face of strong German influence, though Wendish is maintained in two separate literary languages, Upper Wendish, with its center in Budyšin, and Lower Wendish, with its center in Chośebuz. Though these two languages are quite similar, they are not easily mutually intelligible. Lower Wendish is closer on the whole to Polish, whereas Upper Wendish shares features with Slovak and Czech.

The oldest piece of the Wendish language to have come down to us is an oath of loyalty dating from 1532. The oldest continuous literature is a New Testament translation from 1548.

Wendish has characteristic West Slavic stress accent, examples of inherited ablaut patterns, and extensive palatalization of consonants. Morphologically, Wendish is interesting because it preserves the dual in both noun and verb paradigms. Counting the vocative, Wendish has seven cases, with the typical three-gender system. Verbs are special in Wendish because they preserve the old imperfect and aorist tenses, as do Macedonian and Bulgarian.

9.2.3. Czech

Czech is spoken by approximately nine million people in modern-day Czechoslovakia and has served as the standard literary dialect of Prague since the thirteenth century. Its earliest literature, all of it of a religious nature, comes from the thirteenth century. Before that time, only glosses of Czech words in Latin texts are available as evidence of the early language.

Czech has long been under heavy German influence, especially after political events in the seventeenth and eighteenth centuries. The language has undergone a series of extensive changes—many of which have taken place since the time of the earliest documents—including the loss of the dual number and of the aorist and imperfect tenses, features evident in the material from before the sixteenth century. Overall, Czech has innovated in many important categories. Phonologically, Czech underwent a 'vowel mutation' that sets it apart sharply from Slovak, with which it is commonly compared. It has stress accent on the first syllable, but stands alone among the Slavic languages with an intervocalic glottal stop that occurs between words. Examples of ablaut patterns and several other phonological peculiarities divide it from Slovak, especially the vowel mutation. Morphologically, it is fairly typical, with seven cases and three genders. In the verb, tense and aspect distinctions are maintained, though some simplifications have been introduced, even from the time of the early documents (e.g., the loss of the pluperfect tense).

Czech has six main dialect groups: Central (Prague), Northeast, Southwest, the Czecho-Moravian group, the Hanák dialects of Moravia, and the Lach dialects of Silesia.

9.2.4. Slovak

Slovak, considered to be more archaic than Czech, has far fewer speakers (about four million). In Czechoslovakia, the country where Slovak coexists with Czech, the language does not have the same prestige, since Czech is the standard used in Prague. The modern literary language we now call Slovak is not attested until the nineteenth century, but there is evidence of Slovak in Latin documents from as early as the eleventh century from Hungary, where Latin was the official language of the time.

Accent in Slovak is based on first-syllable stress; in general, the overall phonology of Slovak is more conservative than that of Czech. Morphologically, however, it has undergone considerable

simplification, with the elimination of certain cases and the generalization of some endings. The dual has been lost, and inflectional
differences between stem classes are fewer than in Czech. Verbs
in Slovak generally pattern as do verbs in Czech, with certain
morphological differences that need not concern us here.

Slovak dialectologists recognize three main dialect groups:
the Central group, the Western group, and the Eastern group. The
Eastern group is closer to Polish and Ukrainian; the Western
group shares certain features with dialects of Czech. The Central
group serves as the basis of the modern standard language.

9.2.5. Kashubian

Kashubian is considered by many Slavicists to be a dialect of
Polish, and indeed its closeness to Polish cannot be denied. But
there are reasons to consider it separately, the most important
being that it is further away from Polish and is mutually unintel-
ligible with many of the varieties accepted as Polish dialects.

Kashubian has very few speakers, probably fewer than
100,000, and it is almost certain to be displaced by Polish in future
years. It has been subjected to a great deal of influence from
German, being located in Upper Pomerania, a former German
province. Apart from some phonological differences that set
Kashubian off from Polish, the major features of the two are for
the most part similar.

9.3.   East Slavic

The East Slavic languages are Russian (also known as Great
Russian), White Russian, or Belorussian (from the Russian *belyj*
'white'), and Ukrainian.

9.3.1. Russian

Russian is certainly the best known of the Slavic languages
and has the largest number of speakers. We generally divide Russian into three main historical periods: Old Russian (1100–1500),
Middle Russian (1500–1700), and Modern Russian (since 1700).
Old Russian is clearly characterized by certain phonological and
morphological divergences from OCS. Middle Russian, the language of the princes of Muscovy, became the standard language
with an officially accepted style. Though some formal differences
occur between the two, Middle Russian is generally described as

being of a more fixed form than Old Russian. Modern, or Great Russian, the most expansive of the Slavic languages, is spoken in all corners of the Soviet Union and beyond by about 230 million people, though for many of these millions it is an official language, not a native one.

Russian is characterized by the phonemic contrast of palatalization in consonants, a strong free-stress accent, and the reduction of unstressed vowels. Traces of Indo-European ablaut can be found, as in the other Slavic languages.

Morphologically, Russian maintains a seven-case system (nominative, genitive, dative, accusative, instrumental, locative, and a vestigial vocative that survives only in a few words) and three genders, but has lost the dual in all but a few relic forms. In the verb system a number of simplifications have taken place— for example, the loss of the old imperfect and aorist tenses, and some derived verbal forms found in OCS (supine, pluperfect tense, and some others). As in the other Slavic languages, the old mediopassive has been lost, having been replaced by either compound tenses with 'to be' or impersonal reflexive constructions. The use of compounding in tense formation is widespread, as is the extensive use of aspect, which forms the basis of the entire system of the verb.

There are three main Russian dialect groups: Northern, Southern, and Central. The Northern dialects include most of Russian-speaking Siberia; the Southern group stretches south to the White Russian- and Ukrainian-speaking regions; and the Central group includes most of European Russia and Moscow.

Dating the earliest documents from Great Russian is difficult for several reasons. Old Russian can be considered the ancestor not only of Great Russian, but also of Ukrainian and White Russian. So it is difficult to assign certain classifications as Russian, Ukrainian, or White Russian to the earliest documents, which extend into the eleventh century. Difficulty in classification is further compounded by interference from both Church Slavic and Old Church Slavic.

9.3.2. White Russian

White Russian is the official language spoken in a western area of the Soviet Union called White Russia. The term 'White Russia' is of disputed origin, though the most reasonable explanation is that it results from an association with the area in the south called the Pripet Marshes, where white mists are common and familiar. Long under Polish control and originally a Baltic-speaking area, White Russia has been exposed to considerable linguistic influence from both Lithuanian and Polish. The oldest White Russian document is a biblical translation dated to 1517–1519. White Russian has only about nine million speakers and is losing ground to Great Russian.

Structurally, White Russian is characterized by a free-stress accent and the functional distinction between palatal and non-palatal consonants. Ablaut is well represented. A number of technical phonological distinctions distinguish White Russian from Russian and Ukrainian, but they need not concern us here. Morphologically, White Russian is characteristically East Slavic; it has lost the vocative case and the dual number, but maintains the other six cases and the three-gender system. The verb in White Russian generally follows that of Great Russian, with the main distinction in the system being between perfective and imperfective aspect. There are, however, two new compound tenses, the pluperfect and the future perfect. In most other respects, the White Russian verb is comparable to the Great Russian verb.

There are two White Russian dialect groups: the Northeastern, which is transitional with Great Russian, and the Southwestern, which is transitional with Ukrainian.

9.3.3. Ukrainian

Ukrainian, which was also known as Little Russian, is the official language of the Ukrainian republic. (On the earliest documents, see 9.3.1 above.) The language is not evident as a clear-cut historical unity until the thirteenth or fourteenth century, and there is no significant literature in Ukrainian until the eighteenth century because of the early dominance of Church Slavic as a literary medium.

Although the Russians refused to recognize Ukrainian as a separate language until the beginning of this century (hence its name 'Little Russian'), Ukrainian is vastly more different from Great Russian than is White Russian. It is now spoken by over forty million people as a native language.

Phonologically, Ukrainian is marked by moderate free-stress accent and by palatal consonants, though with certain distributional differences of these latter that set the language off from Great Russian. Traces of Indo-European ablaut can be found, though it is interesting that new vowel-alternation patterns not of Indo-European origin (e.g., *kin'* 'horse', gen. sg. *konyá*) have developed in the language. Morphologically, it has the usual three genders, but no dual. Seven cases are found in some, but not in all, nouns (the nominative and vocative have merged in many declensions). In most ways the declensional patterns are like those of the other East Slavic languages.

The verb is more conservative than the noun in some cases, preserving stem classifications familiar from OCS. In other ways the verbal system has undergone considerable simplification, having given up the dual, the aorist and imperfect, the supine, and a number of participles. The passive voice is characteristically Slavic, with either a reflexive pronoun plus active voice construction or one using a participle plus the verb 'to be'. Aspect separating perfective from imperfective action serves as the fundamental distinction in the verbal system.

There are three main dialect areas in the Ukrainian region: the Northern, the Southwestern, and the Southeastern. Each has a number of complex subdivisions, of concern only to Slavic specialists, and we shall not pursue them here. Standard Ukrainian is based mainly on the Southeastern dialect, which is in many ways close to Russian.

A Brief Structural Sketch of Old Church Slavic   9.4.

9.4.1. Phonology

Old Church Slavic phonology is reasonably well understood, given the obvious limitation that we are entirely dependent on uneven historical documents and indirect evidence in our analysis of the system (e.g., the treatment of OCS loanwords in other languages). The phonological system presented here is based primarily on that found in Schmalstieg (1976b).

9.4.1.1. Vowels

	Front		*Central*	*Back*	
High	i		y	u	
	ь	(ĭ)		ъ	(ŭ)
Mid	e			o	ǫ
		ę			
Low	ě			a	

Note: (a) ь is a 'front jer'; ъ is a 'back jer'. The history and phonemic identity of these two sounds are extremely complex issues. (b) There is no strong evidence for contrastive vowel length in OCS, though it is possible that stressed vowels had contrastive length.

9.4.1.2. Consonants

The consonantal system of OCS is marked by the characteristic Slavic feature of palatalization and by several other innovations, such as increased use of fricatives and affricates, when compared with Proto-Indo-European. The consonants are as follows:

	Labial	Dental	Palatal or Palatalized	Retracted	Velar
Stops					
Voiceless	p	t			k
Voiced	b	d			g
Nasals	m	n	n'		
Fricatives					
Voiceless	f(?)	s		š	x
Voiced	v	z		ž	
Affricates					
Voiceless		c	št'	č	
Voiced		dz	žd'		
Trill		r	r'		
(Lateral)		l	l'		

Historical Slavic phonology is a challenging and interesting field, in large part because of the extensive but traceable changes that have taken place in both the vocalic and the consonantal systems. Several distinctive features stand out: In the development of the vocalic system extensive monophthongization has reduced Proto-Indo-European diphthongs to simple monophthongs; any clear understanding of Slavic historical phonology must be based on an understanding of this process. With the consonants, two interesting features are the general Slavic palatalization, mentioned several times earlier, and the so-called Law of Open Syllables (see Schmalstieg 1976b:45).

9.4.2. Morphology

The outstanding feature of OCS from the Indo-European point of view is its conservative morphology, especially in the nouns, adjectives, and other substantives. There are the typical three genders of masculine, feminine, and neuter, and seven cases—nominative, genitive, dative, accusative, instrumental, locative, and vocative. Nouns are divided into various classes according to whether the stem ends in a vowel or a consonant; several subtypes occur within the vocalic stems. The dual number is preserved in OCS, though not in a fully differentiated paradigm.

Adjectives in OCS are divided into two groups, the declinables and the indeclinables, the latter group being fairly restricted. Within the declinables is a further subdivision of so-called hard stems and soft stems according to the final consonant of the stem, and a distinction between definite and indefinite declensions. Pronouns in OCS follow similar patterns.

The OCS verb is characterized primarily by the distinction between perfective and imperfective aspect, marked both by verbal derivatives and by preverbs. In addition to the two aspectual distinctions are three simple tenses (present, imperfect, and aorist), four periphrastic tenses (perfect, pluperfect, conditional, and future perfect). There are five separate participles, and a verbal substantive, all of which are declinable, and a series of indeclinables such as the infinitive and the supine. There is also an imperative form. Verbs are generally classified according to the vowel that follows the stem, the two main classes being marked by either -e- or -i-. OCS has no inherited passive or middle voice, and, apart from the conditional, which is new in Slavic, the elaborate Indo-European mood system has been eliminated.

9.4.3. Syntax

As a richly inflected language, OCS relies heavily on morphology in expressing syntactic functions. The seven-case noun system is reminiscent of many of the other old Indo-European languages: the nominative is a grammatical case expressing 'subject of sentence' and other grammatical functions; the genitive indicates possession, comparison, the direct object of a negated verb, and many other functions; the dative case marks the indirect object and expresses the so-called dative absolute (= the Lat. ablative absolute, Gk. genitive absolute) as in Lat. *his rebus confectis* 'these things having been done', OCS *i abьe ešte glagoljǫštu emu, vъzglasi kurъ* (Luke 22:60) 'And while he still spoke, the cock crowed'. In this sentence *glagoljǫštu emu*, lit. 'speaking—him', is in the dative case (Lunt 1959:131). The accusative case marks the object of the verb, the object of certain prepositions, and extent of time and space; the instrumental case expresses a function of relation or 'in respect to'; the locative is the case to express location without motion; and the vocative is the case of address.

OCS is of highly variable word order, though some dominant patterns are VSO (with alternate SOV), Noun + Adj., Noun + Rel., and Noun + Gen. Prepositions are found almost exclusively, with only the postposition *radi* 'for the sake of' surviving.

9.5.   A Sample Old Church Slavic Text

The following selection from Old Church Slavic is from the Gospel according to St. Matthew 5:1–3. The text is based on an extract of the Codex Zographensis (transliteration from Schmalstieg 1976b:193):

(1) Uzьrěvъ	že	narody	vъzide	na gorǫ.	i
Having seen	(intensive)	people	he went up	on a mountain	and

ěko	sěde	pristǫpišę	kъ	nemu	učenici	ego.	(2) i
when	he sat down	(they) approached	to	him	disciples	his	and

otvrъzъ	usta	svoě	učaaše	ję	glagolę	(3)	Blaženi	ništii
having opened	mouth	his	he taught	them	saying		blessed	the poor

duxomь.	ěko	těxъ	estъ	cěsarьstvo	nebesьskoe.
in spirit	since	theirs	is	kingdom	of heaven

'Seeing the people he went up on a mountain, and when he sat down his disciples approached him, and opening his mouth, he taught them, saying: Blessed are the poor in spirit, for theirs is the kingdom of heaven.'

9.6.   Balto-Slavic

As stated repeatedly elsewhere, it is not always clear in what way we should view points of correspondence and points of divergence between languages or language groups. The issue of common Balto-Slavic is certainly germane to this question, since we have here two language groups sharing a number of characteristics in phonology, lexicon, and word formation that seem to set them apart from the other Indo-European languages and that possibly point to a period of commonality between the two. The similarities are quite strong (in any case stronger than the purported Italo-Celtic common features), and have been taken by many as firm proof of a Balto-Slavic unity. But the divergences are equally compelling, suggesting early parallel development between the two groups, or points of common retention, and not necessarily historical unity.

The notion of a common Balto-Slavic language goes back to Schleicher, who listed it as one of the nodes on his family-tree diagram of the Indo-European languages. It is maintained by Brugmann, who noted seven characteristics shared by the two groups (see Brugmann 1903:18). The concept of unity was dealt a serious blow by Meillet, who expressed his opposition by listing and criticizing Brugmann's shared features (see Meillet 1922 [1967]). It has been revived, killed, and brought back to life again with a regularity that suggests a lack of common methodology among the linguists who have investigated the issue. Brugmann's basic data list has been expanded (especially by Szemerényi), but agreement has remained elusive. In one recent paper, the methodology used in making such judgments has been called into question (Schmid 1976). Schmid points out (1) the number of similarities in words and in forms cannot be used as a measuring stick for genetic relationship, because nobody can say what degree of affinity is constituted by six, ten, or twenty similarities on various grammatical levels; and (2) the discovery of Hittite and the recognition of its extreme archaism weaken the belief that common features shared by older languages such as Indo-Iranian and Greek necessarily point the way to archaic features inherited from PIE; this doubt then lessens the impact of points of comparison between 'Balto-Slavic' and PIE as reconstructed before Hittite.

We might add to Schmid's points the issue of what we mean by 'period of unity' or 'proto-system' or 'common language'. Do we actually mean that the two languages were at one time completely undifferentiated and that both are outgrowths of this period? Many linguists now reject such a notion altogether, claiming that it is simply a convenient fiction stemming from our family-tree metaphors handed down to us by Schleicher. Until we have a better idea of what we are dealing with in terms of prehistory, as well as a better understanding of how pidginization (language mixing) takes place, issues such as the nature of Balto-Slavic will certainly remain unsolved.

9.6.1. Shared Characteristics of Baltic and Slavic

1. The vocalic liquids and nasals $*r̥$, $*l̥$, $*m̥$, $*n̥$ give in Baltic *ir, il, im, in,* and sometimes *ur, ul, um, un,* with parallel distribu-

tion in Slavic. Cf. OCS *devętŭ*, Lith. *deviñtas*, OPruss. *newīnts* 'nine'. (The further development to *ę* in Slavic is a proto-Slavic development.)

2. Both Baltic and Slavic simplify geminate consonants.

3. Both Baltic and Slavic have a definite adjective built on a stem **yo-;* cf. Lith. *geràs-is*, OCS *dobrŭ-jĭ* 'the good'.

4. Masculine active participles in **-nt-* (cf. Lat. *ama-nt-em* 'loving') have given way to a **-yo-* inflection; cf. Lith. gen. sg. *vēžančio*, OCS *vezǫšta*, Lat. *'vehens'* ('carrying').

5. Slavic and Baltic both insert an *-i-* in certain cases of some nouns—for example, Lith. instr. pl. *akmen-i-mìs*, OCS *kamen-ĭ-mi* 'stones'.

6. The Indo-European demonstratives **so*, **sā* (cf. Skt. *sá*, *sā́*, Gk. *ho, hē*, Goth. *sa, so*) are replaced by a demonstrative **to-*, **tā-* in both Slavic and Baltic; cf. Lith. *tàs, tà*, OCS *tŭ, ta*.

7. In both Baltic and Slavic we find the genitive singular used as a basis for pronominal inflection, a feature unique to these two; cf. Lith. dative *mánei* (gen. *manè*), OCS *mŭně* (gen. *mene*). (It is the form *men-* (*mun-*) that reflects this innovation, but the Slavic equations of the genitive and dative stems are highly problematical.)

8. Slavic and Baltic show an **o-* stem ending deriving from **-āt* in the genitive singular; cf. Skt. abl. *vŕkāt*, Lith. gen. *vìlko*, OCS gen. *vlŭka* (with regular loss of final *t*).

9. We may also add here a few of the cognates shared by Baltic and Slavic, but not found elsewhere: OCS *blŭxa*: Lith. *blusà* 'flea'; Slavic *lipa* (cf. Russ. *lipa*): Lith. *líepa* 'linden tree'; Slavic *(d)zvězda* (cf. Pol. *gwiazda*): Lith. *žvaigždē̃* 'star'.

Such are the main points of comparison adduced by Brugmann. Meillet takes each singly and adduces counterevidence and counterarguments to the list. He rejects the notion of Balto-Slavic unity, claiming that most of the points of similarity between the two languages are the result of either parallel development or common retention, but not of common innovation.

The Balto-Slavic issue was debated for the next thirty or so years, and in 1957 Szemerényi addressed it critically once again. Reevaluating Meillet's arguments, Szemerényi argued that Meillet had essentially misinterpreted the evidence. Szemerényi provides highly suggestive arguments in favor of unity. At the end of his long survey, Szemerényi lists the following fourteen points that, he says, "prove a period of common language and life" (1957:120):

1. The Balto-Slavic palatalization (see Kuryłowicz 1956:235 et seq.).
2. The development of *i*, and after velars *u*, from PIE *$*\r̥$, *$*\l̥$, *$*\m̥$, *$*\n̥$ (see no. 1 on p. 120).
3. The change of *s* > *š* after *i, u, r, k*.
4. Accent innovations too complicated to be coincidental.
5. The change in the definite adjective (see 3 on p. 120).
6. The innovation in the participial inflection in *-yo-* (see 4 on p.120).
7. The genitive singular of *o-* stems in *-ā(t)* (see 8 on p. 120).
8. The establishment of a new comparative/superlative construction based on the forms *ē-yos*, *-ē-is* (the use of the *ē* here is the innovation).
9. The use of the genitive form *men-* (*mun-*) in pronouns; see also the accompanying plural formation *nōsōm* (this is an expanded and refined form of that in 7 on p. 120).
10. The use of *tos*, *tā* for PIE *so*, *sā* (see 6 on p. 120).
11. Certain verb forms in both Baltic and Slavic have been reshaped on an identical analogy.
12. Identity of certain preterites in both Baltic and Slavic in *-ē-, -ā-*.
13. Identity in certain verb formations in which Baltic (Lith.) denominatives in *-áuju* correspond to Slavic formations in *-ujǫ*.
14. Lexical correspondences (see 9 on p. 120, with additional words).

9.6.2. Differences between (Proto-) Baltic and (Proto-) Slavic

The following is a list of arguments that have been advanced as evidence against the Balto-Slavic unity. These sometimes come in the form of pure differences, sometimes as objections to the list of similarities (see Klimas 1973:19–22; Klimas' list is shortened here to eliminate questionable points of difference):

1. PIE *ā*, *ō* are maintained in Baltic, but merged in Slavic (as well as in Germanic and Indo-Iranian); cf. Lith. *mótė*, OCS *mati* 'mother'.
2. Proto-Baltic preserves PIE *sr*, which in Slavic changes to *str* (as in Germanic, Albanian, Thracian, and Phrygian). Cf. Lith.

srovĕ̃, Skt. *srávati* 'flows', but OCS *o-strovŭ* 'island'. (Later [?] Baltic changes of *sr-* to *str-* tend to cloud this picture.)

3. Baltic uses the suffix *-mo-* in ordinal numbers, Slavic uses *-wo-;* cf. Lith. *pìrmas* 'first', OCS *prĭvŭ.*

4. Baltic shows evidence of the 1st sg. pres. verb ending *-mai,* but Slavic does not; cf. OPruss. *asmai* 'I am'. (This is a point of controversy, however.)

5. The infix *-sto-,* frequent in Baltic (cf. Lith. *dýgsta: dýgti* 'to germinate') is not found in Slavic (with the possible exception of OCS *rastǫ* 'I grow').

6. Proto-Baltic did not distinguish third-person singular and plural verb forms; proto-Slavic did.

7. The Baltic adjectival formative *-inga* (cf. Lith. *protìngas* 'clever, intelligent') is unknown in Slavic.

8. The Baltic diminutive suffix *-l-* (cf. Lith. *sūnēlis* 'son') is not found in Slavic.

9. The Slavic agentive suffix *-telĭ* (cf. Hitt. *-talla*) is not found in Baltic (cf. OCS *dĕlatelĭ*).

10. Proto-Slavic used a stem *-es* in words for body parts (cf. OCS *oko, očese* 'eye'); this is unknown in Baltic.

11. The proto-Slavic participial formative *-lo-* (OCS *neslŭ*) is not found in Baltic.

12. The so-called Law of Open Syllables (see Schmalstieg 1976b:45) operates only in Slavic, not in Baltic; cf. OCS *osĭ*, Lith. *ašìs* 'axis'.

13. The sigmatic aorist (cf. Gk. *epaídeusa* 'I taught'), present in Slavic, does not exist in Baltic. Cf. OCS *nĕsŭ* 'I carried'.

14. Proto-Slavic uses the suffix *-tĭ* in the formation of abstract numerals, but Baltic does not; cf. OCS *pętĭ*, Lith. *penkì* 'five'.

We can see from the listing of the similarities and differences between the two stocks that the evidence is quite detailed and open to interpretation. Szemerényi obviously goes very far in his assertion about "common language and life," but the similarities are strong. On the other hand, the differences between the two and the overall dissimilar characters of the two languages cannot be lightly dismissed. Since we have at present no effective way of weighing similarities and differences between languages, this and other subgrouping issues will continue to be debated.

References

I. Grammars and Historical Works

de Bray 1980
Diels 1932
Kiparsky 1963–1967
Leskien 1909
Leskien 1914
Leskien 1962
Lunt 1959

Meillet 1934
Miklosich 1926
Schmalstieg 1976b
Shevelov 1964
Vaillant 1950–1966
Vaillant 1964
Vondrák 1924–1928

II. Dictionaries

Berneker 1924
Czech Academy
   Dictionary of Old
   Church Slavic 1958–

Sadnik and
   Aitzetmüller 1955
Vasmer 1950–1959

III. Balto-Slavic

Klimas 1973
Meillet 1922 [1967]
Schmalstieg 1974b

Schmid 1976
Senn 1966b
Szemerényi 1957

IV. Works Cited in the Text

Brugmann 1903
Klimas 1973
Kuryłowicz 1956
Lunt 1959

Meillet 1922 [1967]
Schmalstieg 1976b
Schmid 1976
Szemerényi 1957

10   Germanic

10.0.   Introduction

Of all the Indo-European languages, none has been studied so intensively as those of the Germanic group. The reasons for this are many. First, the Germanic languages offer extensive and homogeneous documentation from a relatively early period (ca. A.D. 400). Second, the Germanic languages have very clear-cut and readily identifiable features distinguishing them from the other Indo-European stocks; indeed, no other group in the Indo-European family has such clear characteristics. Finally, because the Germanic languages are the ones closest to the epicenter of comparative Indo-European studies—that is, Germany—they have always attracted considerable attention in that country.

The proto-Germanic peoples probably started out somewhere in Scandinavia and northern Germany, having settled in these areas several centuries before the Christian Era. They started to expand rapidly during the Roman period, primarily to the detriment of Celtic languages; migrations took them east into former Baltic and Slavic areas in the first and second centuries A.D., and west as far as Iceland and Greenland in the ninth and tenth centuries. (The later sixteenth-century migrations into North America, South Africa, and Australia had a massive effect on the linguistic composition of the world, but as these migrations are of no consequence for Indo-European studies, we shall ignore them here.) These wanderings left the European continent dotted with Germanic dialects, and the study of these dialects gave rise to the field of dialect geography, which to this day finds its center in Marburg. The Germans are frequently mentioned in ancient historical texts, especially those of Julius Caesar and Tacitus, where we find isolated Germanic words and names. Our oldest monuments of the Germanic languages are the Runic inscriptions. These one hundred or so inscriptions in a special alphabet called

Runic date from the third or fourth centuries A.D. and are representative of the North, or Scandinavian, group of Germanic languages.

Numerous groupings of the Germanic languages have been proposed throughout the nineteenth and twentieth centuries, beginning effectively with the grammar of Jacob Grimm in 1819. The exact delineation of the Germanic family is an extremely difficult undertaking for many reasons, not the least of which are the chronological disparities among the many dialects and the changing methods of interpreting geographical isoglosses. We shall as usual take a neutral course on these issues, following in the main the traditional division of the Germanic languages into East, West, and North subgroupings before turning to a more recent scheme.

East Germanic (Gothic) 10.1.

Gothic provides us with our oldest literary record of the Germanic languages. The corpus is a biblical translation into Gothic (actually Visigothic, or West Gothic) of a Greek original by Bishop Wulfila in the fourth century A.D. The translation includes a large part of the New Testament and parts of Nehemiah from the Old Testament. Wulfila's translation was carried out in Moesia (now northern Bulgaria). Since it is the work of a cultivated man with a knowledge of Greek and Latin, the Gothic Bible is extremely regular and consistent.

A large part of the Gothic corpus is contained in the Codex Argenteus, a beautiful gold, silver, and purple manuscript with rich ornamentation now in the library at Upsala, Sweden. The Codex Argenteus contains 187 leaves (plus one recently discovered). Other major resources of Gothic are the Codex Ambrosianus A, which has 190 leaves, B with 154 leaves, C with two leaves, and D with three; the Codex Carolinus, which contains four leaves; and several other manuscript sources. Codex Argenteus is the most beautiful and is considered to be the most important, but the others are in many ways more interesting.

In 1560 a Flemish diplomat named Busbecq reported about sixty to one hundred words that he took from two speakers in the Crimean peninsula. Because of certain unmistakable phonological characteristics, the language Busbecq recorded was identified as

Gothic, thus extending the language into the seventeenth century. This so-called Crimean Gothic has been a focus of activity for many Germanic scholars, some holding it in very high regard and others dismissing it altogether (see Braune-Ebbinghaus 1981: 1–2).

Of the remaining East Germanic dialects, including Ostrogothic (or East Gothic), we have only names in Greek and Roman authors. In any case, all the East Germanic dialects seem to have been very much alike. More will be said about the structure of Gothic below.

10.2.   West Germanic

West Germanic is without doubt the least unified of the three major groups. Our records are relatively late, and they are very uneven both in chronology and in content. Moreover, each of the individual languages is highly inconsistent and dispersed into various dialects. In the Western group we can grossly identify two main branches: the English group, which is usually considered with Frisian as Anglo-Frisian; and the German group, including High and Low German.

10.2.1. Anglo-Frisian

10.2.1.1. Frisian

The oldest records of Frisian are a series of legal documents dating from the tenth to the sixteenth centuries. As with all the Germanic languages, we divide Frisian into the Old (roughly up to 1400), Middle (1400–1600), and Modern (since 1600) periods. The Modern Frisian dialects are spoken mainly in northern Holland in the province of Friesland and on some adjacent islands, and a few are spoken in the low (coastal) areas of Germany. Frisian is receding in the face of strong German and Dutch influence, but a concerted literary and cultural movement is aiding a reemergence of the language, especially in Holland.

Frisian has the standard Anglo-Frisian characteristics—for example, the loss of Proto-Germanic nasals before fricatives (cf. OFris. *mūth,* Germ. *Mund* 'mouth').

Frisian comprises numerous dialects. Within Friesland three main dialects are recognized: East, West (Standard), and Southwest. Other dialects are found on the Frisian-speaking islands and in certain cities of both Holland and Germany.

10.2.1.2. English

The earliest significant monuments of English are dated to the mid-eighth century. There are three main dialects of Old English—Kentish, Saxon, and Anglian—in addition to Northumbrian, Mercian, and West Saxon. Most of the Old English literature is written in the West Saxon dialect, which is considered the standard dialect of the Old English period. West Saxon follows the usage of Winchester, a cultural center of the period; indeed, one of the most significant and best-known early documents of English, *Beowulf,* is written in West Saxon (though it has Anglian elements as well). The traditional divisions of English are, somewhat arbitrarily, Old English (700–1100), Middle English (1100–1500), and New, or Modern, English (since 1500).

Needless to say, the modern expansion of the English language has been nothing short of enormous. It is the first language of most of the people not only of England and the British Isles, but also of most of North America, Australia, parts of Africa, the Hawaiian Islands, and elsewhere around the world. English is also the most frequently acquired second language in the world. Because of the ready availability of material on English and its literary and linguistic history, we shall now leave this topic.

10.2.2. German

10.2.2.1. Low German

The term 'Low German' is essentially a geographical term that refers to the coastal, or lowland, area of the German region, as opposed to the High German region, or the interior. Our oldest documents in this group come from Old Saxon, dating roughly from the ninth century A.D. Old Saxon, the language from the lowlands of Germany, has given rise to the modern Low German dialects. The Low German group contains, in addition to Old Saxon, Low Franconian, the ancestor of modern Dutch-Flemish, and Afrikaans, a sixteenth-century import into South Africa brought by Dutch colonialists.

10.2.2.2. High German

Somewhat apart linguistically from the Low German languages are the High German ones. In the High German base, we find Old High German, attested in glosses as early as the eighth century A.D. and in continuous religious texts from the ninth century. The entire Old High German period is usually dated 750–1050. Next is Middle High German, with a wealth of epic and poetic literature, dated 1050–1500. Since 1500 we speak of Modern German (New High German), which overtook Low German as the main official and literary language in Germany in the early sixteenth century. High German usage was especially favored at this time because of Martin Luther's High German Bible. The principal High German dialects are Bavarian and Alemannic, the latter including Swiss German and Franconian.

10.2.2.3. Yiddish

Yiddish is a High German language spoken by East European Jews who migrated from Germany in the fourteenth to sixteenth centuries. Because of geographical separations between East and West European Jews, two varieties of Yiddish developed, each under different external influences (the East from Slavic and the West from German). We have Yiddish documents dating back to the thirteenth century, and a continuing Hebrew influence is evident throughout the history of the language.

10.3.   North Germanic

As mentioned earlier, our oldest Germanic monuments are the Runic inscriptions from the third century A.D. However, the continuous Northern Germanic literature occurs considerably later. The North Germanic peoples were quite expansive from the time of the Vikings (from about 800 A.D.). During this time parts of England and Ireland, Greenland, Iceland, and the Faroe Islands came under their control, and these early conquests are reflected in the languages (e.g., English pronouns were remade in part on the North Germanic pronouns). We refer to the oldest North Germanic language as Old Icelandic, or Old Norse, a term that signifies the texts composed before about 1350. The bulk of the literature in Old Icelandic was composed between the twelfth and the fourteenth centuries, though some as far back as 830 is attested (Skaldic poetry). The literature is principally prose in the form of sagas and was produced mostly in Iceland.

The North Germanic languages are commonly divided into two groups, East and West. The East group is represented by Old Swedish, which is first recorded in about 2,000 Runic inscriptions from the eleventh and twelfth centuries, and in continuous texts (mainly legal) from the thirteenth century. Next is Old Danish, where we find a few early inscriptions and continuous literature after the thirteenth century. Finally, we have Gutnish, first attested in a fourteenth-century legal document. All three—Swedish, Danish, and Gutnish—are spoken today.

The West group of North Germanic is represented by Norwegian, Faroese, and Icelandic (and Old Norse). We may speak of Old Norwegian, but very little can be said about it. Middle Norwegian (after 1350) is greatly simplified, and modern Norwegian is in the main very close to Danish and Swedish. Faroese is essentially an archaic variety of North Germanic isolated during the Viking expansion. Faroese has few speakers, but a lively national literature. Icelandic is the most conservative of them all, owing not only to its geographical isolation, but also to the fierce purism of the Icelanders. There is a rich literature in Icelandic dating from the thirteenth century to the modern era.

It was mentioned above that other groupings of the Germanic languages have been proposed. The most plausible suggestion is by Lehmann (1966), who claims that there is no linguistic basis for the division of the Germanic languages into three groups. He proposes a two-way split into Northeast and West. These two groups are distinguished by their treatment of the sequences -*ww*- and -*jj*-. In the Northeast group, -*ww*- developed into -*ggw*-, and -*jj*- developed into -*ggj*- or -*ddj*-. In the West group, -*ww*- was maintained, as was -*jj*-. Examples are Goth. *triggw-s* 'faithful', OIc. *trygg-r*, but OHG *(gi-)triuwi,* OE *(ge-)treowe*. Other phonological distinctions between the two groups occur as well.

Other classifications are possible also, but we need not consider them here. Germanic dialectology has been the basis for many developments in our knowledge of language change and dialect differentiation, giving rise to several schools of thought and even theoretical positions. Its importance in our understanding of the Indo-European family, and of general processes of change, cannot be overestimated.

General Characteristics of Germanic   10.4.

It was noted above that Germanic occupies a special place in Indo-European studies because of its wealth of distinctive characteristics that set it apart from the other Indo-European languages. It may be helpful if we identify some of those characteristics:

1. The systematic shift of the Indo-European consonant system into Proto-Germanic known as Grimm's Law. In this shift, the PIE plain voiceless stops and voiceless aspirated stops (if such existed) changed to the corresponding voiceless fricatives: PIE *p, *t, *k, *kʷ and *ph, *th, *kh, *kʷh > PGmc. *f, *þ, *x, *xʷ; the voiced stops changed to voiceless stops: PIE *b, *d, *g, *gʷ > PGmc. *p, *t, *k, *kʷ; and the voiced aspirated stops shifted to voiced fricatives: PIE *bh, *dh, *gh, *gʷh > PGmc. *β, *ð, *γ, *γʷ (these voiced fricatives later changed to voiced stops).

Voiceless Stops to Voiceless Fricatives

*p > *f	Skt.	*páśu-* 'cattle'	Skt.	*nápāt-* 'descendent'
	Lat.	*pecus*	Lat.	*nepōs* 'grandson, nephew'
	Goth.	*faíhu*		
	OIc.	*fē*	OIc.	*nefe* 'relative, nephew'
	OE	*feoh*	OE	*nefa*
	OHG	*fihu*	OHG	*nefo*
*t > *þ	Skt. (Vedic)	*trí-* 'three'	Skt.	*vártate* 'he turns'
	Lat.	*tria*	Lat.	*vertō*
	Gk.	*tría*		
	Goth.	*þriya*	Goth.	*waírþan* 'become'
	OIc.	*þriū*		
	OE	*ðrēo*	OE	*weorðan*
	OS	*thriu*	OS	*werthan*
*k > *x(h)	Skt.	*śatám* '100'	Skt.	*śván-* 'dog'
	Lat.	*centum*	Lat.	*canis*
	Gk.	*he-katón*	Gk.	*kúōn*
	Goth.	*hund*	Goth.	*hunds*
	OE	*hund*		
			OIc.	*hundr*
	OHG	*hunt*	OHG	*hunt*
*kʷ > *xʷ(hʷ)	Skt.	*katará-* 'which of the two'	Lat.	*linquō* 'I leave'
	Gk.	*póteros*	Gk.	*léipō*
	Lith.	*katràs*	Lith.	*liekù*
	Goth.	*hwaþar*	Goth.	*leihwan* 'lend'
	OIc.	*huaþarr*		
	OE	*hwæðer*		
	OS	*hweðar*		
	OHG	*hwedar*		

Voiced Stops to Voiceless Stops

*b > *p	Lith.	dubùs 'deep'	Lith.	trobà 'building'
	Goth.	diups	Goth.	þaurp 'village'
	OIc.	diūpr		
			OWel.	treb 'house'
	OE	dēop	OFris.	therp, thorp
*d > *t	Skt.	dántam 'tooth'	Skt.	pádam 'foot'
		(acc.)		(acc.)
	Lat.	dentem (acc.)	Lat.	pedem (acc.)
			ˈ Gk.	podá (acc.)
	Goth.	tunþus	Goth.	fõtus
	OS	tand	OIc.	fõt
	OE	tōð	OE	fõt
*g > *k	Skt.	jā́nu- 'knee'	Skt.	ájra- 'country'
	Lat.	genu	Lat.	ager 'field'
	Gk.	gónu	Gk.	agrós
	Goth.	kniu	Goth.	akrs
	OE	kneo	OIc.	akr
			OS	akkar
*gʷ > *kʷ	Skt.	gnā́- 'woman'		
	Gk. (Boeotian)	banā́		
	Gk. (Attic)	gunḗ		
	OPruss.	genna		
	OCS	žena		
	Goth.	qino		
	OHG	quena		

Voiced Aspirated Stops to Voiced Fricatives

*bh > *β	Skt.	bhárāmi 'I carry'	Skt.	bhrā́tar- 'brother'
	Lat.	ferō	Lat.	frāter
	Gk.	phérō	Gk.	phrā́tēr
	Goth.	baíran	Goth.	brōþar
	OIc.	bera	OIc.	brōðir
	OHG	beran	OHG	bruoder
*dh > *ð	Skt.	dhṛṣṇóti 'he dares'	Skt.	rudhirá- 'red'
			Lat.	ruber
	Gk.	thrasús 'bold'	Gk.	eruthrós
	Goth.	(ga-)dars 'he dares'	Goth.	rauþs
	OE	dear(r)	OIc.	rauðr
	AS	(ge-)dyrst	OHG	rōt (OHG d > t)
*gh > *γ	Skt.	haṁsá- 'goose, swan'	Skt.	stighnóti 'climbs'
	Lat.	(h)anser		
	Gk.	khḗn	Gk.	steíkhō
			Goth.	steigan

OIc.	*gās*		OIc.	*stīga*
OE	*gōs*			
OHG	*gans*		OHG	*stīgan*

*gʷh > *γʷ	Lat.	*ninguit* 'it snows'
		(*nix, nivis* 'snow')
	Gk.	*nípha* 'snow'
	Av.	*snaēžáiti* 'it snows'
	Goth.	*snáiws*
	OHG	*snēo*
	AS	*snāw*

(**γʷ* itself later splits into *g* and *w*)

Taken all together, the shift looks like this:

PIE	PGmc.
*p, t, k, kʷ (*ph, th, kh, kʷh)	> **f, þ, x, xʷ*
*b, d, g, gʷ	> **p, t, k, kʷ*
*bh, dh, gh, gʷh	> **β, ð, γ, γʷ*

It is interesting to note that the net phonological effect of Grimm's Law on Proto-Germanic (PGmc.) is relatively slight. Note that in PGmc. there is still a voiceless series and a voiced series. The overall difference between the two systems is that in PIE the aspirated stops were differentiated from the plain voiced stops by the feature of aspiration, whereas in PGmc. the voiceless stops are now in opposition with the voiceless fricatives, which are opposed to the voiced fricatives. The number of phonemes has remained the same, but their distribution and interrelatedness in the phonological system has changed.

Also part of the Germanic consonant shift is the famous Verner's Law, named after its author, Karl Verner. Verner accounted systematically for a number of apparent exceptions to Grimm's Law by an ingenious explanation. The basic problem was that many of the consonants that should have been voiceless fricatives in Germanic—that is, *f, þ, x, xʷ* as well as *s*—were instead found as voiced fricatives—namely, *β, ð, γ, g* or *w*, and *z*. Note, for example, the differences in the Germanic forms for 'brother' and 'father' where the other languages show a *t:*

'Brother'			'Father'	
Skt.	*bhrátar-*		Skt.	*pitár-*
Gk.	*phrátēr*		Gk.	*patḗr*
Goth.	*brōþar*		Goth.	*faðar*
OS	*brōther*		OE	*fæder*
			OS	*fader*

Nothing in Germanic accounts for this difference between the voiceless /þ/ of 'brother' and the voiced /ð/ or /d/ of 'father'. Verner explained the voiced variants by the position of the accent in Proto-Indo-European. Note in the Sanskrit and Greek 'father' above that the accent is on the second syllable, the one *following* the shifted sound, whereas in 'brother' it *precedes* the shifted sound. Since the Germanic stress rule always calls for stress on the first, that is, root syllable, the Germanic forms cannot be explained internally. But Verner's brilliant reconstruction of the PIE stress and the concomitant explanation of these exceptions to Grimm's Law as a result of stress placement in the parent language was one of the most significant discoveries in the history of linguistics. Verner's Law is as follows: when the accent followed the sound in question in Proto-Indo-European and when it was in a voiced environment, the voiced fricative resulted, not the voiceless one as Grimm's Law predicts. Verner's Law provided a means of formulation for exceptions to the First Shift and introduced new criteria and techniques of analysis. It provided the main thrust for the regularity principle (also known as the Neogrammarian Hypothesis), which in its simplest form states that sound change is regular and that no changes take place without a discoverable rule regulating them.

2. The change of the Indo-European pitch accent to a stress or expiratory accent on the first syllable of the root.

3. (a) The merger of PIE *o and *a to a: cf. Goth. *akrs,* OIc. *akr,* OHG *achar:* Lat. *ager,* Gk. *agrós,* Skt. *ájra-* 'field, acre'; Goth. *ahtau,* OIc. *átta,* OHG *ahto:* Lat. *octo,* Gk. *oktṓ,* OIr. *ocht* 'eight'. (b) The merger of PIE *ō and *ā into *ō.* Cf. Skt. *bhrā́tar-,* Lat. *fräter,* Gk. *phrā́tēr:* Goth. *brōþar,* OIc. *brōðir,* OS *brōther,* OHG *bruoder* 'brother'; Lat. *flōs,* Goth. *blōma,* OIc. *blōme,* OS *blōme,* OHG *bluomo* 'flower'.

4. The shift of *ŗ, *ḷ, *ṃ, *ṇ to ur, ul, um, un. Cf., for example, Skt. *tŗṣú-* 'thirsty, eager', OIc. *þurr,* OHG *durri.*

5. Extensive reduction of short vowels in final syllables.

6. The systematic use of the inherited Indo-European vowel alternations in strong verbs (ablaut, or vowel gradation). These vowel alternations were a basic Indo-European morphological characteristic and were of the type *e : o : ø,* as well as other combinations. The alternation between these three grades, as they are called, is found sporadically in all the Indo-European languages, and is seen clearly in verbs such as Gk. 1st sg. pres. *léipō* (*e*)

'leave', 1st sg. perf. *léloipa* (*o*) 'left', 1st sg. aor. *élipon* (*∅*) 'left'. This system is found extensively in Germanic, and remains in seven basic classes of strong verbs. We see it clearly in Gothic verbs such as the following:

hilpan (< **help-*)	*halp* (< **holp-*)	*hulpun* (< **h̥lp-*)
'to help'	'he helped'	'they helped'
giban (< **geb-*)	*gaf* (< **gob-*)	*gēbun* (< **gēb-*)
'to give'	'he gave'	'they gave'
beitan	*báit*	*bitun*
'to bite'	'he bit'	'they bit'
baíran	*bar*	*bērun*
'to carry'	'he carried'	'they carried'

Cf. English *drive, drove, driven; ride, rode, ridden; sing, sang, sung,* and so on. This list could be greatly expanded, but it seems that the point is made. Ablaut is a far more important feature in Germanic than in any other Indo-European language.

7. Certain changes in the verbal system involving the loss of many formal categories: for example, the reduction of the complex tense and aspect system to one distinguishing only past and present; simplification of the complex mood system, reducing it from as many as six moods to only three (indicative, imperative, and subjunctive, the latter two with much narrower range than in PIE); reduction of the earlier voice system of active and mediopassive to active (with some remnants of the passive in Gothic and Old English).

8. Simplification of the earlier inflectional system from a system of eight cases to one with five (with remnants of a sixth—the instrumental—in Old English). Germanic eliminates the earlier ablative and locative, and all but eliminates the instrumental. It maintains the nominative, genitive, dative, accusative, and vocative (though the vocative is extremely rare as a separate form).

9. The creation of the so-called weak preterite with the dental (t, d, ð, þ) suffix. The origin of this suffix (seen in Goth. *salboda,* OHG *salbōta,* OIc. *kallaða*) is highly debated and has at least three plausible historical explanations; the question of its origin is a recurring issue in Germanic linguistics.

There are several other special Germanic characteristics, all of a more technical nature and of interest primarily to the specialist, that set this group off by itself. There are also some interesting lexical peculiarities relating to inherited vocabulary, loanwords, and independent internal developments.

A Brief Structural Sketch of Gothic   10.5.

As the Germanic language with the earliest literary documentation, Gothic has figured significantly in the reconstruction of Proto-Indo-European and Proto-Germanic. Gothic has a structure generally reminiscent of the other old Indo-European languages, with detailed noun, verb, and adjective inflection. However, this rich inflectional structure is in some ways misleading from the general Germanic point of view, since Gothic was heavily influenced by Greek in Wulfila's translation of the Bible. A difficult question in Gothic studies centers on the extent of linguistic contamination in Gothic from Greek. This influence is especially evident in the lexicon, where scores of words were either directly borrowed from Greek (cf. Goth. *aíwaggēljō,* Gk. *euaggélion* 'gospel'; Goth. *gaíaínna,* Gk. *géenna* 'hell') or where words were modeled on Greek originals (these are called 'calques' or 'loan translations'; cf. Goth. *wailamērjan* 'to preach, bring good tidings', Gk. *euaggelídzomai* 'I preach', where Gothic *waila* = Gk. *eû* 'good, well', and Goth. *mērjan* = Gk. *-aggelídzomai* 'announce'); the final type of lexical borrowing is a 'blend', where the parts of a compound are from both Greek and Gothic, as we see in the word *daimōnareis* 'one possessed with the devil', which is based on Gk. *daímōn* 'devil' with a Gothic suffix *-areis.*

Evidence of Greek influence on Gothic is plentiful elsewhere in the language, especially in matters of word order and syntax. A notable example of syntactic influence is to be found in the absolute constructions, those in which parenthetical material is added to a sentence in the form of a nonfinite verb form in a specified case, such as the ablative in Latin or the genitive in Greek. Absolutes are most easily viewed as reduced full sentences; for example, instead of 'After Bill arrived at the show, the theater was closed', we find something like 'Bill having arrived at the show, the theater was closed'. These constructions are of interest in Gothic for several reasons: first, they are not reconstructible for Proto-Germanic, since they are not found outside Gothic; second, they are found in every case (nominative, genitive, dative, and accusative). Both these facts point to a definite foreign basis for the construction, the first for obvious reasons, the second for the simple reason that the Greek genitive absolute was not consistently rendered into Gothic. Had the construction already existed in Gothic it would most certainly have been properly transferred from Greek into the specified case form. An example of a dative absolute from Gothic is the following: *jah usleiþandin Iēsua in skipa, gaqēmun sik manageins filu du imma* 'and Jesus having passed over [*Iēsua usleiþandin* dat. sg. masc.] in the ship, there came together to him a great multitude'.

10.5.1. Phonology

10.5.1.1. Vowels

Gothic has a complex vowel system that has undergone many changes from both Proto-Indo-European and Proto-Germanic times. There are five short vowels, five long vowels, and three diphthongs:

i, ei (= ī) | u, ū   ⋀

aí (= e), ē   Ⲙ   aú (= o), ō   ◊

a, ā   ⋀

Diphthongs: ái, áu, iu

Note: *aí* (*e*) and *aú* (*o*) do not continue PGmc. **e* and **o*. Also, **e* merged with the reflexes of **i* (cf. Goth. *wigs*, OHG *weg* 'way'), and **o* merged with the reflexes of **u* (cf. Goth. *juk*, OHG *joh* 'yoke'). The *e* found in Gothic (written *aí*) comes from an earlier **i* by a process called 'breaking', as is also the case with *o* (written *aú*). (For details consult either Wright 1954 or Braune-Ebbinghaus 1981.)

Gothic makes systematic use of inherited ablaut, with seven different ablaut classes based on the vowel of the four principal stems: the present, the preterite singular, the preterite plural, and the past participle. A few examples are the following:

	Present	Preterite Singular	Preterite Plural	Past Participle
(Series I)	ei	ái	i (aí)	i (aí)
('to thrive')	þeihan	þáih	þaíhum	þaíhans
(Series IV)	i (aí)	a	ē	u (aú)
('to take')	niman	nam	nēmum	numans
(Series VI)	a	ō	ō	a
('to strike')	slahan	slōh	slōhum	slahans

10.5.1.2. Consonants

Gothic consonantal phonology is fairly uniform and presents no special problems to the student of Germanic languages. One noteworthy characteristic is that Verner's Law, by which some of the expected voiceless outcomes of Grimm's Law became voiced under certain accentual conditions, is highly irregular. The general noneffect of Verner's Law in Gothic has been variously explained as either the result of extensive East Germanic leveling of paradigmatic alternants created by Verner's Law (e.g., OE *weorþe* 'I become', with *þ* vs. *wurdon* 'they became', with *d* [< *ð]) or that Verner's Law simply did not spread through the entire Gothic lexicon and that the inconsistency with which it occurs may show not the results of leveling, but rather of the incomplete spread of the rule. In any case, the synchronic Gothic consonantal inventory is as follows:

	Labial	Interdental	Dental	Velar	Labiovelar
Stops					
Voiceless	p		t	k	k^w (q)
Voiced	b (β)	(ð)	d (ð)	g (γ)	
Fricatives					
Voiceless	f	þ	s	x, h	x^w (hw)
Voiced		(ð)	z		
Nasals	m		n	ŋ	
Liquids			l, r		
Semivowels	w, j				
	(palatal)				

Note: the exact phonemicization of the voiced stops as either stops or fricatives is somewhat problematical. Note further that the fricatives listed with the stops (e.g., *b* [β]), are not stops; stops became fricatives under certain conditions.

10.5.2. Morphology

Gothic noun morphology recalls that of other old Indo-European languages. There are three genders: masculine, feminine, and neuter; two numbers: singular and plural; and four systematically used cases: nominative, genitive, dative, and accusative. The vocative case is regularly modeled on either the nominative or the accusative. Nouns are divided into the two main classes of vocalic stems (those whose stem ends in a vowel) and consonantal stems (those whose stem ends in a consonant), with major subdivisions in each category.

Adjectives in Gothic inflect as do nouns, though the two basic divisions in this class are different from those of the noun class. Adjectives are based either on nominal endings or pronominal endings, with some adjective classes a mix of the two.

Pronouns in Gothic are like those of the other Indo-European languages, with first- and second-person forms not marked for gender and with the third person marked for masculine, feminine, or neuter. Interestingly, the first and second persons have fairly complete paradigms of the dual number. Other pronouns, such as the reflexive, relative, possessive, and so on, are generally unremarkable.

The verb in Gothic is divided into two major classes, traditionally called 'strong' and 'weak'. The strong group comprises those in which the preterite is formed by (1) ablaut, or vowel gradation: cf. *nima* 'I take', *nam* 'I took'; *beida* 'I await', *báiþ* 'I awaited'; (2) by reduplication, which involves the repetition of the first consonant of the root and some vowel (this is a pan-Indo-European phenomenon reconstructible for the proto-language): cf. *háita* 'I call', *haíháit* 'I called'; *máita* 'I cut', *maímáit* 'I cut'; or, finally, (3) by both reduplication and ablaut: cf. *tēka* 'I touch', *taítōk* 'I touched'; *lēta* 'I let', *laílōt* 'I let'. Other subdivisions of the strong verbs also exist.

Weak verbs in Gothic reflect a special Germanic formation in which the preterite ends in the so-called dental suffix, usually *-t-* or *-d-,* the origin of which is disputed. There are four weak groups. Several examples of weak verbs are *nasja* 'I save', *nasida* 'I saved'; *sōkja* 'I seek', *sōkida* 'I sought'; *salbō* 'I annoint', *salbōda* 'I annointed'. The weak class eventually became the productive one in Germanic.

Gothic shows significant remnants of the mediopassive voice in the form of a passive (occurring in the present tense of the indicative and subjunctive). There are three numbers (singular, plural, and dual); the indicative, subjunctive, and imperative moods; an infinitive; and several participles. Strikingly, the complex tense system found in the other Indo-European languages is reduced to a simple system with a present and a preterite tense.

Nominal compounding, a defining characteristic of modern languages such as German, is not found extensively in Gothic.

10.5.3. Syntax

Gothic syntax is a difficult topic, primarily because of the large amount of Greek influence evident in the language. Case functions generally parallel the uses found in other Indo-European languages. Gothic is prepositional and has adjective-noun concord (as expected). Participles do not enjoy the same status as in other stocks such as Greek and Baltic, but the absolute constructions do increase their use. Word order in Gothic is highly variable: Noun-Poss. seems to be the rule, with dominant Adj. + Noun and Gen. + Noun. Though prepositions dominate, SOV seems to be the standard order of the three major sentence constituents. How much of these patterns is due to Greek and how much is inherited from Germanic is a question we shall leave open here.

A Sample Gothic Text   10.6.

The following Gothic text is from the Gospel according to St. Matthew 6:25:

Duþþē	qiþa	izwis:	ni	maúrnáiþ		sáiwalái	izwarái	hwa	matjáiþ
Therefore	I say	to you	not	be anxious for		life	your	what	you eat

jah	hwa	drigkáiþ,	nih	leika	izwaramma	hwē	wasjáiþ;	niu
and	what	you drink	nor	body	your	by what	you clothe	not

sáiwala	máis	ist	fōdeinái	jah	leik	wastjōm?
life	more	is	than meat	and	the body	than clothing

'Therefore I say to you: do not be anxious for your life, what you eat and what you drink, nor how you clothe your body; is not life more than meat and the body more than clothing?'

References

I. General Germanic Grammars

Dieter et al. 1900
Grimm 1819–1837
  (1870–1898)
Hirt 1931–1934
Kluge 1913
Krahe and Meid
  1967–1969
Loewe 1933

Meillet 1937
Noreen 1894
Prokosch 1938
Streitberg 1896
Streitberg et al. 1936
Van Coetsem and
  Kufner 1972
Wilmanns 1893–1909

II. Gothic Grammars

Braune and
  Ebbinghaus 1981
Jellinek 1926

Kieckers 1928
Kluge 1911
Krahe 1948

Krause 1953
Mossé 1956
Streitberg 1920

von der Gabelentz and
   Loebe 1843–1846
Wright 1954

III. North Germanic Grammars

Fritzner and Seip 1954
Gordon 1957
Gutenbrunner 1951
Heusler 1931

Noreen 1904
Noreen 1913
Noreen 1923

IV. Old English Grammars

Brunner 1965
Campbell 1959
Luick 1921–1940

Mossé 1950–1959
Sievers 1886

V. Old Frisian Grammars

Siebs 1901
Steller 1928
Van Helten 1890

VI. Old Saxon Grammars

Cordes 1973
Gallée 1910
Holthausen 1921

VII. Old High German Grammars

Braune and Mitzka
   1953
Franck 1909

Schatz 1907
Schatz 1927

VIII. Dictionaries (All Languages)

Bosworth and Toller
   1972
Cleasby and Vigfusson
   1957
de Vries 1962
Feist 1939

Graff 1835–1846
Hall and Meritt 1960
Holthausen 1925
Holthausen 1934
Holthausen 1963
Jóhannesson 1956

Nauta 1926
Oxford English
    Dictionary 1933–
Schönfeld 1911
Schützeichel 1969

Seebold 1970
Torp and Falk 1909
von der Gabelentz and
    Loebe 1843–1846
von Richthofen 1961

IX. Works Cited in the Text

Braune and
    Ebbinghaus 1981
Grimm 1819–1837
    (1870–1898)

Lehmann 1966
Wright 1954

Tocharian

11.0.   Introduction

Around the turn of this century, a large amount of material written in a previously unknown language was discovered in the Chinese Turkestan (Tarim Basin) region of Central Asia. Since the language was recorded in a known writing system (a north Indian syllabary called Brāhmī), decipherment of the documents proceeded rapidly, and before long the language was identified as belonging to the Indo-European group. It was given the name Tocharian, since it was linked with a central Asian people referred to in classical texts as *Tócharoi,* or *Tochari.* There has been much debate over the name itself, with some specialists claiming that the term *Tuγrien* would be more appropriate, since in Uigur, a Turkic language of the region, the name for these people is *Twγry.* Others have denied outright that the people who spoke and used the language are the same as the *Twγry,* or *Tócharoi,* maintaining that these people were actually Iranians. In any case, the name Tocharian has survived and is well rooted in the scholarly tradition as the name for the language, if not for the people who spoke it.

But even if the Tócharoi were the speakers of this language, then we still know precious little about them. Original attempts to link them with ancient Iranians have been discredited by the recognition that the bulk of Iranian words in Tocharian are borrowings. It is now generally held that the speakers of Tocharian were part of a very early migration from the central Indo-European area, possibly as early as 2000 B.C. But, as is often the case in such matters, our evidence is fragmentary and our conjectures are highly tenuous.

The texts themselves are considerable. They were probably composed between A.D. 500 and 1000, with the best estimates focusing on the seventh and eighth centuries. Many of the texts are bilingual (with Sanskrit) and are the work of Buddhist missionaries. Material other than that of a religious nature was also found, including commercial documents, caravan passes, and medical and magical texts.

Though Tocharian is clearly Indo-European, a large part of the vocabulary defies precise etymology. That it does is due not only to the great time interval since the separation from the Indo-European area, but also to the effect of neighboring languages, both Indo-European and non-Indo-European. On the Indo-European side, there is considerable influence from Sanskrit and Iranian (mostly of a religious or technical nature); on the non-Indo-European side, there is influence from Tibetan, some Chinese, and Uigur, though these have not had the same effect on the Tocharian lexicon as have Sanskrit and Iranian.

Tocharian Dialects   11.1.

Tocharian is of importance in Indo-European studies for several reasons. The first of these is its clear dialect divisions. There are two clearly marked forms of Tocharian, which have been infelicitously named Dialect A and Dialect B. A is also known as Tourfan and as East Tocharian, while B is also known as Kuchean and as West Tocharian. But, in fact, the A and B labels are most commonly found in the literature. This division is quite marked, and it is the position of most specialists that the two should be considered separate languages, closely related, rather than dialects of the same language. A few examples illustrate this point (from Lane 1966):

11.1.1. Phonology

1. A *e* = B *ai;* A *o* = B *au.* Cf. A *tre,* B *trai* '3'; A *pekat,* B *paiykāte* 'wrote'; A *klots,* B *klautso* 'ear'.

2. A *a* = B *e.* Cf. A *ak,* B *ek* 'eye'; A *kam,* B *keme* 'tooth'.

3. A has apocope in final vowels; B does not. Cf. A *kam,* B *keme* 'comb'; A *pekat,* B *paiykāte* 'wrote'; A *śäṃ,* B *śana* 'woman, wife'.

4. A and B have differences in the location of accent, with accompanying vowel syncope.

11.1.2. Morphology

There are rather radical differences in morphology, more radical than can be shown with simple correspondences. For ex-

ample, each language uses widely differing plural morphemes in
cognate words, where one would expect the same morpheme-
class endings; the same is true for other case endings—all of
which suggests reanalysis and differentiation on the part of these
two languages when they were not in extreme close contact. Also
noteworthy here is the fact that A seems to have borrowed extensively from B in vocabulary. Simple parallel borrowings between
two similar dialects of the same language would usually be remade phonologically in the receiving language. But the fact that
these have not been simply assimilated with appropriate sound
substitutions is strongly suggestive of more considerable differences than is normally indicated by the word 'dialect'.

11.2.   The Impact of Tocharian

The mere addition of a wealth of new Indo-European data is
bound to have an effect on the bases of the discipline, and Tocharian proved to be no exception in this respect. Former airtight
isoglosses crumbled; for example, the *-r* as a marker of the
deponent-passive found in Italic and Celtic is found in Tocharian
as well (1st sg. deponent passive A *-mār,* B *-mar;* cf. A *klyosmār,*
B *klyausemar* 'hear'; cf. Lat. *loquitur,* OIr. *labrithir* 'speaks').
However, there have never been enough parallels established
between Tocharian and any other Indo-European stock to justify
a subdivision (early attempts to link it with Hittite and Iranian
have been discredited). It stands alone as a separate branch of
Indo-European.

Another important development resulting from the Tocharian
discoveries was brought about by the Tocharian reflexes of the
Proto-Indo-European velar consonants. Before Tocharian was
discovered and analyzed, the Indo-European languages showed a
neat and practically airtight distinction between those languages
that had velar reflexes (*k, x,* etc.) of the Proto-Indo-European
velars and those that had sibilants (*s, š,* etc.). Despite some minor
problems (such as the fact that Lithuanian seems to be a mixed
type), the distinction between the so-called *centum* languages
(after the Latin word for '100' with initial *k*) and *satem* languages
(after Avestan *satəm* '100' with initial *s*) was as secure as isoglosses can be. A few examples of the *centum-satem* division
follow:

'10' (*$dek\bar{m}$)

Satem: Skt. *dáśa,* Av. *dasa,* Arm. *tasn,* OCS *desętĭ,* Lith. *dĕšimt*
Centum: Gk. *déka,* Lat. *decem,* OIr. *deich,* Goth. *taíhun* (Gmc. *h* = [x])

'100' (*$k\bar{m}tom$)

Satem: Skt. *śatám,* Av. *satəm,* OCS *sŭto,* Lith. *šiṁtas*
Centum: Gk. *he-katón,* Lat. *centum,* OIr. *cēt,* Goth. *hund*

The convenient feature of the *centum-satem* division was that it provided not only a phonological division, but also a geographical one: all the eastern languages were *satem,* whereas all the Western languages were *centum.* This geographical distribution prompted all sorts of speculation concerning East-West ethnography (which was empty) and early Indo-European migrations. The *satem* group was seen as the innovating group that had started out eastward from the central Indo-European area at an early stage, splitting along the way. Tocharian changed all that; it is the easternmost Indo-European language, and it is *centum!* Cf. A *känt,* B *kante :* Skt. *śatám* '100'; A *okät,* B *okt :* Skt. *aṣṭaú* 'eight'.

Tocharian overall has been a puzzlement to many Indo-European scholars. In many features it is extremely archaic, frequently sharing ancient features with Hittite (especially in noun morphology) and with Sanskrit and Greek (e.g., its preservation of the mediopassive voice, the presence of both subjunctive and optative moods, and some others). Of course, it should be pointed out that the scaled-down noun morphology of Tocharian and Hittite (and Greek and Germanic) may not be an innovation at all, but may instead reflect an older, more conservative system. In many other respects, Tocharian is so changed from the reconstructed parent language that its value for the advancement of knowledge about the proto-language is not very great. Its greatest contribution to our understanding of Indo-European phonology is in its treatment of the so-called laryngeal consonants, where it has firmed up many hypotheses (but see Van Windekens 1976–1979, 1:4), and in verb morphology, where it has clarified some points concerning ablaut in the parent language. But the continuing difficulty of providing a simple table of correspondences for the Tocharian phonemes makes the language quite difficult to use in comparative Indo-European work. Thus the overall impact of Tocharian has been essentially negative in that it has provided evidence against hypotheses concerning Proto-Indo-European made before its discovery.

11.3.   A Brief Structural Sketch of Tocharian A

11.3.1. Phonology

11.3.1.1. Vowels

Tocharian A has a triangular vowel system with functional length distinctions present in the nonmid vowels. The only vowel of uncertain quality and historical origin is the *ä*, which may have a palatal quality, but is most often compared to Slavic ъ. Historically, *ä* is usually derived from Indo-European *$*ə_2$ ('schwa secundum'), itself a sound of uncertain status in the reconstructed proto-language. The Tocharian A vowel system takes the following diagrammatic shape:

Tocharian A has monophthongized the inherited Indo-European diphthongs, which are, however, maintained in B (*ai, au, āu, oy*). There are two semivowels, *y* and *w*, which occur in morphophonemic alternation with *i* and *u*.

The Indo-European ablaut system is greatly reduced in Tocharian, primarily because of internal phonological changes such as the weakening of unstressed syllables. It is recoverable in a number of words, principally in the form of *i : e* alternation (cf. A *pikäṣ* 'writes': *pekat* 'wrote'); also found is a *u : ō* series (cf. A *lutkäṣ* 'lets become': *lotäk* 'became') and a *ä : a* series, which probably continues the Indo-European *e : o* series (examples are quite complex). The essential point about Tocharian ablaut is that it is of no productive morphological significance in the language. All forms are phonological relics and reflect no ongoing morphological process.

Accent in Tocharian A is very poorly understood; B provides more systematic evidence of the rules of accent placement. In any case, the considerable vowel reduction in the language suggests an emphatic syllable accent rather than a musical one.

11.3.1.2. Consonants

The most striking aspect of the Tocharian A (and B) consonantal inventory is the elimination of the voiced stops *b, *d, *g, as well as the aspirated consonants *bh, *dh, and *gh. These have all merged together with the reflexes of the plain voiceless stops *p, *t, *k into Tocharian p, t, k. If we assume the voiceless aspirates *ph, *th, *kh for the proto-language then these too must be counted with the Tocharian voiceless stops p, t, k. There are no voiced obstruents in Tocharian.

The basic distinction in the Tocharian consonantal inventory is between palatal and non-palatal consonants. In simple form, it is as follows:

	Liquids	Nasals	Fricatives	Occlusives
Nonpalatal	r, l	n, ṅ, ṃ, m	s	p, t, k
Palatal	ly	ñ	ṣ	c, ts, ś

Note: (a) ṅ indicates [ŋ]; ṃ shows nasalization of the preceding vowel, equivalent to Skt. *anusvāra*. (b) c indicates [č]; ś (also written ç) is of undetermined quality (possibly tš). Historically it shows palatalization of *k or *ts.

Sandhi is quite pervasive in the Tocharian texts, especially at word boundaries. But careful analysis by specialists suggests that Tocharian sandhi, while superficially similar to that of Sanskrit, is in fact a metrical technique used to arrange verses in the proper number of feet by adding or eliminating syllables. A few examples will serve to illustrate the basic process: *-i > -y: ñi anapär > ñy anapär; o + o > o: wiyo oki > wiy oki*. Tocharian sandhi is in general a fairly simple assimilatory process.

11.3.2. Morphology

The Tocharian noun is interesting from the Indo-European viewpoint for many reasons. There are the typical three genders of masculine, feminine, and neuter (though in adjectives the neuter is absent). There are, however, at least four, and possibly five, different formal categories of number. These are the singular, plural, and dual, which we have seen elsewhere, the paral, which marks a naturally occurring pair, and perhaps also a plurative, which marks a distributive plural (i.e., where there is a noun belonging to more than one person, e.g., 'The boys broke their *legs'*). This final category and the paral are the sources of some controversy among specialists (see Winter 1962).

Nouns in Tocharian are generally divided into two main subclasses according to whether they end in a vowel (the thematic class) or a consonant (the athematic class). Within each there are subdivisions of considerable complexity.

Inflectionally, the Tocharian noun is a source of some confusion, especially from the Indo-European viewpoint. Each noun in Tocharian is divided into two declensional groups made up of the primary and the secondary cases. The primary cases are the nominative, the genitive, and the oblique, the last of which assumes the (accusative) function (in Tocharian B there is also a distinct vocative). The secondary cases are formed on the oblique stem by the suffixation of a variety of postpositions. The secondary cases are the instrumental, perlative, comitative, allative, ablative, locative, and causal, each with fairly specific syntactic and semantic functions. Such a distribution of nominal inflections is fairly unique among the Indo-European languages. It should also be noted in this respect that some fairly extensive reductions and losses of final consonants in Tocharian resulted in part in the radical reshaping of the inflectional system.

Adjectives in Tocharian follow various noun paradigms, with the above-noted exception that the neuter is not formally marked. Pronouns are similar to those in the other languages, with personal, demonstrative, interrogative, and relative forms, as well as some suffixed or enclitic personal forms. Pronouns maintain the three-gender system.

The Tocharian verb maintains the Indo-European distinction between active and mediopassive voice, the latter marked by the -*r* found in Italic, Celtic, and elsewhere. There is a further distinction between the so-called basic form, which marks the intransitive passive, and the causative form, which marks the transitive active forms of the verb—for example, A basic form *tsälpātär* 'goes over, becomes lost' and A causative *tsalpästär* 'lets go over, loses'.

In the verb only the singular, plural, and (rarely) the dual are found. The tenses of the verb are the present, imperfect, and preterite (with an intensive preterite in B), and several periphrastic tenses formed with participles, gerunds, and the copula. There are three moods as well: the conjunctive, which has a variety of functions, including the marking of futurity, the optative, and the imperative. There are several participles (active and middle), a gerund, and various other nominal categories derived from verbs.

11.3.3. Syntax

Because of the elaborate nominal inflecting system of primary and secondary cases, most higher-order syntactic functions in Tocharian are subsumed under the category of 'case function'. Nonetheless, there is more to the syntax of a language than its cases, as is true of Tocharian. Agreement between noun and modifiers is maintained. The order of modifying elements is typically Adj. + Noun and Gen. + Noun, though the order for relative pronouns is Noun + Rel. Postpositions dominate, providing of course the basis of the secondary cases, though some prepositions are to be found as well. Sentence-level word order is consistently SOV.

A Sample Tocharian A Text   11.4.

The following short text from Tocharian A comes from the Puṇyavantajātaka, a Buddhist tale modeled on the Buddhistic Sanskrit version of the Mahavāstu (from Lane 1947, 1948; incorporates reconstructions of Krause-Thomas 1964, vol. 2, p. 18):

kāsu	ñom-klyu	tsraṣiśśi	śäk	kälymentwaṃ	sätkatär:	yärk
good fame		of the strong	in six	directions	spreads out	reverence

ynāñmune	nam	poto	tsraṣṣuneyā	p^{u}käṣ	kälpnāl:
respect	obeisance	honor	by strength	by everyone	are to be attained

yuknāl	ymāräk	yäsluñcas	kälpnāl	ymāräk
to be conquered	quickly	(are) enemies	to be obtained	quickly (is)

yātlune:	tsraṣiśśi		mäk	niṣpalntu	tsraṣiśśi
prosperity	of the strong	(there are)	much	riches	of the strong

	mäk	śkaṃ	ṣñaṣṣeñ.
(there are)	much	and	relatives

'The good fame of the strong spreads in ten directions. Reverence, respect, obeisance, and honor are to be attained through strength by everyone. To be conquered quickly are enemies; to be obtained quickly is prosperity. Of the strong there are great riches; of the strong there are also many relatives.'

References

I. Grammars and Historical Works

Krause 1952
Krause and Thomas
  1960–1964
Pedersen 1941

Sieg et al. 1931
Van Windekens 1944
Van Windekens
  1976–1979

II. Dictionaries

Van Windekens 1941
Van Windekens 1976, vol. 1

III. Works Cited in the Text

Krause-Thomas 1964,
  vol. 2
Lane 1947
Lane 1948

Lane 1966
Van Windekens 1976,
  vol. 1
Winter 1962

Anatolian 12

Introduction 12.0.

If the discovery of Tocharian stirred Indo-European studies with its delivery of new resources, the discovery of the Anatolian languages, especially Hittite, shook the discipline so deeply that the reverberations are still being felt. The discovery of Hittite was startling enough; and the demonstration that it was an Indo-European language was even more shocking. But the later realization, achieved after much careful analysis, that the language contained many archaic Indo-European features that had been lost in the other languages, or were simply hypothetical constructs proposed by comparativists of exceptional foresight, was simply momentous, and provided a vindication of the methods of comparative analysis.

The Discovery 12.1.

In the late nineteenth century a large amount of material written in cuneiform script was discovered in Middle Egypt at Tell el-Amarna. (The cuneiform is a wedge-shaped script developed by the ancient Sumerians in the fourth millenium B.C. and borrowed by the Akkadians, Hittites, and other groups in Asia Minor.) It was written for the most part in Akkadian, an East Semitic language, and was concerned chiefly with certain diplomatic affairs between Egypt and the kingdom of Heta. Contained in this material were several cuneiform letters written in two languages: the Akkadian, which could be confidently read, and a second, unknown language. There were some early suggestions that this unknown language might be Hittite, but they were not well received. The issue rested for about ten years, when excavations were begun at Boğazköy, about ninety miles to the east of Ankara, Turkey, in northcentral Anatolia. Here the archives of the Hittite kings of the fourteenth and thirteenth centuries B.C.

were found in 1906 by Winckler, and they contained references to the Heta mentioned in the Egyptian documents. It soon became clear that the unknown language of the Tell el-Amarna discoveries and that of the Boğazköy discoveries were the same, namely, Hittite. This was the language of the Heta referred to by the Egyptians and the Hatti referred to in Akkadian. Interestingly, the Amarna tablets also show that the Hittites called themselves 'Nesites', from the city of Neša (see Neu 1974:132–35).

The Boğazköy Tablets, which numbered about 10,000 at first, to increase to about 25,000 with continued excavation, were dated to about 1500–1200 B.C., with some reaching as far back as 1800 B.C. Because they were written in several languages, some confusion arose at first. Akkadian and Assyrian, two languages known at the time, are prevalent in the texts, but the bulk are in the third language. Decipherment proceeded quickly, since most of the material of the Boğazköy discoveries was written in cuneiform, and, in the second decade of this century, Bedřich Hrozný posited (1915) that the third language of the Boğazköy texts, Hittite, was an Indo-European language.

Hrozný's assertion was met with widespread skepticism for many reasons. First is that the texts contain evidence of pervasive influence from other languages; this greatly complicated the initial analysis. Things were further complicated by the discovery at the Boğazköy site of hieroglyphs written in the same script that had already been identified from elsewhere (incorrectly, as it turned out) as Hieroglyphic Hittite. But further analysis showed that Hieroglyphic Hittite is not Hittite, but rather Luwian, an Anatolian language closely related to Hittite. The interspersion of Luwian and the poorly known Palaic, another Anatolian language, within the Hittite texts was another complicating factor in the final unraveling. (While we are on the subject of related languages, we should mention here Lycian, dated to the fifth century B.C. and known from about 150 inscriptions and some coin legends, and Lydian, which is contained in about sixty inscriptions dated to the fourth century B.C. These six—Hittite, Hieroglyphic Hittite, Luwian, Palaic, Lydian, and Lycian—make up the Anatolian branch of the Indo-European family.)

The linguistic confusion in the Boğazköy texts certainly did not lend support to Hrozný's claim concerning the Indo-European character of Hittite. And the fact that the texts contain numerous

Akkadian and Sumerian words did not help matters, either. If these circumstances were not enough to cast doubt on Hrozný's assertion, there were even more reasons for the Indo-Europeanists of the day to doubt its correctness. First, Asia Minor was not a familiar territory for Indo-European peoples; second, Hrozný guarded the texts covetously, and they were generally not available for investigation by Indo-European scholars at that time; finally, even after the unraveling of many of the mysteries of the texts, the language that emerged, Hittite, seemed thoroughly unlike any known Indo-European language.

Archaism in Hittite   12.2.

The correlation of the Tell el-Amarna texts with the Boğaz-köy texts, the unraveling of the Hieroglyphic Hittite texts, the claim that the cuneiform texts of Boğazköy were written in an Indo-European language, the assertion that this language was that of the Hittites, who are found throughout ancient history and even in the Old Testament—all this did not provide any final solutions. In fact, the more that was learned about Hittite, the more complicated the problems became. To be sure, its Indo-European nature was evident (cf. Hitt. *genu-*, Gk. *gónu*, Lat. *genu*, Skt. *jǎnu-*, Goth. *kniu*, Arm. *cunr* 'knee'; Hitt. *newaš*, Skt. *náva-*, Lat. *novus*, Gk. *né(w)os*, Lith. *naũjas* 'new'; Hitt. *ḫaštai*, Gk. *ostéon*, Lat. *os* 'bone', and similar lexical correlations; nominative endings in *-s;* 1st- and 3rd-person verb forms in the characteristic Indo-European *-mi, -zi* [< *ti*]; and many more points of comparison). But the fundamental problem was that Hittite was simply so different from the other Indo-European languages. For example, Hittite has two genders, animate and inanimate, whereas the rest of the older Indo-European languages have three (masculine, feminine, neuter); the Hittite verb has only two moods, indicative and imperative, whereas the older Indo-European languages have, in addition, such categories as optative and subjunctive, and traces of ones such as injunctive and precative; instead of the impressive array of tenses found in Latin, Greek, and Sanskrit verbs such as present, imperfect, future, aorist, perfect, and pluperfect, in Hittite we find only a simple present-future and a preterite, though there are also periphrastic perfect and pluperfect formations. Hittite makes systematic use of certain neuter noun

types (in particular the *r/n* stems) found only occasionally in the
other languages (e.g., *watar* 'water', gen. *wetenaš*). Most curious
among the many divergences between Hittite and the other languages is the lack of symmetry between singular and plural cases
in the noun: the plural has only four cases in some inflectional
stems, as opposed to a maximum of eight in the singular. Another
outstanding feature is the fact that Hittite is by most accounts
exclusively postposing (e.g., *É-ri anda* 'in the house'), whereas
the majority of the older languages are preposing (e.g., Lat. *in
urbe* 'in the city'), though some others such as Umbrian and Vedic
are predominantly postposing.

Based on these and a number of other phonological and morphological features, it was posited first by Forrer (1921), but later
championed by Sturtevant (see Sturtevant 1962b for chronology),
that the extensive differences between Hittite and the other
Indo-European languages were indicative of extreme archaism.
So archaic was it held to be, in fact, that it was suggested that the
simplest explanation was the assumption that Hittite had broken
away from the parent language before the separation of Latin,
Greek, Sanskrit, and the other Indo-European languages. This
hypothesis led to a position associated ever since with Sturtevant's name, the *Indo-Hittite Hypothesis*. Sturtevant's basic position was that there were numerous innovations common to the
Indo-European languages that are not found in Hittite; the most
straightforward way to explain such facts is by the assumption
that the Indo-European languages innovated after Hittite and the
other Anatolian languages had separated from the parent stock. In
Sturtevant's view, Anatolian is a daughter of Indo-Hittite and a
sister of Indo-European, as represented in fig. 1 below (see Sturtevant 1962b:109; see also, for contrast, the family tree of Indo-
European languages).

The Indo-Hittite hypothesis is very much out of vogue today
in the United States (it never caught on at all in Europe); those
American specialists who favored the theory seemed to lose their
enthusiasm after Sturtevant's death in the mid-1950s (though
Cowgill 1975, 1979 has revived it). Among those who consider
Hittite simply a branch of Indo-European, it is thought to have no
really close connections with other Indo-European stocks, though
Tocharian and Greek affinities have been noted.

Hittite and the Indo-Hittite hypothesis forced linguists to
confront as never before the recurring issue of archaism versus

innovation in historical reconstruction. In early programmatic papers Sturtevant argued forcefully that the idiosyncrasies of Hittite were archaisms and that the other Indo-European stocks were the innovators. But this is far from clear in all cases; in the noun, for example, Hittite shows no dual number, a category systematically found in some Indo-European languages (e.g., Greek, Sanskrit, Lithuanian) and residually in many others. What should we make of this? The dual is certainly limited enough in its internal makeup (it typically has only a few fully differentiated cases) that it could be an innovation; but is it not possible that Hittite simply lost it? Similarly with the noun: do the reduced plural systems indicate loss, or are they indicative of a still earlier stage when both singular and plural had fewer cases, and when perhaps Hittite had added new cases in the singular, but not (yet) in the plural? Under these circumstances, the eight-case system of Sanskrit would be seen as a later system with an increased number of cases, rather than as an older system that was preserving the situation before the breakup of the cases (see Fairbanks 1976). It is clear that in some instances Hittite definitely is older, as in its gender system. For example, the Indo-European feminine -$\bar{a}$ stems (e.g., Lat. *puella* 'girl') seem to be developed from the plural of neuter collectives in -*a* (e.g., Lat. *castra* 'camp'); yet in other ways (e.g., the verb system), it seems to have innovated considerably. We shall now turn to a particular instance in which Hittite is demonstrably older than its Indo-European sisters, or cousins, a feature that has earned it a good deal of its reputation as the oldest and generally most archaic language of the entire family.

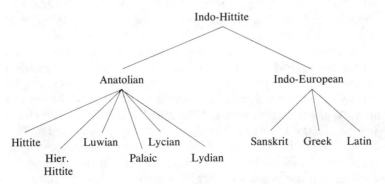

Fig. 1. *Indo-Hittite*

12.3.   The Laryngeals

One of the most famous events in the history of all linguistics centers on a feature of Hittite phonology. To understand the impact of this event, we must go back to 1879, when a Swiss linguist, Ferdinand de Saussure, made several proposals concerning the sound system of Indo-European. At the young age of twenty-one, Saussure proposed a brilliant reconstruction of Indo-European consonant structure to account for certain unexplained and seemingly unexplainable vowel alternations in Greek and Sanskrit (Saussure 1879). Saussure noted that the vowel alternation in pairs such as Greek *hístāmi* 'stand': *statós* 'stood' (*ā : a*) is parallel to that found in pairs such as *leípō* 'leave': *élipon* 'left' or *peíthō* 'trust': *épithon* 'trusted' (*e : ɸ*). But how to explain the long vowel (*ā*) in *hístāmi?* Saussure was working in the spirit of the regularity hypothesis, which states, in its simplest form, that sound change is regular and consistent; sounds do not simply develop individually at random (see 10.4, no. 1). In the *ā : a* pairs we seem to have such a random development. Saussure was also investigating the alternations between such pairs as Gk. *ágō* 'drive' and *ógmos* 'furrow', where the *a : o* alternation is called into question. Saussure assumed that a similarity such as that in *(s)ékhō* 'have': *éskhon* 'had' (*e : ɸ*); *leípō: élipon* (*e : ɸ*); alongside *hístāmi: statós* (*ā : a*) and *ágō: ógmos* pointed the way to a stage when perhaps all these morphemes had parallel structures. In particular, he suggested that the form *hístāmi* (which is a reduplicated form of a pre-Greek **sístāmi;* cf. Lat. *sistō,* Skt. *sthā̆-*) derived from a root **steA-,* with short *e* followed by *A* (where *A* stands for a lost sound that he called a 'coefficient sonantique'). His claim was that the *A,* which was lost later, had the effect of changing the vowel length and vowel color in *hístāmi.* In this way it would be entirely parallel to the *e* of *leípō, (s)ékhō,* and so on. Saussure postulated the existence of two such 'coefficients sonantiques' for Proto-Indo-European, arguing that they were justified on the basis of the traces found in the attested languages. He did not speculate on the phonetics of these sounds (though he seemed to view them as resonants), but argued instead that they were justified on the basis of the evidence found in the descendent languages. What is most remarkable (and controversial) about the early Saussurean position is the fact that he was postulating the existence in the proto-language of a feature not found in any of the daughter languages. Such a hypothesis went very much against the prevailing attitudes, since many linguists felt then, and do now, that we should never assign features to proto-systems for which we have no *direct* evidence in the descendent systems. Saussure, in fact, was the first abstract phonologist, since he was working strictly with indirect evidence.

Saussure's hypotheses caused a mixed reaction. Some scholars utterly rejected the idea of lost sounds from Proto-Indo-European, while others embraced it so fervently that they did more to discredit than help it by making wild proposals concerning the number of lost sounds (which came to be called 'laryngeals'); some proposed as many as twelve! Another source of speculation propelled by the laryngeal theory concerned possible antecedent relationships between the Indo-European languages and other groups, in particular Semitic, which also has laryngeal sounds. All these speculations tended to weaken the impact of the theory and to reduce its attractiveness to the Indo-European scholars of the day, all of whom were working comfortably in the prevailing nineteenth-century tradition and required hard proof in order to be convinced. The proof came in 1927, when Kuryłowicz published a study in which he demonstrated that the consonant *ḫ* in Hittite occurs in exactly those positions where Saussure had postulated a 'coefficient sonantique'. This clear and forthright analysis, in which Kuryłowicz offered a number of rules to account for the behavior of these sounds in different phonetic and morphological environments, shook the field of Indo-European studies once again. Here at last was the *direct* proof in Hittite of the elements Saussure had suggested on the basis of the *indirect* evidence found in the other languages. Hittite was now given prominence as a most archaic Indo-European stock, and, more importantly, the methods of reconstruction linguists had been using for decades were given solid verification. This was truly a momentous event.

Among the words found to have *ḫ* in Hittite where Saussure had posited the lost sounds based on indirect comparative evidence are the following:

Hittite *ḫa-an-na-aš*	'grandmother':	Lat. *anus*
ḫa-an-ti	'front':	Lat. *ante*
ḫar-ki-iš	'white':	Gk. *argés*
ḫa-aš-ši-i	'hearth':	Lat. *āra*

In these first four examples Saussure had postulated a laryngeal on the basis of his theory about the Indo-European root. Systematically worked out later by Benveniste (see Benveniste 1935), this theory states essentially that every root was of the type *CeC-* (C = consonant); in those roots where an initial vowel is found in the other languages (Lat. *ante*, Gk. *antí*, etc.), a laryngeal had been lost. In these four words above, we see that Hittite has preserved the laryngeal. Consider also the following:

Hittite	*pal-ḫi-i-iš*	'broad':	Lat. *plānus*
	pa-aḫ-ša-an-zi	'they protect' (3rd pl. pres.):	Lat. *pāscō*
	me-e-ḫu-e-ni	'time' (dat. sg.):	Goth. *mēl*
	pa-aḫ-ḫu-e-ni	'fire' (dat. sg.):	Gk. *pûr*
	wa-aḫ-an-zi	'they turn' (3rd pl. pres.):	Skt. *vāya-* 'weaving'

Here the laryngeal had been postulated on the basis of otherwise unexplained vocalic length and quality in the words on the right. It is commonly believed that the Hittite evidence confirms the reconstruction.

The archaism and conservatism of Hittite was thus clearly demonstrated, but it would be inaccurate if we left this topic with the impression that all was well. To begin with, many Hittitologists and Indo-Europeanists simply do not accept the laryngeal theory at all. They have searched for and provided, with varying degrees of success, alternate explanations for Hittite *ḫ*. And other explanations are available—for instance, that it was a 'hiatus breaker' between vowels or that its presence in many words is due to analogical forces operating in Hittite. These explanations are not without merit; the laryngeal hypothesis has often been used as a *deus ex machina* to explain away numerous problems where a more careful analysis using traditional reconstructions would yield identical results. And we cannot overlook the fact that adherents to the theory have often hurt their own cause by pushing it to ridiculous extremes. But here we can only say that the majority of Indo-European scholars accept it, largely because of the Hittite evidence.

The value of Hittite in our reconstruction of the protolanguage cannot be overestimated. On the other hand, until (if ever) means are available to the historical linguist for clearly differentiating archaism from innovation in problematic cases, many of the difficulties of comparative Indo-European linguistics that Hittite might have solved will remain points of contention between different schools. The issue has surfaced again recently in reference to new work being done in the reconstruction of Proto-Indo-European syntax: are the Hittite postpositions archaic, and, if so, what do they tell us about word order and syntax of the proto-language? (Some would ask whether they are postpositions at all; see Starke 1977.) It is not an easy question.

A Brief Structural Sketch of Hittite   12.4.

12.4.1. Phonology

Because Hittite is written in a highly imprecise cuneiform syllabary, the phonology of this language cannot be determined with the same accuracy we enjoy with that of the other Indo-European languages. The syllabary as a writing system is often deficient in its marking of vowels, and the situation is worsened by the presence in Hittite writing of so-called pleonastic vowels, which are extra vowels not involved in the pronunciation of the word. All of this makes the determination of the precise phonetics of Hittite a rather hazardous undertaking. Nonetheless, specialists agree on a few generalizations, and we will turn to these now.

12.4.1.1. Vowels

Hittite has at least four, and possibly five, vowels: *a, e, i, u,* and *ú* (the issue of how many vowels centers on whether *u* stands for [o] and *ú* stands for [u]). Orthographic variation between *a* and *e* and between *e* and *i* further confuses the phonetic interpretation of the texts.

It is undecided whether Hittite had contrastive vowel length or not. Vowels are commonly doubled in the texts, and some specialists argue that this doubling, along with other internal evidence, indicates contrastive length. But others assert that the doubling represents orthographic variation, is the result of stress placement (about which we know nothing), or is the result of a contraction (viz., VCV > VV). The issue remains undecided.

Hittite had, in addition to these vowels, two diphthongs, *ai* and *au*, and two semivowels *w* and *y*. The *y* is in frequent positional variation with *i*, as *w* is with *u*.

Ablaut is common in Hittite in certain verb classes and is residually evident throughout the language. Several noteworthy examples are *kuenzi* 'he strikes', *kunanzi* 'they strike'; cf. Skt. *hánti, ghnánti* (Hitt. *e < *e, a < *o; *e, *o, *a > a* in Skt. [see 4.2.1]); but the development of the *h* and *gh* show the prior existence of the *e* in *hánti* and the *ø* in *ghnánti*). Another Hittite example is *kuerzi* 'he cuts', *kuranzi* 'they cut'.

12.4.1.2. Consonants

The most conspicuous feature of Hittite consonantal phonology from the Indo-European point of view is the elimination of the voiced/voiceless contrast and the preservation of *h* mentioned in 12.3 above. Like most of the other languages, Hittite also dropped the aspirated stops. Thus the Hittite stop system contains only *p, t, k* (*p* < **p, *b, *bh, *ph* [?]; *t* < **t, *d, *dh, *th* [?]; *k* < **k, *g, *gh, *kh* [?]). As a general rule, the inherited voiceless stops are written in Hittite with a double consonant, whereas the voiced stops and voiced aspirates are written with a single consonant (**ph, *th, *kh* are of uncertain status in the proto-language; see 1.3.1.2.a).

Besides *p, t, k,* we find in Hittite the nasals *m* and *n,* as well as *r, l, s* (which is written *š,* but is probably phonetically [s]), *z* (= [ts]), and *h.*

The frequent double stops in Hittite are of uncertain phonological status. Sometimes they exist as simple variants of single forms (e.g., *peššiyazi, pišiyazzi* 'he throws'). There are, however, a few minimal pairs based on the single-double contrast (e.g., *a-ša-an-zi* 'they are', *a-aš-ša-an-zi* 'they remain behind').

There is evidence of sandhi in Hittite, though surely not to the extent that it is found in Sanskrit or in Old Irish. Assimilations such as *halkin pianzi* > *hal-ki-im pi-an-zi* 'they give cereals', and *kuššan-šet* > *kuššaššet* 'his remuneration' illustrate the basic process.

12.4.2. Morphology

Hittite morphology is remarkably different from that of other old Indo-European languages in many crucial features, some of which are mentioned in 12.3 above. In the noun, for example, only two genders are found, animate and inanimate (also called 'masculine' and 'common'); there are only a few traces of the dual number, and the singular and plural are often interchanged, especially because of the incomplete morphological differentiation of the two. There are more cases in the singular than in the plural, and, although the endings are for the most part comparable to parallel forms in the other languages, the reshaping (or retention) of the inflectional system makes point-by-point comparison quite difficult.

Nouns are classified according to the same general principles of stem class as in the other languages, the major distinction being between consonant stems and vowel stems. There are some differences, however. Since *a and *o merged into a in Hittite, the two noun classes marked by these vowels (actually *o and *ā) have become indistinguishable. Also, the productive use of the r/n stems such as watar, wetenaš (cf. Lat. iter, itineris 'road') is unusual, as is the Hittite development of an ḫ-stem noun class.

The Hittite cases are, as mentioned above, a matter of controversy. A composite singular paradigm yields eight cases: nominative, vocative, accusative, genitive, dative, locative, ablative, and instrumental. In most noun classes there is considerable overlap between case endings. In the plural the system is greatly reduced (or not fully developed), with at best four cases for which differentiated case endings are found: nominative, accusative, genitive, and dative-locative.

Adjectives follow nominal patterns. Pronouns exist in two varieties, fully declined forms and unemphatic (or reduced) forms that are encliticized to the governing word (e.g., kateme 'with me'). Besides the personal pronouns, there are also possessives, indefinites, relatives, and interrogatives that are more or less comparable to those found in the other languages.

The Hittite verb has only two moods, indicative and imperative, and two tenses, present-future and preterite. This verbal system is in marked contrast to that of languages such as Latin, Greek, and Sanskrit, where the number of tenses and moods is considerably greater. Interestingly, though, some periphrastic formations in Hittite are remarkably similar to constructions in the later Indo-European languages, especially in the periphrastic perfect, which is formed with the verb ḫar(k)- 'have' (e.g., antuḫšan kuinki parā ḫuittiyan ḫarmi 'I have given preference to some person or other'). We also find a periphrastic used with eš- 'be', as in lamniyan ešdu 'it should be named'. Though such constructions are occasionally found in the older languages (e.g., Lat. habeō id factum 'I have done it'), they are more typical of a much later stage of development within the Indo-European family.

There are two main verbal conjugations in Hittite, the -mi conjugation and the -ḫi conjugation. The -mi type is an old athematic type comparable to such forms as Lat. sum 'I am' (Hitt. ešmi), though it is far more common in Hittite than elsewhere. The -ḫi type is of great comparative interest because it strongly recalls the reconstructed Indo-European perfect (cf. Hitt. memaḫi 'I said', Lat. meminī 'I remember', Skt. bubudhé 'I awoke'). The

-*ḫi* conjugation has recently served as the focal point for a renewed interest in the Indo-Hittite debate (see Cowgill 1975, 1979).

There are two voices in Hittite, the active and the mediopassive, the latter with primarily middle meaning. The mediopassive is morphologically of interest because it can employ the morpheme -*r* as an inflectional marker (e.g., *ešari* 'he sits'). We have seen this -*r* marker before in Italic, Celtic, and Tocharian mediopassive endings.

Along with several participles, verbal nouns, and two derived verbal types (the iterative and the causative), the foregoing captures the major components of the Hittite verb.

12.4.3. Syntax

Hittite syntax follows mainly the requirements of inflected languages, with the cases serving to mark most higher-order syntactic functions. That the agreement between noun-adjective and subject-verb is not nearly so rigid in Hittite as elsewhere may be indicative of an archaic state when both gender and number categories were not discretely and precisely separated. Most cases follow more or less conventional usage, with special morphological and syntactic relations in the form of overlapping endings or of equivalent meaning existing between the dative and locative and between the ablative and instrumental.

Hittite makes extensive use of particles, which are encliticized and which serve to mark a variety of semantic and syntactic functions such as introducing a quotation, showing coordination, and others. Though Hittite makes use of adverb-preverb constructions, it is otherwise exclusively postposing. Typologically Hittite is quite consistent, with dominant Adj. + Noun, Gen. + Noun, Rel. + Noun, and SOV order to go with its postpositions.

12.5.   A Sample Hittite Text

The following brief Hittite text is from the *Keilschrift-Urkunden aus Boghazköi* (commonly cited as *KUB*) 6:45, reproduced in Held and Schmalstieg (in preparation), with interlinear translation. The text introduces a Prayer to be Spoken in an Emergency (free translation at end follows mainly Pritchard 1969: 397). (Note: the following orthographic conventions are used in the text: capital letters indicate Sumerian logograms; italicized capital letters indicate Akkadian words; italicized lowercase letters indicate Hittite material; the dot (.) represents a syllable division in Sumerian and Akkadian; the hyphen (-) represents a syllable division in Hittite; raised small caps (M, F, D) mark determinatives for masculine, feminine, or divine entities.)

1. *UM-MA* *ta-ba-ar-na*   MNIR.GÁL LUGAL. GAL LUGAL KUR
   Thus   Tabarnas (speaks) Muwatallis king   great king (of) land

   URU   *Ḫa-at-ti*
   city Hatti

2. DUMU M*mur-ši-li* LUGAL. GAL LUGAL KUR URU   *Ḫa-at-ti*
   son (of) Mursilis   king   great king (of) land city Hatti

   UR.ŠAG *ma-a-an* UKÙ-*ši*
   hero   if   to a man

3. *me-mi-aš* *ku-iš-ki* *na-ak-ki-ya-aš-zi*   *nu* - *za*   *ar-ku-wa-ar*
   affair   any   become burdensome   then (prt.) refl. prayer

4. DÙ - *zi* *šu-uḫ-ḫi-kan* *še - ir* D*UTU-i* *me-na-aḫ-ḫa-an-da* 2 GIŠ
   makes   roof   prt.   on   sky   close to   2 wood

   BANŠUR AD.KID
   tables   wickerwork

5. *da-a-ri-ya-an-da* *da-a-i* 1 GIŠ   BANŠUR *A-NA* D*UTU*   URU
   covered   sets up 1 wood table   to   goddess (of) city

   TÚL-*na* *A-NA* DINGIR.MEŠ.
   Arinna   to   (other) gods

'Thus speaks the Tabarnas [title of a Hittite king] Muwatallis, the Great King, the king of the land of the Hatti, the son of Mursilis, the Great King, the king of the land of the Hatti, a hero: if any affair becomes too burdensome for a man, then he offers a prayer, and sets up two covered tables of wickerwork on the roof close to the sky; he sets up one table to the goddess of the city of Arinna, and one table to all the other gods.'

References

I. Grammars and Historical Works

Benveniste 1962
Friedrich 1960
Friedrich et al. 1969
Kammenhuber 1959
Kronasser 1956

Laroche 1960
Meriggi 1966–1967
Neu and Meid 1979
Sturtevant 1951

II. Dictionaries

Friedrich 1952–1954
Friedrich and
  Kammenhuber
  1975–
Gusmani 1964
Güterbock and
  Hoffner 1980–

Hoffner 1967
Laroche 1959
Meriggi 1962
Sturtevant 1931
Tischler 1977–

III. Laryngeal Theory

Keiler 1970
Lehmann 1952
Lindeman 1970

Puhvel 1960
Szemerényi 1973
Winter, ed. 1965

IV. Indo-Hittite

Cowgill 1975
Cowgill 1979

Sturtevant 1942
Sturtevant 1962b

V. Works Cited in the Text

Benveniste 1935
Cowgill 1975
Cowgill 1979
Fairbanks 1976
Forrer 1921
Held and Schmalstieg
  (in preparation)

Hrozný 1915
Kuryłowicz 1927
Neu 1974
Pritchard 1969
Saussure 1879
Starke 1977
Sturtevant 1962b

Minor Indo-European Languages 13

Introduction 13.0.

In addition to the 'major' Indo-European languages described in the foregoing chapters, a group of 'minor' languages, which are known to us only in the form of inscriptions, place and personal names, and glosses, deserve our attention. Many of these languages (especially Illyrian) have been the source of repeated controversy in Indo-European studies, mostly as regards their closer affinities within the family. Some have not been accepted by all scholars as definitely Indo-European. The controversies are due not only to the paucity of substantial data, but also to the analysis of the data and, often, to the interpretation of ancient historical accounts of both the peoples and their languages.

Following our practice of not becoming involved in these controversies, we shall proceed here with a list of essential facts and information, together with a list of necessary bibliographical items that the interested (and intrepid) reader might consult to investigate these languages more deeply.

Ligurian 13.1.

Judging from occasional references in ancient history, the Ligurians at one time were spread across a fairly wide area in western Europe. But by the time for which we have detailed documentation of these people, their area had been narrowed considerably by Etruscan, Gaulish, and Roman conquests. The Ligurians are only imperfectly known, and it is hazardous to speak of them as a coherent ethnic unit.

Soon after discovery, Ligurian was judged to be Indo-European, but the evidence is so meager that some recent analyses suggest that the Ligurians belong to the ancient Mediterranean substratum already mentioned in connection with Greek as Pelasgic. The Ligurian linguistic evidence consists mostly of place names, some of which are almost certainly Indo-European. We have, for example, *Berigiema* 'snow-mountain' (?), *Comberanea;* also *Roudelius, Quiamelius, lebēris* '(a form of) rabbit', *saliunca* 'valerian', and a fair number of nouns with the characteristic *-sc-* suffix (e.g., *Vinelasca*). Though probably Indo-European, Ligurian does not have close affinities with any other Indo-European languages, including Italic and Celtic, with which it has been often connected.

13.2.   Lepontic

The so-called Lepontic dialect has never been classified beyond a doubt. Most of the inscriptional evidence we have is onomastic, which can sometimes be deceiving in historical studies. Most scholars agree that Lepontic was Indo-European, but its closer affinities are more difficult to ascertain. The most popular practice is to group it with Celtic, with which it shares several phonological features. Other scholars, less sure, have suggested a Ligurian connection, but this is fanciful speculation. Even its Celtic affinities are questionable, since it diverges from that group in several key diagnostic features. In its treatment of the Indo-European labiovelars, for example, it is ambiguous, and this ambiguity contributes to the difficulty. Some specialists have chosen to view the Lepontic and Celtic parallels as indicative of Celtic influence rather than of common retention.

13.3.   Sicel

Once again we find in Italy a few inscriptions, some glosses, and some onomastic evidence of a language seemingly distinct from all the others. This language has been called Sicel, and, though it is now generally held to be closely affiliated with Italic, other connections have been proposed as well, especially the Illyrian one. The Italic connection is surely the strongest, with the glosses providing the best evidence: *kámpos* 'hippodrome': Lat. *campus; arbínē* 'flesh': Lat. *arvina; gela* 'frost': Lat. *gelu;* and others. Sicel is relevant to Indo-European studies only in its connection with the subgrouping issue.

13.4.   Raetic

Raetic is customarily omitted from all but the most detailed discussions of ancient Italic prehistory. The evidence is so meager that no valid conclusions on its subgrouping can be made. It is found to the north and west of Venetic, and has certain parallels with Illyrian, but also with Germanic and Etruscan! Needless to say, most discussions of Raetic are extremely brief.

Thraco-Phrygian   13.5.

13.5.1. Thracian

Thracian is a clearly Indo-European language known to us from a substantial number of names (personal, botanical, and geographical), some glosses, and a few inscriptions. A few examples are as follows: Thracian *pinon* 'barley drink' : cf. OCS *pivo* 'drink', Skt. *píbati* 'he drinks', Lat. *bibō* 'drink'; the geographical name *Strumón*, which is usually connected with OCS *ostrovŭ*, Gk. *hréō* 'flow', Latv. *straũma,* and ultimately English *stream.*

The Thracian material covers a considerable period of time, thereby making the classification and interpretation more difficult. We know from the evidence of modern archaeology that Thracian was spoken over a fairly wide area in eastern and central Europe, as well as on some coastal islands and into Asia Minor. Such wide territorial expanse promotes dialect divisions, and, despite the meagerness of the data, we can grossly distinguish the area north of the Danube as representing the Dacian dialect and that to the south as representing the Thracian dialect proper.

The Thracians came under early Greek and later Roman influence, and, though we have some accounts of the language surviving into the Middle Ages, they are highly suspect. By some accounts, Thracian exerted a considerable influence on Albanian.

13.5.2. Phrygian

Phrygian is known to us in the form of several early inscriptions (perhaps as old as the eighth century B.C.), a substantial number of later inscriptions, a wealth of names, and several glosses. Its Indo-European character and close connections with Thracian are well accepted, though it is clear that the language came under heavy Greek influence, and even the inscriptions show the unmistakable signs of Phrygian-Greek bilingualism.

The Thraco-Phrygian branch is seen by many scholars to constitute the intermediate stage between Indo-European itself and Armenian, but that classification is not universally accepted, and it is not followed in this book.

13.6.   Illyrian and Messapic

13.6.1. Illyrian

Among the lesser-known languages, none has surfaced so consistently in discussions of Indo-European prehistory and subgrouping as Illyrian. During the 1930s a wave of 'pan-Illyrianism', or 'Illyromania', occurred in Indo-European studies, with investigators pointing to evidence of Illyrian throughout the European area, especially on the Dalmatian coast. Such claims were based chiefly on analysis of hydronymic evidence, but their impact has been greatly muted in recent years. Nonetheless, the confirmed Illyrian names across Europe are impressive, and the expansiveness of these people cannot be denied. Among the names generally accepted as Illyrian are *Amantia, Apsias, Segesta,* and *Egesta,* the last two containing the characteristic Illyrian suffix *-est-*. But place names are all we have of this language, and even these have been modified by the languages of the countries in which they are found. We have no bilingual texts and no syntax at all—just a series of speculations.

13.6.2. Messapic

Closely related to Illyrian is Messapic. This language is much better known than Illyrian and is demonstrably close to that language. In fact, a good deal of what we know, or think we know, about Illyrian is based on Messapic. Our knowledge of Messapic is based on about two hundred inscriptions from the Roman province of Venetia, many of which contain proper names closely related to Illyrian names. We have some glosses as well, so that our statements about Messapic can be made with a degree of certainty impossible for Illyrian.

There have been attempts to link Illyrian and Messapic (Illyro-Messapic) with some other Indo-European groups, notably Germanic and Balto-Slavic. For some time Messapic was thought to be close to Latin, though it is now most closely linked with Albanian. But all these attempts have come under heavy criticism in recent years, and we should remain skeptical of any closer subgroupings for these two languages.

13.7.   Venetic

The Venetic language, which stems from the same area as the later Roman province of Venetia, is known from about two

hundred inscriptions dated from the sixth to the first centuries
B.C. Its closer connections with other Indo-European languages
are a matter of debate. The language shows some very clear parallels to Italic, especially in matters of consonantal phonology and
a few case forms. Some consider its closer affinity to Italic a
foregone conclusion and even suggest its inclusion in the Latin-
Faliscan group. But recent examination of Venetic has cast some
doubt on this position, and it is now suggested that we return
to the older position that Venetic is simply another west Indo-
European dialect that had the misfortune to find itself in the
Latin-speaking area, to which it eventually succumbed.

References

I. General Information on the Lesser Known Languages

Birnbaum and Puhvel,   Haas 1960
    eds. 1966   Krahe 1964
Conway et al. 1933   Whatmough 1937

II. The Individual Languages

A. Ligurian

Schmoll 1959b

B. Sicel

Schmoll 1959a

C. Thraco-Phrygian

Detschew 1957
Friedrich 1932
Reichenkron 1966

D. Illyrian and Messapic

Haas 1962   Mayer 1957
Krahe 1955–1956   Parlangeli 1960

E. Venetic

Beeler 1949   Pellegrini and
Krahe 1950   Prosdocimi 1967
                               Untermann 1961

Bibliography
Index of Words
General Index

BIBLIOGRAPHY

Wherever possible, I have cited only the most recent edition of the works listed below. Although this method may create some chronological disparities, it allows the easiest and most convenient form of referencing.

Adrados, Francisco R. 1975. Lingüística indoeuropea. Madrid: Gredos.

Allen, W. Sidney. 1953. Relationship in comparative linguistics. Transactions of the Philological Society. 1950:180–206.

Anttila, Raimo. 1972. An introduction to historical and comparative linguistics. New York: Macmillan.

Back, Michael. 1978. Die sassanidischen Staatsinschriften (Acta Iranica 18). Leiden: Brill.

Baldi, Philip. 1976. The Latin imperfect in *bā-. Language 52:839–51.

———. 1977a. Remarks on the Latin R-form verbs. Zeitschrift für vergleichende Sprachforschung 90:222–57.

———. 1977b. Morphosyntax and the Latin genitive. Folia Linguistica 11:107–22.

———. 1978. The influence of speech perception on inflectional morphology in Latin. General Linguistics 18:61–89.

Bammesberger, Alfred. 1979. On the origin of the Irish f-future. Bulletin of the Board of Celtic Studies 28:395–98.

Bartholomae, Christian. 1895–1896. Vorgeschichte der iranischen Sprachen und Awestasprache und Altpersisch. Strassburg: Trübner.

———. 1904. Altiranisches Wörterbuch. Strassburg: Trübner.

Bechtel, Friedrich. 1921–1924. Die griechischen Dialekte. Berlin: Wiedmann.

Beeler, Madison. 1949. The Venetic language. Berkeley and Los Angeles: Univ. of California Pr.

———. 1966. The interrelationships within Italic. In Ancient Indo-European dialects, ed. by Henrik Birnbaum and Jaan Puhvel, pp. 51–58. Berkeley and Los Angeles: Univ. of California Pr.

Benveniste, Emile. 1935. Origines de la formation des noms en indo-européen. Paris: Adrien-Maisonneuve.

———. 1962. Hittite et indo-européen. Paris: Maisonneuve.

Berneker, Erich. 1924. Slavisches etymologisches Wörterbuch. Heidelberg: Winter.

Birnbaum, Henrik, and Puhvel, Jaan. 1966. Ancient Indo-European dialects. Berkeley and Los Angeles: Univ. of California Pr.

Bloch, Jules. 1934. L'indo-aryen du Veda aux temps modernes. Paris: Maisonneuve.

Böhtlingk, Otto. 1923–1925. Sanskrit Wörterbuch im kürzerer Fassung. Leipzig: Markert and Petters.

———, and von Roth, Rudolph. 1966. Sanskrit Wörterbuch. Wiesbaden: Harrassowitz.

Boisacq, Émile. 1938. Dictionnaire étymologique de la langue grecque. Paris: Klincksieck.

Bopp, Franz. 1816. Über das Conjugationssystem der Sanskritsprache in Vergleichung mit jenem der griechischen, lateinischen, persischen und germanischen Sprachen. . . . (English version of part of this work prepared in 1820, now available. 1974. Amsterdam: John Benjamins.)

Bosworth, Joseph, and Toller, T. Northcote. 1972. An Anglo-Saxon dictionary. Oxford: Clarendon Press.

Brandenstein, Wilhelm, and Mayrhofer, Manfred. 1964. Handbuch des Altpersischen. Wiesbaden: Harrassowitz.

Braune, Wilhelm, and Mitzka, Walter. 1953. Althochdeutsche Grammatik. 8th ed. Halle: Niemeyer.

———, and Ebbinghaus, Ernst. 1981. Gotische Grammatik. 19th ed. Halle: Niemeyer.

Brugmann, Karl. 1897–1916. Grundriss der vergleichenden Grammatik der indogermanischen Sprachen. Strassburg: Trübner.

———. 1903. Kurze vergleichende Grammatik der indogermanischen Sprachen. Strassburg: Trübner.

———. 1913. Griechische Grammatik. Munich: Beck.

Brunner, Karl. 1965. Altenglische Grammatik nach der angelsächischen Grammatik von Eduard Sievers. Halle: Niemeyer.

Buck, Carl D. 1928. A grammar of Oscan and Umbrian. Boston: Ginn.

———. 1933. Comparative grammar of Greek and Latin. Chicago: Univ. of Chicago Pr.

———. 1951. A dictionary of selected synonyms in the principal Indo-European languages. Chicago: Univ. of Chicago Pr.

————. 1955. The Greek dialects. Boston: Ginn.

Burrow, Thomas. 1965. The Sanskrit language. Glasgow: The University Press.

Bynon, Theodora. 1977. Historical linguistics. Cambridge: At the University Press.

Camaj, Martin. 1969. Lehrbuch der albanischen Sprache. Wiesbaden: Harrassowitz.

Campbell, A. 1959. Old English Grammar. Oxford: Clarendon Press.

Chadwick, John. 1970. The decipherment of Linear B. Cambridge: At the University Press.

Chantraine, Pierre. 1942–1953. Grammaire homérique. Paris: Klincksieck.

————. 1968–1977. Dictionnaire étymologique de la langue grecque. Paris: Klincksieck.

Cleasby, Richard, and Vigfusson, Gudbrand. 1957. An Icelandic-English dictionary. Oxford: Clarendon Press.

Conway, Robert S. 1967. The Italic dialects. Hildesheim: Olms.

————; Johnson, S. E.; and Whatmough, J. 1933. The prae-Italic dialects of Italy. Cambridge: Harvard Univ. Pr.

Cordes, G. 1973. Altniederdeutsches Elementarbuch. Heidelberg: Winter.

Cowgill, Warren. 1970. Italic and Celtic superlatives and the dialects of Indo-European. In Indo-European and Indo-Europeans, ed. by G. Cardona, H. Hoenigswald, and A. Senn, pp. 113–53. Philadelphia: Univ. of Pennsylvania Pr.

————. 1975. More evidence for Indo-Hittite: the tense-aspect systems. In Proceedings of the Eleventh International Congress of Linguistics, ed. by Luigi Heilmann, vol. 2, pp. 557–70. Bologna: Società editrice il Mulino.

————. 1979. Anatolian hi- conjugation and Indo-European perfect: installment II. In Hethitisch und Indogermanisch, ed. by Erich Neu and Wolfgang Meid, pp. 25–39. Innsbruck: Innsbrucker Beiträge zur Sprachwissenschaft.

The Czech Academy Dictionary of Old Church Slavic. (Slovník Jazyka Staroslověnského.) 1958–.

Dambriūnas, L.; Klimas, A.; and Schmalstieg, W. R. 1966. Introduction to Modern Lithuanian. New York: Franciscan Fathers Press.

de Bray, R. G. 1980. Guide to the Slavonic languages. 3 vols. Cambridge: Slavica.

Delbrück, Berthold. 1879. Die Grundlagen der griechischen Syntax. Syntaktische Forschungen 4. Halle: Verlag des Waisenhauses.

———. 1888. Altindische Syntax. Halle: Verlag des Waisenhauses.

———. 1893–1900. Vergleichende Syntax der indogermanischen Sprachen. 3 vols. (Vols. 3–5 of the Grundriss der vergleichenden Grammatik der indogermanischen Sprachen. 1st ed.) Strassburg: Trübner.

Detschew, Dimiter. 1957. Die thrakischen Sprachreste. Vienna: Rudolf M. Rohrer.

de Vries, Jan. 1962. Altnordisches etymologisches Wörterbuch. Leiden: Brill.

Diels, Paul. 1932. Altkirchenslavische Grammatik. Heidelberg: Winter.

Dieter, F., et al. 1900. Laut- und Formenlehre der altgermanischen Dialekte. Leipzig: O. R. Reisland.

Endzelīns, Jānis. 1923. Lettische Grammatik. Heidelberg: Winter.

———. 1944. Altpreussische Grammatik. Riga: Latvju grāmata.

———. 1971. Comparative phonology and morphology of the Baltic languages. Trans. W. R. Schmalstieg and B. Jēgers. The Hague-Paris: Mouton.

Ernout, Alfred. 1961. Le dialecte ombrien. Paris: Klincksieck.

———, and Meillet, Antoine. 1968. Dictionnaire étymologique de la langue latine. Paris: Klincksieck.

Evans, D. Simon. 1964. A grammar of Middle Welsh. Dublin: Institute for Advanced Studies.

Fairbanks, Gordon. 1976. Case inflections in Indo-European. Journal of Indo-European Studies 4:101–31.

Feist, Sigmund. 1939. Vergleichendes Wörterbuch der gotischen Sprache. Leiden: Brill.

Forrer, Emil. 1921. Ausbeute aus den Boghazköi-Inschriften. Mitteilungen der deutschen Orient-Gesellschaft 61.20–39.

Fleuriot, Léon. 1964. Le vieux breton: éléments d'une grammaire. Paris: Klincksieck.

Fraenkel, Ernst. 1955. Litauisches etymologisches Wörterbuch. Heidelberg: Winter; Göttingen: Vandenhoeck and Ruprecht.

Franck, J. 1909. Altfränkische Grammatik. Göttingen: Vandenhoeck and Ruprecht.

Friedrich, Johannes. 1932. Kleinasiatische Sprachdenkmäler. Berlin: de Gruyter.

———. 1952–1954. Hethitisches Wörterbuch. Heidelberg: Winter.

———. 1960. Hethitisches Elementarbuch. Heidelberg: Winter.

————, and Kammenhuber, Annelies. 1975–. Hethitisches Wörterbuch. Heidelberg: Winter.

————, et al. 1969. Altkleinasiatische Sprachen. Leiden and Cologne: Brill.

Friedrich, Paul. 1975. Proto-Indo-European syntax: the order of meaningful elements. Journal of Indo-European Studies, Monograph No. 1.

Frisk, Hjalmar. 1954–1972. Griechisches etymologisches Wörterbuch. Heidelberg: Winter.

Fritzner, J., and Seip, D. 1954. Ordbog over det gamle norske Sprog. Oslo: Moller.

Gallée, Johan H. 1910. Altsächische Grammatik. Halle: Niemeyer.

Giacomelli, Gabriella. 1963. La lingua falisca. Florence: L. S. Olschki.

Gimbutas, Marija. 1970. Proto-Indo-European culture: the Kurgan culture during the fourth, fifth, and third millenia B.C. In Indo-European and Indo-Europeans, ed. by G. Cardona, H. Hoenigswald, and A. Senn, pp. 155–97. Philadelphia: Univ. of Pennsylvania Pr.

————. 1973. The beginning of the Bronze Age in Europe and the Indo-Europeans: 3500–2500 B.C. Journal of Indo-European Studies 1:163–214.

Godel, Robert. 1975. An introduction to the study of Classical Armenian. Wiesbaden: Reichert.

Gordon, E. V. 1957. An introduction to Old Norse. Oxford: Clarendon Press.

Graff, E. J. 1835–1846. Althochdeutscher Sprachsatz. Berlin: Beim Verfasser und in commision der Nikolaischen Buchhandlung.

Grassman, Hermann. 1964. Wörterbuch zum Rig-Veda. Wiesbaden: Harrassowitz.

Greenberg, Joseph. 1966. Some universals of grammar with reference to the order of meaningful elements. In Universals of language, ed. by J. Greenberg, pp. 73–113. 2d ed. Cambridge: MIT Pr.

Grimm, J. 1819–1837 (1870–1898). Deutsche Grammatik. Göttingen: Dietrich; Berlin: Dümmler; Gütersloh: Bertelsmann.

Gusmani, Roberto. 1964. Lydisches Wörterbuch. Heidelberg: Winter.

Gutenbrunner, Siegfried. 1951. Historische Laut- und Formenlehre des Altisländischen. Heidelberg: Winter.

Güterbock, Hans G., and Hoffner, Harry A. 1980–. The Hittite dictionary of the Oriental Institute of the University of Chicago. Chicago: Oriental Institute.

Haas, Otto. 1960. Das frühitalienische Element. Vienna: Notring der Wissenschaftlichen Verbände Österreichs.

————. 1962. Messapische Studien. Heidelberg: Winter.

Haebler, Claus. 1965. Grammatik der albanischen Mundart von Salamis. Wiesbaden: Harrassowitz.

Hall, J. R. Clark, and Meritt, H. D. 1960. A concise Anglo-Saxon dictionary. Cambridge: At the University Press.

Hamp, Eric. 1966. The position of Albanian. In Ancient Indo-European dialects, ed. by Henrik Birnbaum and Jaan Puhvel, pp. 97–121. Berkeley and Los Angeles: Univ. of California Pr.

Heilmann, Luigi. 1963. Grammatica storica della lingua greca. Turin: Società editrice internazionale.

Held, Warren, and Schmalstieg, William R. Beginning Hittite grammar. (In preparation.)

Heusler, Andreas. 1931. Altisländisches Elementarbuch. Heidelberg: Winter.

Hirt, Herman, 1912. Handbuch der griechischen Laut- und Formenlehre. Heidelberg: Winter.

————. 1921–1937. Indogermanische Grammatik. Heidelberg: Winter.

————. 1931–1934. Handbuch des Urgermanischen. Heidelberg: Winter.

Hoenigswald, Henry M. 1960. Language change and linguistic reconstruction. Chicago: Univ. of Chicago Pr.

Hoffner, Harry A. 1967. An English-Hittite glossary. Revue hittite et asianique, vol. 25.

Hoffmann, Karl, et al. 1958. Iranistik (Linguistik). Leiden and Cologne: Brill.

Hofmann, J. B. 1930–1956. Lateinisches etymologisches Wörterbuch. Heidelberg: Winter.

Holder, Alfred. 1961–1962. Alt-Celtischer Sprachsatz. Graz: Akademische Druck-und Verlagsanstalt.

Holthausen, Ferdinand. 1921. Altsächisches Elementarbuch. Heidelberg: Winter.

————. 1925. Altfriesisches Wörterbuch. Heidelberg: Winter.

————. 1934. Gotisches etymologisches Wörterbuch. Heidelberg: Winter.

————. 1963. Altenglisches etymologisches Wörterbuch. Heidelberg: Winter.

Hopper, Paul. 1973. Glottalized and murmured occlusives in Indo-European. Glossa 7: 141–66.

Hrozný, Bedřich. 1915. Die Lösung des hethitischen Problems. Mitteilungen der deutschen Orient-Gesellschaft 56.17–50.

Hübschmann, Heinrich. 1875. Über die Stellung des Armenischen im Kreise der indogermanischen Sprachen. Weimar: n.p.

———. 1962. Armenische Grammatik. Hildesheim: Olms.

Jellinek, M. H. 1926. Geschichte der gotischen Sprache. Berlin and Leipzig: de Gruyter.

Jensen, Hans. 1959. Altarmenische Grammatik. Heidelberg: Winter.

———. 1964. Altarmenische Chrestomathie. Heidelberg: Winter.

Jóhannesson, A. 1956. Isländisches etymologisches Wörterbuch. Bern: Francke.

Joynt, Maud, et al. 1939–. Contributions to a dictionary of the Irish language. Dublin: Royal Irish Academy.

Kammenhuber, Annelies. 1959. Esquisse de grammaire palaïte. Bulletin de la Société de Linguistique de Paris 54:18–45.

Keiler, Allan R. 1970. A phonological study of the Indo-European laryngeals. The Hague: Mouton.

Kent, Roland. 1945. The sounds of Latin. Baltimore: Waverly Press.

———. 1946. The forms of Latin. Baltimore: Waverly Press.

———. 1953. Old Persian. New Haven: American Oriental Society.

Kieckers, Ernst. 1928. Handbuch der vergleichenden gotischen Grammatik. Munich: Huber.

Kiparsky, Valentin. 1963–1967. Russische historische Grammatik. Heidelberg: Winter.

Klimas, Antanas. 1973. Baltic and Slavic revisited. Lituanus 19:7–26.

Kluge, Friedrich. 1911. Die Elemente des Gotischen. Strassburg: Trübner.

———. 1913. Urgermanisch: Vorgeschichte der altgermanischen Dialekte. Strassburg: Trübner.

Krahe, Hans. 1948. Historische Laut- und Formenlehre des Gotischen. Heidelberg: Winter.

———. 1950. Das Venetische. Heidelberg: Winter.

———. 1955–1956. Die Sprache der Illyrier. Wiesbaden: Harrassowitz.

———. 1962. Indogermanische Sprachwissenschaft. Berlin: de Gruyter.

———. 1964. Unsere ältesten Flussnamen. Wiesbaden: Harrassowitz.

———, and Meid, W. 1967–1969. Germanische Sprachwissenschaft. Berlin: de Gruyter.

Krause, Wolfgang. 1952. Westtocharische Grammatik. Heidelberg: Winter.

———. 1953. Handbuch des Gotischen. Munich: Beck.

————, and Thomas, Werner. 1960–1964. Tocharisches Elementarbuch. Heidelberg: Winter.

Kronasser, Heinz. 1956. Vergleichende Laut- und Formenlehre des Hethitischen. Heidelberg: Winter.

Kuryłowicz, Jerzy. 1927. ə indo-européen et ḫ hittite. Symbolae grammaticae in honorem Ioannis Rozwadowski. Cracow: Drukarnia Uniwersytetu Jagiellońskiego.

————. 1956. L'apophonie en indo-européen. Wrocław: Polska Akademia Nauk.

————. 1968. Indogermanische Grammatik. Band II. Akzent-Ablaut. Heidelberg: Winter.

Lane, George S. 1947. The Tocharian Puṇyavantajātaka: text and translation. (Publications of the American Oriental Society, Offprint Series No. 21.) New Haven: American Oriental Society.

————. 1948. Vocabulary to the Tocharian Puṇyavantajātaka. (Publications of the American Oriental Society, Offprint Series No. 25.) New Haven: American Oriental Society.

————. 1966. On the interrelationships of the Tocharian dialects. In Ancient Indo-European dialects, ed. by Henrik Birnbaum and Jaan Puhvel, pp. 213–33. Berkeley and Los Angeles: Univ. of California Pr.

Lanman, Charles W. 1884. A Sanskrit reader. Cambridge: Harvard Univ. Pr.

Laroche, Emmanuel. 1959. Dictionnaire de la langue louvite. Paris: Maisonneuve.

————. 1960. Les hiéroglyphes hittites. Paris: Klincksieck.

Lehmann, Winfred P. 1952. Proto-Indo-European phonology. Austin: Univ. of Texas Pr.

————. 1966. The grouping of the Germanic languages. In Ancient Indo-European dialects, ed. by Henrik Birnbaum and Jaan Puhvel, pp. 13–27. Berkeley and Los Angeles: Univ. of California Pr.

————. 1973. Historical linguistics: an introduction. New York: Holt, Rinehart, and Winston.

————. 1974. Proto-Indo-European syntax. Austin: Univ. of Texas Pr.

Lehmann, R. P. M., and Lehmann, W. P. 1975. An introduction to Old Irish. New York: Modern Language Association.

Lejeune, Michel. 1964. Index inverse du grec mycénien. Paris: Centre national de la recherche scientifique.

Leskien, August. 1909. Grammatik der altbulgarischen (altkirchenslavischen) Sprache. Heidelberg: Winter.

————. 1914. Grammatik der serbo-kroatischen Sprache. Heidelberg: Winter.

————. 1919. Litauisches Lesebuch. Heidelberg: Winter.

————. 1962. Handbuch der altbulgarischen (altkirchenslavischen) Sprache. Heidelberg: Winter.

Leumann, Manu. 1977. Lateinische Laut- und Formenlehre. Munich: Beck.

Levin, Saul. 1964. The Linear B controversy reexamined. New York: State Univ. of New York Pr.

Lewis, Henry, and Pedersen, Holger. 1937. A concise comparative Celtic grammar. Göttingen: Vandenhoeck and Ruprecht.

Lindeman, Fredrik O. 1970. Einführung in die Laryngaltheorie. Berlin: de Gruyter.

Lindsay, William M. 1894. The Latin language. Oxford: Clarendon Press.

Loewe, Richard. 1933. Germanische Sprachwissenschaft. Leipzig: de Gruyter.

Luick, Karl. 1921–1940. Historische Grammatik der englischen Sprache. Leipzig: Tauchnitz.

Lunt, Horace. 1959. Old Church Slavonic grammar. The Hague: Mouton.

McCluskey, S.; Schmalstieg, W. R.; and Zeps, V. 1975. The Basel epigram: a new minor text in Old Prussian. General Linguistics 15: 159–65.

Macdonell, Arthur A. 1968. Vedic grammar. Varanasi and Delhi: Indological Book Services.

Marstrander, Carl, et al. 1913–. Dictionary of the Irish language. Dublin: Royal Irish Academy.

Mayer, Anton. 1957. Die Sprache der alten Illyrier. Vienna: Rudolf M. Rohrer.

Mayrhofer, Manfred. 1953–. Kurzegefasstes etymologisches Wörterbuch des Altindischen. Heidelberg: Winter.

Meillet, Antoine. 1913. Altarmenisches Elementarbuch. Heidelberg: Winter.

————. 1922 [1967]. The Indo-European dialects. Trans. Samuel N. Rosenberg. University: Univ. of Alabama Pr.

————. 1928. Esquisse d'une histoire de la langue latine. Paris: Klincksieck.

————. 1931. Grammaire du vieux perse. Paris: Champion.

————. 1934. Le slave commune. Paris: Champion.

————. 1936. Esquisse d'une grammaire comparée de l'arménien classique. Vienna: Pp. Mekhitharistes.

————. 1937. Caractères généraux des langues germaniques. Paris: Hachette.

————. 1964. Introduction à l'étude comparative des langues indo-européennes. University: Univ. of Alabama Pr.

————, and Vendryes, Joseph. 1927. Traité de grammaire comparée des langues classiques. Paris: Champion.

Meriggi, Peiro. 1962. Hieroglyphisch-hethitisches Glossar. Wiesbaden: Harrassowitz.

————. 1966–1967. Manuale di eteo geroglifico. Rome: Edizione dell' Ateneo.

Meyer, Gustav. 1883–1892. Albanesische Studien. Vienna: Philosophisch-historische Classe.

————. 1888. Kurzegefasste albanesische Grammatik. Leipzig: Breitkopf and Härtel.

————. 1891. Etymologisches Wörterbuch der albenesischen Sprache. Strassburg: Trübner.

Miklosich, Franz. 1926. Vergleichende Grammatik der slavischen Sprachen. Heidelberg: Winter.

Mossé, Fernand. 1950–1959. Manuel de l'anglais du moyen âge des origines au XIVe siècle. Paris: Aubier.

————. 1956. Manuel de la langue gotique. Paris: Aubier.

Nauta, G. A. 1926. Oudfriesche Woordenlijst. Haarlem: Tjeenk Willink.

Neu, Erich. 1974. Der Anitta-Text. (Studien zu den Boğazköy Texten, vol. 18.) Wiesbaden: Harrassowitz.

————, and Meid, Wolfgang. 1979. Hethitisch und Indogermanisch. Innsbruck: Innsbrucker Beiträge zur Sprachwissenschaft.

Newmark, Leonard. 1957. Structural grammar of Albanian. Bloomington: Indiana University Research Center in Anthropology, Folklore, and Linguistics.

Noreen, Adolf. 1894. Abriss der germanischen Lautlehre. Strassburg: Trübner.

————. 1904. Altschwedische Grammatik. Halle: Niemeyer.

————. 1913. Geschichte der nordischen Sprachen. Strassburg: Trübner.

————. 1923. Altisländische und altnorwegische Grammatik. Halle: Niemeyer.

O'Rahilly, Cecile, ed. 1967. Táin Bó Cúalnge, from the Book of Leinster. (Irish Texts Society, vol. 49.) Dublin: Institute for Advanced Studies.

Oxford English Dictionary. 1933–.

Palmer, L. R. 1954. The Latin language. London: Faber and Faber.

Parlangeli, Oronzo. 1960. Studi messapici. Milan: Istituto lombardo di scienze et lettere.

Pedersen, Holger. 1909–1913. Vergleichende Grammatik der keltischen Sprachen. Göttingen: Vandenhoeck and Ruprecht.

––––––. 1941. Tocharisch vom Gesichtspunkt der indoeuropäischen Sprachvergleichung. Copenhagen: Munksgaard.

––––––. 1959. The discovery of language: linguistic science in the nineteenth century. Trans. John W. Spargo. Bloomington: Indiana Univ. Pr.

Pellegrini, G. B., and Prosdocimi, A. L. 1967. La lingua venetica. Padua: Istituto di glottologia dell' Università.

Pipa, Fehime. n.d. Elementary albanian. Rome(?): Vatra.

Pisani, Vittore. 1960–1964. Manuale storico della lingua latina. Turin: Rosenberg and Sellier.

––––––. 1961. Glottologia indeuropea. Turin: Rosenberg and Sellier.

Pischel, Richard. 1900. Grammatik der Prakrit-Sprachen. Strassburg: Trübner.

Pokorny, Julius. 1951–1959. Indogermanisches etymologisches Wörterbuch. Bern and Munich: Francke.

Polomé, Edgar. 1979. Creolization and linguistic theory. In A Festschrift for Oswald Szemerényi, ed. by B. Brogyanyi, pp. 679–90. Amsterdam: John Benjamins.

Poultney, James W. 1959. The Bronze Tables of Iguvium. Baltimore: American Philological Association.

Pritchard, James B., ed. 1969. Ancient Near-Eastern texts relating to the Old Testament. Princeton: Princeton Univ. Pr.

Prokosch, Eduard. 1938. Comparative Germanic grammar. Baltimore: Linguistic Society of America.

Puhvel, Jaan. 1960. Laryngeals and the Indo-European verb. Berkeley and Los Angeles: Univ. of California Pr.

Reichelt, Hans. 1967. Awestisches Elementarbuch. Heidelberg: Winter.

Reichenkron, Günter. 1966. Das Dakische. Heidelberg: Winter.

Renou, Louis. 1930. Grammaire sanscrite. Paris: Maisonneuve.

Ridgway, David. 1981. The forgers and the fibula. Times Literary Supplement, 19 June 1981, p. 691.

Sadnik, L., and Aitzetmüller, R. 1955. Handwörterbuch zu den altkirchenslavischen Texten. The Hague: Mouton.

Saussure, Ferdinand de. 1879. Mémoire sur le système primitif des voyelles dans les langues indo-européennes. Leipzig: Vieweg.

Schatz, Joseph. 1907. Altbairische Grammatik. Göttingen: Vandenhoeck and Ruprecht.

————. 1927. Althochdeutsche Grammatik. Göttingen: Vandenhoeck and Ruprecht.

Schmalstieg, William R. 1973. New thoughts on Indo-European phonology. Zeitschrift für vergleichende Sprachforschung 87:99–157.

————. 1974a. An Old Prussian grammar. University Park: Pennsylvania State Univ. Pr.

————. 1974b. A question without a clear answer: one aspect of the relations between Baltic and Slavic. In Suvažiavimo Darbai VIII, ed. by A. Liuima, S. J., pp. 181–88. Rome: Lietuvių Katalikų Mokslo Akademija.

————. 1976a. Studies in Old Prussian. University Park: Pennsylvania State Univ. Pr.

————. 1976b. An introduction to Old Church Slavic. Cambridge: Slavica Publishers.

————. 1980. Indo-European linguistics: a new synthesis. University Park: Pennsylvania State Univ. Pr.

————, and Klimas, Antanas. 1967. Lithuanian reader for self-instruction. New York: Franciscan Fathers Press.

Schmid, Wolfgang P. 1976. Baltisch und Indogermanisch. Baltistica 12: 115–22.

Schmidt, Karl H. 1976. Der Beitrag der keltiberischen Inschrift von Botorrita zur Rekonstruktion der protokeltischen Syntax. Word 28. (Special Issue: Celtic Linguistics, p. 51–62.)

Schmoll, Ulrich. 1959a. Die vorgriechischen Sprachen Siziliens. Wiesbaden: Harrassowitz.

————. 1959b. Die Sprache der vorkeltischen Indogermanen Hispaniens und das Keltiberische. Wiesbaden: Harrassowitz.

Schönfeld, M. 1911. Wörterbuch der altgermanischen Personen- und Völkernamen. Heidelberg: Winter.

Schützeichel, Rudolf. 1969. Althochdeutsches Wörterbuch. Tübingen: Niemeyer.

Schwyzer, Eduard, and Debrunner, Albert. 1934–1950. Griechische Grammatik. Munich: Beck.

Seebold, E. 1970. Vergleichendes und etymologisches Wörterbuch der germanischen starken Verben. The Hague-Paris: Mouton.

Senn, Alfred. 1966a. Handbuch der litauischen Sprache. Heidelberg: Winter.

———. 1966b. The relationships of Baltic and Slavic. In Ancient Indo-European dialects, ed. by Henrik Birnbaum and Jaan Puhvel, pp. 139–51. Berkeley and Los Angeles: Univ. of California Pr.

Shevelov, George. 1964. A prehistory of Slavic. Heidelberg: Winter.

Siebs, Theodor. 1901. Geschichte der friesischen Sprache. Strassburg: Trübner.

Sieg, Emil; Siegling, Wilhelm; and Schulze, Wilhelm. 1931. Tocharische Grammatik. Göttingen: Vandenhoeck and Ruprecht.

Sievers, Eduard. 1886. Angelsächische Grammatik. Halle: Niemeyer.

Solta, G. R. 1960. Die Stellung des Armenischen im Kreise der indogermanischen Sprachen. Vienna: Mechitharisten-Buchdr.

Sommer, Ferdinand. 1914. Handbuch der lateinischen Laut- und Formenlehre. Heidelberg: Winter.

Stang, Christian S. 1966. Vergleichende Grammatik der baltischen Sprachen. Oslo: Bergen; Tromsö: Universitetsforlaget.

Starke, Frank. 1977. Die Funktionen der dimensionalen Kasus und Adverbien im Althethitischen. Wiesbaden: Harrassowitz.

Steller, Walther. 1928. Abriss der altfriesischen Grammatik. Halle: Niemeyer.

Strachan, John. 1949. Old Irish paradigms and glosses. 4th ed. (Revised by Osborn Bergin, 1970.) Dublin: Royal Irish Academy.

Streitberg, Wilhelm. 1896. Urgermanische Grammatik. Heidelberg: Winter.

———. 1920. Gotisches Elementarbuch. Heidelberg: Winter.

———; Michels, V.; and Jellinek, M. H. 1936. Die Erforschung der indogermanischen Sprachen. Vol. 2. Germanisch. Berlin: de Gruyter.

Sturtevant, Edgar. 1931. Hittite glossary. Baltimore: Waverly Press.

———. 1942. The Indo-Hittite laryngeals. Baltimore: Linguistic Society of America.

———. 1951. A comparative grammar of the Hittite language. New Haven: Yale Univ. Pr.

———. 1962a. Linguistic change. Chicago: Univ. of Chicago Pr.

———. 1962b. The Indo-Hittite hypothesis. Language 38:105–10.

Szemerényi, Oswald. 1957. The problem of the Balto-Slavic unity: a critical survey. Kratylos 2:97–123.

———. 1970. Einführung in die vergleichende Sprachwissenschaft. Darmstadt: Wissenschaftliche Buchgesellschaft.

————. 1972. Comparative linguistics. *In* Current trends in linguistics, ed. by Thomas Sebeok. Vol. 9. Linguistics in western Europe, pp. 119–95. The Hague-Paris: Mouton.

————. 1973. La théorie des laryngals de Saussure à Kuryłowicz et à Benveniste: essai de réévaluation. Bulletin de la Société de Linguistique de Paris 68:1–25.

Taraporewala, Irach Jehangir Sorabji. 1962. Elements of the science of language. Calcutta: Calcutta University.

Thesaurus linguae latinae. 1904–.

Thumb, Albert, et al. 1909–1959. Handbuch der griechischen Dialekte. Heidelberg: Winter.

————; Hirt, Hermann; and Hauschild, Richard. 1958–1959. Handbuch des Sanskrit. Heidelberg: Winter.

Thurneysen, Rudolf. 1946. A grammar of Old Irish. Dublin: Institute for Advanced Studies.

Tischler, Johann. 1977–. Hethitisches etymologisches Glossar. Innsbruck: Innsbrucker Beiträge zur Sprachwissenschaft, 20–.

————. 1979. Zu den syntaktischen Grundlagen der Nominalkomposition: die Reihenfolge der Teilglieder. *In* A Festschrift for Oswald Szemerényi, ed. by B. Brogyanyi, pp. 853–68. Amsterdam: John Benjamins.

Torp, A., and Falk, H. 1909. Wortschatz der germanischen Spracheinheit. Göttingen: Vandenhoeck and Ruprecht.

Trautmann, R. 1910. Die altpreussischen Sprachdenkmäler. Göttingen: Vandenhoeck and Ruprecht.

Untermann, Jürgen. 1961. Die venetischen Personennamen. Wiesbaden: Harrassowitz.

Vaillant, André. 1950–1966. Grammaire comparée des langues slaves. Lyon and Paris: Editions IAC.

————. 1964. Manuel du vieux slave. Paris: Institut des études slaves.

Van Coetsem, Frans, and Kufner, Herbert L., eds. 1972. Towards a grammar of Proto-Germanic. Tübingen: Niemeyer.

Van Helten, W. L. 1890. Altostfriesische Grammatik. Leeuwarden: Kuipers and Wester.

Van Windekens, A. J. 1941. Lexique étymologique des dialectes tokhariens. No. 11. Louvain: Bibliothèque du Muséon.

————. 1944. Morphologie comparée du tokharien. Louvain: Bibliothèque du Muséon.

————. 1976–1979. Le tokharien confronté avec les autres langues indo-européennes. Louvain: Centre internationale de dialectologie générale.

Vasmer, Max. 1950–1959. Russisches etymologisches Wörterbuch. Heidelberg: Winter.

Vendryes, Joseph. 1959–1960. Lexique étymologique de l'irlandais ancien. Dublin: Institute for Advanced Studies.

Vetter, Emil. 1953. Handbuch der italischen Dialekte. Heidelberg: Winter.

Vilborg, Ebbe. 1960. A tentative grammar of Mycenaean Greek. Göteborg: Almqvist and Wiksell.

von der Gabelentz, H. C., and Loebe, J. 1843–1946. Ulfilas: Veteris et novi testamenti versionis gothicae fragmenta quae supersunt. Leipzig: Hirzel.

Vondrák, Wenzel. 1924–1928. Vergleichende slavische Grammatik. Göttingen: Vandenhoeck and Ruprecht.

von Planta, Robert. 1892–1897. Grammatik der oskisch-umbrischen Dialekte. Strassburg: Trübner.

von Richthofen, K. 1961. Altfriesisches Wörterbuch. Göttingen: Dietrich.

Wackernagel, Jacob, et al. 1896–1964. Altindische Grammatik. Göttingen: Vandenhoeck and Ruprecht.

———. 1926–1928. Vorlesungen über Syntax. Basel: Birkhäuser.

Watkins, Calvert. 1966. Italo-Celtic revisited. *In* Ancient Indo-European dialects, ed. by Henrik Birnbaum and Jaan Puhvel, pp. 29–50. Berkeley and Los Angeles: Univ. of California Pr.

———. 1969. Indogermanische Grammatik. Band III. Formenlehre. Heidelberg: Winter.

Whatmough, Joshua. 1937. The foundations of Roman Italy. London: Methuen.

Whitney, William D. 1889. Sanskrit grammar. Cambridge: Harvard Univ. Pr.

Wilmanns, W. 1893–1909. Deutsche Grammatik. Strassburg: Trübner.

Winter, Werner. 1962. Nominal and pronominal dual in Tocharian. Language 38:111–34.

———, ed. 1965. Evidence for laryngeals. The Hague: Mouton.

———. 1966. Traces of early dialectal diversity in Old Armenian. *In* Ancient Indo-European dialects, ed. by Henrik Birnbaum and Jaan Puhvel, pp. 201–11. Berkeley and Los Angeles: Univ. of California Pr.

Wright, Joseph. 1954. Grammar of the Gothic language. Oxford: Clarendon Press.

INDEX OF WORDS

The index is arranged by language according to the order of appearance in the text. All entries have been alphabetized according to the order of letters in the Roman alphabet. Numbers refer to pages.

Italic

Oscan

Umbrian

Celtic

Hellenic (Greek)

Armenian

Albanian

Baltic

Slavic

Germanic

Tocharian

*nokʷt-, 88

*pekʷ-, 88
*peŋkʷe, 48

*so, *sā, 120, 121

*to-, *tā-, 120
*tos, *tā, 121

*wirī (nom. pl.), 42
*wl̥kʷ-, 88

Non-Indo-European Languages

(Estonian) tagiyas, 95

(Finnish) taivas, 95

(Parthian) ma(r)h, 80

GENERAL INDEX

An Introduction to the Indo-European Languages

Designed by John DeBacher
Composed at Village Typographers, Inc.
in VIP Times Roman
Printed by Edwards Brothers, Inc.
on International Bookwhite

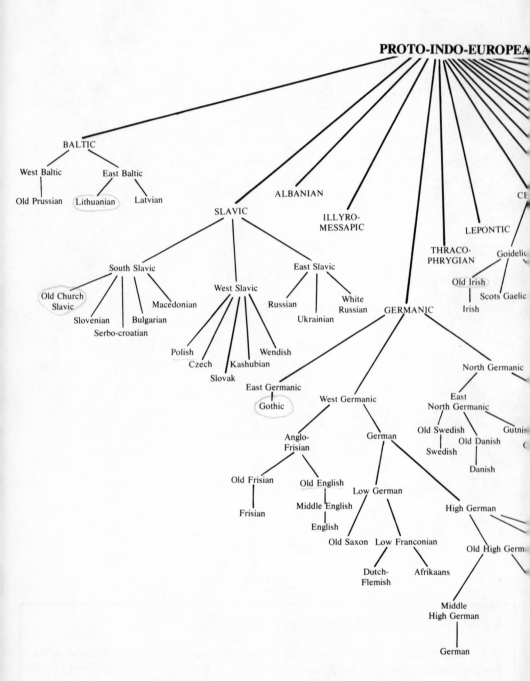

PROTO-INDO-EUROPEAN

BALTIC

West Baltic

Old Prussian Lithuanian Latvian

East Baltic

SLAVIC

ALBANIAN

ILLYRO-
MESSAPIC

LEPONTIC

THRACO-
PHRYGIAN

CE

Goidelic

Old Irish

Scots Gaelic

Irish

South Slavic

Old Church
Slavic

Slovenian Bulgarian

Serbo-croatian

Macedonian

West Slavic

Russian

Ukrainian

East Slavic

White
Russian

GERMANIC

Polish Wendish

Czech Kashubian

Slovak

East Germanic

Gothic

West Germanic

North Germanic

East
North Germanic

Old Swedish Gutnis

Old Danish

Swedish

Danish

Anglo-
Frisian

German

Old Frisian Old English

Frisian Middle English

English

Low German

High German

Old Saxon Low Franconian

Dutch- Afrikaans
Flemish

Old High Germ

Middle
High German

German

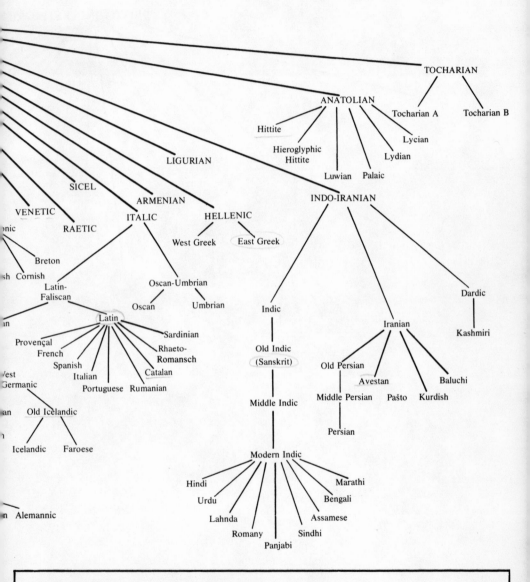

TOCHARIAN

ANATOLIAN

Tocharian A   Tocharian B

Hittite

Lycian

Hieroglyphic
Hittite

Lydian

LIGURIAN

Luwian   Palaic

INDO-IRANIAN

SICEL

VENETIC

ARMENIAN

ITALIC

HELLENIC

onic

RAETIC

West Greek   East Greek

Breton

sh   Cornish

Oscan-Umbrian

Dardic

Latin-
Faliscan

Oscan   Umbrian

Indic

Iranian

Kashmiri

un

Latin

Sardinian

Provençal

Rhaeto-
Romansch

Old Indic

Old Persian

French

(Sanskrit)

Spanish

Catalan

Avestan

Baluchi

Vest
Germanic

Italian

Portuguese   Rumanian

Middle Indic

Middle Persian   Pašto   Kurdish

an

Old Icelandic

Persian

Icelandic   Faroese

Modern Indic

Marathi

Hindi

Bengali

Urdu

Alemannic

Lahnda

Assamese

Romany   Sindhi

Panjabi

A Family Tree of the Indo-European Languages

Note: The branches of this family tree are not arranged in any geographical order.
For the geography of the Indo-European stocks, see the map on inside front cover.